Giovanni Gabrieli

Interior of St. Mark's. (*Mansell Collection, London*)

Giovanni Gabrieli

and the music of the Venetian High Renaissance

DENIS ARNOLD

London
OXFORD UNIVERSITY PRESS
New York Melbourne
1979

Oxford University Press, Walton Street, Oxford OX2 6DP

OXFORD LONDON GLASGOW NEW YORK
TORONTO MELBOURNE WELLINGTON
IBADAN NAIROBI DAR ES SALAAM CAPE TOWN
KUALA LUMPUR SINGAPORE JAKARTA HONG KONG TOKYO
DELHI BOMBAY CALCUTTA MADRAS KARACHI

ISBN 0 19 315247 9

PRINTED AND BOUND IN ENGLAND BY
HAZELL WATSON AND VINEY LTD
AYLESBURY, BUCKS

Introduction

ONE of the earliest great musicological studies was devoted to the life and works of Giovanni Gabrieli. It was written by Carl von Winterfeld, a German scholar of such extraordinary percipience and industry that even nearly a century and a half after his book first appeared in 1834, any successor venturing to discuss Venetian music must not only acknowledge his indebtedness to it but must also consider how his views are being shaped by the attitudes of the early part of the nineteenth century. Winterfeld's study has an air of authority which is rare. He transcribed virtually all Gabrieli's church music; he knew enough of Schütz's work to trace the relationship between the two; he was by no means ignorant of the 'moderns' such as Monteverdi, which allowed him to put Gabrieli into historical perspective; he was tireless in discovering documents so that the main facts about the music of St. Mark's helped not only in assembling the biography of the composer, but in describing the conditions under which his music was produced and performed. It is an astonishing work of scholarship, and it is not surprising to find no other published major attempt at a reappraisal of Gabrieli until the last twenty years, when the discovery of much late Renaissance music has given impetus to its performance. Even then, the next study to be published, Egon Kenton's *Life and Works of Giovanni Gabrieli* (American Institute of Musicology, 1967), began as an attempt to translate Winterfeld's into English.

Winterfeld was in a sense an amateur musicologist. Born of a noble family in 1784, he was educated mainly in Berlin, studying law at university; but in 1809 he joined the Berlin Singakademie, an organization devoted to the performance of music by Handel and Bach, and together with other members of his family he became an enthusiast for choral music. Then in 1812 he went on his own Grand Tour to Italy, where, as an incidental amusement, he looked for 'old' music which might interest the Singakademie and its conductor Zelter. He found a great deal, mainly of the Roman school of the sixteenth and seventeenth centuries, although later composers such as Ziani and Leonardo Leo were also to his taste.

Strangely enough, he never went back to Italy after this trip; on returning home, he married and in 1816 became a civil servant in the city of Breslau. By a fortunate chance, Breslau, like Berlin, had an institution devoted to the study of church music, the Königliche Akademische Institut für Kirchenmusik, which came into Winterfeld's care in his official capacity about 1818. Breslau also had a splendid library, the Klosterbibliotek, which had been made available to the public on the secularization of the monasteries in 1810. So the way was open for Winterfeld to become a musical scholar. In 1830, he founded the Schlesische Gesellschaft für Vaterländische Kultur, a 'British Academy' style institution, at which scholars read papers. Winterfeld's contributions dealt with the beginnings of the oratorio, the significance of Viadana, and the basso continuo—and on Giovanni Gabrieli. In 1832 he published a short study of Palestrina, and then finished his great work on Gabrieli after nearly twenty years of research. He returned to Berlin, where his main battles were fought trying to persuade protestant churches to revive 'old' music in the teeth of Calvinistic objections. He died of a stroke in February 1852, while playing chorales on his harmonium.

To praise his scholarly achievement is almost an impertinence for a later scholar. Amateur though he was, Winterfeld played a major part in changing attitudes to 'old' music. Indeed, his very amateur status helped to give his work the authority which is stamped all over it. At a time when Leopold von Ranke was benefiting from the opening of the archives, enabling him to write his major history of the Papacy, Winterfeld was doing the same for areas of musical history. Such men loved facts, and gave them in plenty. They were products of an age when scientific techniques were coming into fashion; they were civil servants who loved documentation. Winterfeld was also a man who saw musicians as part of society. It is not difficult to imagine his delight in studying a Venetian composer, born of a proud state to which the paternalism of nineteenth-century Prussia must have seemed akin. He was a religious man, a serious Christian, for whom music had a major role in worship. Gabrieli, like Palestrina, was, so it seemed, principally a composer of church music, and as one who served both church and state was an even more attractive figure to Winterfeld.

It is precisely because of the strength of Winterfeld's musical portrait of Gabrieli that a new interpretation, however daunting it must seem after such a musicological classic, is necessary. For Winterfeld's interests in music for church and state made him stress those facets of Gabrieli's work rather than others. Gabrieli, after all, wrote three dozen madrigals; more important still, he composed over forty splendid works for instrumental ensemble and nearly fifty for keyboard. Taken together they form nearly half Gabrieli's total *oeuvre*, and while it could be held that the madrigals and some of the organ pieces are not of the greatest significance in musical history, this certainly cannot be said of the music for instrumental ensemble, which is of the highest aesthetic quality and of unique importance for its epoch. This excellence in instrumental music can teach us a great deal about Gabrieli and must be taken into account in any re-assessment of his work.

It tends to be forgotten that Gabrieli was never *maestro di cappella* at St. Mark's, but one of its organists. It is a profession which makes its own special demands and develops its own preferred character of musicianship, especially when divorced from the post of *magister cori*. It demands the requisite keyboard skills, as well as the capacity to accompany and support the choir. It does not necessarily require a grasp of intellectual or literary concepts. In this, it stood against the trends of the later sixteenth century, where it was the *literati* among musicians, the noble amateurs and their professional colleagues, who became interested in humanist ideas of combining words and music and were the most distinguished and progressive figures of musical life. At the same time, it was secular music which provided the major developments in musical idioms. Again Gabrieli went against the trends.

Thus Winterfeld's picture of the composer, though a classic and irreplaceable, today needs supplementation. The present study aims to do this in several ways. Firstly it brings together newly discovered documents: most notably those in the account books of St. Mark's, which tell us of the details of the instrumental ensemble and the choir strengths at various times during Gabrieli's lifetime; and those in the minute books and receipts of the Scuola Grande di S. Rocco, Gabrieli's work for which has gone unnoticed until recently. The background of the music for this confraternity has been given in some detail, partly because it helps to show that the composer's music was not designed solely for the special conditions at St. Mark's, partly because it is interesting in itself, and enlightens a hitherto dark corner of Renaissance music-making. Secondly, by comparing Gabrieli's music with that of his teachers, colleagues, and pupils, it is possible to gain a clear picture of his development and tastes. From this process, it emerges that Gabrieli was not a cheerful extrovert as were his colleagues Croce and Bassano (both excellent composers); nor was he a musical polyglot as were his teacher Lasso and his uncle Andrea. But though conservative, he was not a stick-in-the-mud as is shown by his pupils, and we can see the pattern of his changing style. As well as revealing the complexity of his nature, I hope this process will shed light on a major school of composition which, though famous, still lacks a major study of its music in any language.

If this adds up to a view which hardly fits in with that of the conventional historians who see Gabrieli as one of the earliest composers of the emerging Baroque it will be no bad thing. In fact, he is difficult to include in the mainstream of Italian music, a religious composer in a secular age and a purely instrumental one at a time when the most important genres are impure combinations of diverse arts. A mixture of conservatism and progressive ideas makes for a distinctive voice. Certainly, the quality of sound evoked by Gabrieli is unmistakable: the flair in gaining the maximum effect from the ensemble, the crisp, anacrusic rhythms, the basic simplicity yet encrusted decorativeness of the harmony, all unique to him. Though it is a less universal voice than those of Lasso or Monteverdi, it is, as Winterfeld defined it, comparable with those of some singleminded geniuses such as Palestrina or Victoria; and compared with the extremes of Gesualdo or the clever sophistication of Marenzio, Gabrieli's honest musicality seems serious and devout. It is these virtues which give his music its value today, when Venice no longer holds the East in fee, nor is national pride held to be a supreme concept. While superficially he may seem a composer to impress the members of the Grand Council, he is in fact very much a musician's composer, to be treasured by those who enjoy the craft as well as the grandeur of splendid music.

Acknowledgements

RESEARCH for this book has been spread over many years, during which I have had the good fortune of help and encouragement from colleagues, pupils, and friends, as well as the staffs of many institutions. I must thank the Queen's University of Belfast for grants of money and time at the beginning of my work. My visits and enquiries from the following libraries and archives have always been received with immense kindness: that of the Conservatorio G. B. Martini in Bologna; the Biblioteca Marciana, Venice; the Murhardsche und Landesbibliothek, Kassel; the Österreichische Nationalbibliothek and Gesellschaft der Musikfreunde, both in Vienna; the Biblioteca comunale Ariostea, Ferrara; the Archivio di Stato, Venice.

On a more personal note, Professor Brian Pullan has generously put at my disposal his discoveries concerning the Venetian confraternities, especially the material he found in the archive of the Scuola Grande di S. Rocco. My friend and former pupil Mrs. Margaret Monk prepared the reduced scores and copied the musical examples in their present form. In Venice, the hospitality of the late Mario Gasparoni and his wife Tullia has not only left me with pleasant memories but has also helped to penetrate the mysteries of certain customs of Venetian society; to which must be added Cav. John Cherry's kindness in the loan of his house on the Grand Canal from time to time. Lastly my greatest debt is, as always, to my wife who has not only typed the book from a horrifyingly difficult manuscript, compiled the index, read the proofs, checked documents cited against the originals—in other words, done all the less agreeable tasks—but has been a constant companion at all times, no matter how fraught or difficult.

Oxford, 1979 — Denis Arnold

List of Plates

Interior of St. Mark's *Frontispiece*

Between pages 160–1

1 The Scuola Grande di S. Rocco
2 The 'great' organ of St. Mark's
3 Doge Marino Grimani

Between pages 192–3

4 The procession at the coronation of the Dogaressa in 1597
5 One of the wind players of the Doge
6 One of the singers in the choir of St. Mark's

The procession in the Piazza San Marco (*Galleria dell'Accademia, Venice*) *Jacket*

Abbreviations used in the footnotes

A.S.V.: Archivio di Stato, Venice.
Caffi: *Storia della musica sacra nella già cappella ducale di San Marco in Venezia dal 1318 al 1797*, 2 vols (1854–55 R/1931).
CMM: *Corpus Mensurabilis Musicae*.
DTÖ: *Denkmäler der Tonkunst in Österreich*.
IMAMI: *Instituzioni e Monumenti dell'Arte Musicale in Italia*.
Kenton: *Giovanni Gabrieli* (American Institute of Musicology, 1967).
MGG: *Die Musik in Geschichte und Gegenwart*.
Pullan: *Rich and Poor in Renaissance Venice* (Oxford, 1971).
Sansovino: *Venetia Città Nobilissima* (1663 edition).
Winterfeld: *Johannes Gabrieli und sein Zeitalter* (Berlin, 1834).

Contents

Introduction v

CHAPTER 1 THE FORMATIVE YEARS 1

CHAPTER 2 SERVICE AT ST. MARK'S 18

CHAPTER 3 THE ORGANIST 40

CHAPTER 4 THE EARLY MUSIC FOR VENETIAN FESTIVALS 69

CHAPTER 5 THE MADRIGALS 107

CHAPTER 6 THE EARLY INSTRUMENTAL MUSIC 128

CHAPTER 7 THE GRAND CEREMONIAL MUSIC 163

CHAPTER 8 THE SCUOLA GRANDE DI S. ROCCO 188

CHAPTER 9 THE PUPILS 211

CHAPTER 10 THE LATER INSTRUMENTAL MUSIC 231

CHAPTER 11 THE LATER CHURCH MUSIC 258

Envoi 295

Bibliography 304

Index 309

For Elsie

CHAPTER ONE

The Formative Years

WE do not know when or even where Giovanni Gabrieli was born. The entry in the register which records his death[1] in the summer of 1612 tells us that he was then fifty-six years of age (or maybe fifty-eight—the stroke of the pen is none too clear). But the scribe was not necessarily reliable, for his successor thirty years later managed to make an error in recording the death of an even greater composer, Claudio Monteverdi. So the best we can do, until more documentary evidence is discovered, is to believe that Gabrieli was born in the years around 1555.[2] As to the place of his birth the likeliest guess is that he was born in Venice itself, where most of his life was spent.

This uncertainty is not very surprising. If Gabrieli was born into a noble family, as some have suggested, it was probably a very minor branch. Even his uncle was not at this time a man of any great reputation. Andrea Gabrieli was probably in his mid-thirties or approaching forty when his nephew was born. He was certainly a Venetian, born in the district of Cannareggio (not then as unfashionable as now, since the social distribution about the city was more even than it is today). At some time in his early years Andrea was a singer in St. Mark's, but how long he remained in that post, or how valued a member of the Doge's *cappella* he was, is not recorded.[3] When his nephew was a baby he was organist at the parish church of S. Geremia, a modest enough position which gives no idea of the glory to come.

But when Giovanni was still a small child, an act of Andrea's shaped both their futures: Andrea went away to work in Munich, at the court of Duke Albrecht of Bavaria. Again exact dates are lacking, but it is known[4] that Andrea was there in 1562, and that he was one of the musicians who in that year accompanied the Duke to Nuremberg, Prague, Bamberg,

[1] A.S.V., necrology of the Provveditori alla Sanità, under the date.
[2] For the arguments in favour of the various dates, see the article 'Gabrieli' in *MGG*, Vol. 4.
[3] Caffi I, p. 166, says he was a singer in St. Mark's in 1536 without quoting his source. I have not managed to trace the entry in A.S.V.
[4] Wolfgang Boetticher, *Orlando di Lasso und seine Zeit* (Kassel and Basel, 1958), p. 166.

Würzburg, and Frankfurt for the coronation of the Holy Roman Emperor. Such a change of service obviously meant a great deal to Gabrieli. From being an organist at a minor Venetian church, who had contributed to a few madrigal anthologies, he became soon after his return home one of the most productive, published, and popular composers of his time. From about 1565, scarcely a year passed without some works of his coming from the Gardano press, either contributions to anthologies or complete volumes of his own music. Somebody or something had acted as a catalyst in those few years across the Alps.

The musical atmosphere of the Bavarian court must have been one factor.[5] The establishment there was quite large, about thirty-five musicians of various kinds, though it was not yet as grand as it was shortly to become. More important, it offered a new kind of ambience, one centred round the opulent celebration of worldly events, where the Duke and his family took first place. The Duke loved music and was himself something of a lutenist. When he travelled, his retinue might include some two dozen musicians, from Italy, various parts of Austria and Germany, and especially the Netherlands. Some of them were virtuosi, chosen for the agility of their voices or fingers and their power of ornamenting melody. Several were composers, and of these the greatest was undoubtedly the Hofkapellmeister, Orlando di Lasso.

Lasso, teacher of both Gabrielis

Lasso, born at Mons in about 1532, was probably a younger man than Andrea Gabrieli, but one of infinitely more experience. Tradition has it that he was kidnapped three times as a boy for the beauty of his voice, and by the time he was appointed to his eminent position in Munich at the age of about twenty-five, he had seen not only his native Low Countries, but a good deal of Italy, including Naples, Milan, and Rome. A period as *maestro di cappella* at St. John Lateran had given him an insight into the writing of modern church music; Naples had taught him the art of dialect songs; his homeland had shown him what the polyphonic chanson had to offer. He was apparently as much at home in German as in French or Italian. Musically he was equally polyglot. His chansons seem the essence of the genre, as it had developed in the middle of the sixteenth century: sometimes witty, sometimes gently sentimental, his music captures the overall meaning of the words without going into the detail of word-

[5] For the most ample account of conditions at the court see A. Sandberger, *Beiträge zur Geschichte der bayerischen Hofkapelle unter Orlando di Lasso* (Leipzig, 1894–5).

painting which is characteristic of the madrigal. He was master of an art as realistic as Dutch painting, and both his *chansons* and *villanelle* show a keen eye for character and situation. Lasso was fully at home in the artifice of the post-Rore madrigal, capable of reflecting each image of the verse without disturbing the sense of its unity. In this genre itself, Lasso's range is immense. There are madrigals for connoisseurs, the disciples of that *musica reservata* of which the Bavarian court was so proud. Whatever its exact meaning, the term certainly implies a subtle relationship between words and music, as well as an understanding of the new-fangled devices of *note nere* and of chromaticism. At this stage of his life at least Lasso was a modern, in touch with the latest developments at Ferrara. He was equally a master of the grand manner, writing ceremonial madrigals for the large forces he was gradually assembling at Munich. These are written for eight, ten, or more parts, weaving a complex contrapuntal web, often giving rise to virile rhythms, always with changing sonorities to astonish and delight the ear. In addition Lasso was already a complete composer of church music, writing motets and masses for the ducal *cappella* and for the sumptuous monasteries which Duke Albrecht encouraged. The composer well practised in secular music has the power to please in church too. Lasso has a gift for memorable phrases accompanied by comparatively simple harmonies, which is the antithesis of learnedness, even if it by no means lacks learning. The diatonic style which first revealed itself in the popular music of the first half of the century permeates his church music, showing itself in bass lines which move naturally in fourths and fifths to give the strong cadential progressions which dominate the harmony. The rhythms of the words inspire musical rhythms, and as phrases are repeated so do they remain in the mind. There is no wonder that Lasso's motet books were reprinted time and again, and that publishers were happy with his fluency which gave them new collections at frequent intervals. But Lasso's fecundity did not stop there. He composed teaching pieces, or *bicinia*, for master and pupil to sing or play, not to mention boozy German songs. Like Mozart, Lasso had the ability to tackle any genre and discover its essence. He was an astonishing figure in sixteenth century music.

Relationship between Lasso and Andrea Gabrieli

Lasso's biographer, Wolfgang Boetticher,[6] suggests that the relationship between Lasso and Andrea Gabrieli was by no means one-sided, and that

[6] op. cit.

the younger man may well have learned from his older Italian colleague. If this was so, it surely remains true that the Italian's debt was enormous. For when he came back home, to be appointed organist of St. Mark's in 1564, he embarked on the same path as his illustrious Bavarian colleague. Within the next few years he too showed that he could excel in all known musical genres. His first publication of note was a book of *Cantiones Sacrae* for five voices, dedicated to Duke Albrecht and modelled on a similar volume of Lasso's which had come out a few years earlier. At the same time he was writing dialect songs, *giustiniane*, in the same vein of caricature as Lasso's *villanelle*, with a distinct Venetian humour but no less 'realistic' in their depiction of their *commedia dell'arte* characters.[7] Madrigal books followed and quickly became very popular, to judge by their reprints; in these the differences between the two composers become apparent. Gabrieli acquired the same sensitivity to setting words, but he lacked both Lasso's good taste in poetry and such academic interests as *musica reservata*. He is primarily an entertainer, seeking the widest possible audience rather than one of connoisseurs. There is a gaiety about his short-breathed melodies, the bright sonorities he gains from his coupling of voices, which takes the place of imitative counterpoint, and his diatonic, characteristically clear harmony. There is no hint of the darker side of life which infected Lasso even in his middle years and was to cloud his old age. Gabrieli was undoubtedly a less complex person, perhaps because he was more intrinsically musical. The capers of Lasso in the *intermezzi* at the wedding celebrations of the heir to the throne in 1567, where he was one of the *comici* and a many-sided moving spirit in the uproarious proceedings,[8] can hardly be imagined coming from Gabrieli. And it is significant that Lasso was no great instrumental virtuoso, as Gabrieli was. Andrea's substantial corpus of organ music is the one sphere where Lasso cannot match him.

Andrea Gabrieli's ceremonial music

In one special way, the two composers are very close, and it is tempting to believe that Gabrieli learned directly from Lasso. Their grand ceremonial music is very alike. Circumstances explain why Gabrieli's experience at Munich should have proved valuable in Venice. Willaert, *maestro di cappella* at St. Mark's until 1562, had an interest in the grand manner, par-

[7] A. Einstein, 'The Greghesca and the Giustiniana of the Sixteenth Century', *The Journal of Renaissance and Baroque Music* I (1946), p. 19.

[8] M. Trojano, *Discorsi delli Trionfi, Giostre, Apparati, è delle cose più notabile fatte nelle Sontuose Nozze, dell'Illustr. e Eccell. Signor Duca Guglielmo . . . nell'anno 1568* (Munich, 1568).

ticularly in some of the motets of his *Musica Nova* (1559),[9] where he seems to be deliberately aiming at a simplicity of texture which makes the most impressive use of large resources. His successor, Cipriano de Rore, had less inclination towards such a style; and the man who was in charge of the Doge's music when Gabrieli became one of the organists, Zarlino, was a theorist rather than a composer, apparently a sound administrator (needed in such a post) but hardly with the facility for occasional music which St. Mark's required. Gabrieli's colleague, Claudio Merulo, was admittedly capable of such pieces, though this gift seems to have developed later, when he had examples to follow; in the 1560s he was primarily a virtuoso

[9] For a discussion of the dating of this collection see A. Newcomb, 'Editions of Willaert's *Musica Nova*: new evidence, new speculations', *Journal of the American Musicological Society* XXVI (1973), p. 132.

organist and composer for his instrument. So only Andrea Gabrieli had the experience to produce motets and grandiose madrigals for festivals.

His first published work in the genre was a madrigal, 'Felici d'Adria', probably composed for the visit of the Archduke Charles of Carinthia who was passing through Venice on his way home from Spain in 1567.[10] It is a massive work for eight voices and very much in the manner of Lasso: exciting in rhythms, simple in harmony, yet quite complicated in counterpoint (see Example 1).

If it does not show that flair for sound that Andrea was later to develop and to pass on to his nephew, it helps to explain why he was so deeply involved in the music-making at the various festivals of the 1570s. It was in this decade that Venice recovered, for a time, its former glory and power. The Turkish wars had of late provided no cause for satisfaction and indeed in 1570 Cyprus was lost. Then came the news of the naval victory at Lepanto, which made Christendom once more safe from the infidel. Even the Papacy, never the Most Serene Republic's best friend, saw the merit of Venetian naval might and sent its congratulations. Venice itself went wild with joy. The celebrations went on for days and included processions mounted by all the city's institutions. Predictably Andrea was the composer of the music for the *festa* when decorated floats were pulled around St. Mark's Square, representing the continents making obeisance to the saviour of Christendom.[11] This music included madrigals sung on the floats by appropriately dressed performers. Clearly there was not much room for grand forces here—a quartet of singers perhaps, and a similar number of instrumentalists. Yet Andrea's instinct for sonority is quite obvious. He chooses bright combinations of voices, written simply, but with a sure ear for effect. In the open air this is the way to make some impression, and comparing these works with earlier music for such occasions —there are a number of laudatory madrigals for Venetian festivals by Baldassare Donato, later to be Giovanni Gabrieli's superior as *maestro*, at this time a singer in St. Mark's[12]—we see the result of the broadening of Andrea's horizons (see Example 2).

It is impossible to say precisely when Andrea's music for St. Mark's became similarly splendid, though there are two signs that it came into increasing

[10] Modern editions in *DTÖ* XLI, ed. A. Einstein (Graz, 1934, reprinted 1960), and *Ten Madrigals*, ed. D. Arnold (London, 1970).

[11] A. Einstein, *The Italian Madrigal* (Princeton, 1949), Vol. II, p. 523.

[12] See editions of three of his madrigals, ed. D. Stevens (New York and London). Although it is doubtful whether these madrigals should be considered as a cycle as stated by Stevens, there can be no doubt that they were intended for some such ceremonial occasion.

use there. The first is the number of large-scale motets for the major religious days observed in Venice which were eventually to be published among Andrea's collected works. The second is that the Doge's *cappella* gradually took on the shape of that at Munich. The arrival of instrumentalists shows the trend most clearly; in 1567 the first salaried players were placed on the payroll of St. Mark's, and in the same period payments were also made to others for taking part in the grand festivals. '1568, 21st April, from the treasury paid to S. Jac^{o} Frutariol for 4 *corneti muti*, 2 *corneti alti*, a *cornamusa*, and a flute (*fifero*) who played the concerti in the organ loft on the festival day, 8 *scudi*.'[13] It is no wonder that Andrea's motets began to show a richness of tone-quality hitherto unknown. Some of them are in the Lasso manner, written for eight or more contrapuntal strands, but with richer harmony and the lower registers, now supported by the trombonists, exploited more fully. Others explore the double-choir style, the *cori spezzati* in the galleries near the high altar suggesting various dramatic interchanges and juxtapositions. Even the layman could appreciate these: one noble commentator, Francesco Da Molino, who was not otherwise given to describing musical effects in detail, noted that when Henri III of France attended mass in St. Mark's on his visit in 1574 'the most excellent musicians sang the Te Deum to the sound of both organs . . .'[14] as though this were something not heard elsewhere or very often.

[13] A.S.V., Proc. de Supra, Registro 3, entry for 21 April 1568: 'Per spese p̧ la chiesa // a cassa cõtadi a S.Iac^{o} Frutariol p̧ quatro corneti muti, do corneti alti, una cornamusa et un fifaro p̧ far li concerti nel organo le feste. scudi otto.'

[14] Biblioteca Marciana: MSS Italiani, Classe VII, no. 553 (8812), p. 60: '. . . da Ecc^{mi} Musici fu cantato con tutti dui li organi il Te Deum . . .'.

This visit of the recently crowned French monarch set the seal on Andrea Gabrieli's reputation as a writer of ceremonial music. The *festeggiamento*[15] of the visitor was more than usually lengthy and opulent, and the musicians were busy.

. . . at two o'clock of each [day] the best musicians of Venice, perhaps even of Italy, gave most rare *concerti* and sang many pieces in praise of His Majesty in the Palazzo Ducale, and among other occasions, there was one evening when were assembled large boats, constructed in the form of pyramids and with other decorations, full of musicians, who, to the light of torches, played the most exquisite instruments which could be found, making such marvellous harmony and *concerti* as to give infinite pleasure . . .[16]

There was a play with music by Merulo and Zarlino; and probably some of the work composed for this gay week was contained in those retrospective anthologies, the *Concerti di Andrea Gabrieli* (1587) and the *Dialoghi* assembled by Gardano in 1590.

Relationship between the two Gabrielis

These were the years when Giovanni Gabrieli was becoming a musician, for, as it appears, he was already worthy of note in his late teens.

If Messer Andrea Gabrieli (of blessed memory) had not been my uncle, I should dare to say (without fear of being accused of bias) that, as there are few illustrious painters and sculptors gathered together in the world, so are there few indeed composers and organists as excellent as he is. But since by my consanguinity I am scarcely less than his son, it is not fitting for me to say freely that which affection, guided by truth, would seem appropriate to me.[17]

We can assume that the two were master and disciple, a relationship which may have been valued by the uncle as much as the nephew, since Andrea apparently had no sons. Giovanni's education must have centred round

[15] P. Nolhac and A. Solerti, *Il viaggio in Italia di Enrico III re di Francia, e le feste a Venezia, Ferrara, Mantova e Torino* (Turin, 1890).

[16] Biblioteca Marciana: MSS Italiani, Classe VII no. 553 pp. 59–60: '. . . et alle dui hore di caduna [giorno?] di esse da i primi musici di Ven.ª e forse d'Italia dinanzi al detto Palaggio furono uditi concerti rarissimi, et cantate molte cose in lode della Maestà Sua, e fra l'altre una sera comparve sopra barche grosse, un mausoleo edificato con piramidi, et altri adornamati pieno di Musici, e torci accesti con tutte sorte du più esquiti Instrumenti che si trovassero, che fecero tal armonia e tal concerti maravigliosi, che infinitamente piaquero.'

[17] From the dedication of the *Concerti di Andrea, et di Gio: Gabrieli* (Venice, 1587). The original is to be found in Caffi I, p. 173, Kenton, p. 52, and A. Einstein, *The Italian Madrigal* Vol. II, p. 520.

playing the organ, in view of his future career. As far as composition was concerned, we can gain some idea of Andrea's teaching methods from another pupil, Ludovico Zacconi, who worked with him around 1577 and later wrote

Among the many pupils (among whom I number myself) of Sig. Andrea Gabrieli, most honoured organist of St Mark's, there was one whom I will not name who had made many counterpoints upon a *canto fermo*, and being tired of it, asked the master whether he could change it; and the master looking at him with displeasure [this pupil] said 'Please, Master, let me change this *canto fermo*, for I do not know what more I can do with it', and taking up a pen, he [Gabrieli] composed four or five *fughe*, each one more beautiful than the other, and said 'Do you really think you had done everything possible . . .?'[18]

Such thoroughness (though perhaps the tale must be taken with a grain or two of salt) explains the ease with which both Gabrielis' counterpoint flows. It certainly indicates that Giovanni was expected to be a complete musician, at a time when the decline of what might be called 'clever counterpoint'—the art of using devices such as canon—meant that madrigals could be written even by amateurs. The first two madrigals by young Gabrieli to be published were anything but amateurish.

Giovanni Gabrieli's years in Munich

But these madrigals belong to a further stage of his education and career. When they appeared from the press in 1575, he was already working at Munich under Lasso. His uncle was surely responsible for this essential step forward. Again our exact knowledge of events is sketchy. The Bavarian court was looking for musicians in Venice in 1573, and found a castrato there,[19] and Giovanni may have been another of their finds on this occasion. It is perhaps more likely that he met Lasso himself when he was in Venice in the January or February of the following year,[20] for it is inconceivable that Andrea and Lasso did not renew their acquaintance then. In any case, Giovanni was at the Bavarian court in 1575, all the more fortunately, since there was a serious outbreak of the plague in Venice in the same year.

The trip probably widened Giovanni's horizons just as much as it had for his uncle nearly fifteen years earlier. Music-making had grown in

[18] L. Zacconi, *Prattica di Musica* (Venice, 1592), Cap. 33, p. 83. Facsimile edition (Bologna, 1967). [19] Boetticher, op. cit., p. 433.
[20] ibid, p. 441. For a dissenting view see Leuchtmann I, p. 175.

opulence in Munich as well as in Venice. By the end of the 1560s there were no fewer than sixty musicians on the court payroll, with many distinguished names among them. At one stage in the following decade there were three organists, of whom two were composers of some merit. One of these, Giuseppe Guami, later came to Venice; another was Ivo de Vento, known for his interest in various types of harmonic experiment. There were seven string players, including one Antonio da Bergamo, who was a virtuoso on the treble viol. The group of cornettists and trombonists was also seven strong, and included Guami's brother Francesco, also a composer, and various other musicians who later came back to Venice, perhaps at the prompting of Gabrieli. Of these, there were several members of the Laudis family, Francesco being a virtuoso cornettist of the first order.

One would dearly like to have more information about this period of Gabrieli's life. The few surviving documents[21]—entries in paybooks—tell us that he was a full member of the household, entitled to the summer uniform, probably boarding one of the boys of the *cappella* in his own rooms. But what is probably more instructive is to look at the dedications of his various later publications; they are nearly all to Bavarians. There are the Fuggers, the great family of bankers to whom half Europe was indebted and whose patronage in Augsburg and Nuremberg was especially strong; the Bishop of Bamberg; the merchant and musician Georg Gruber, who was in charge of a club or confraternity which gave music in the Frauenkirche at Nuremberg; the Abbot of SS. Afra and Ulrich, the largest and most impressive church in Augsburg. Clearly Gabrieli met a host of influential men, who were later to send their young musicians to study with him, commission works, and think of him, perhaps, as the greatest composer in Italy: and indeed this association was to influence the course of German music for several decades.

The influence of the Bavarian court probably made him more conservative than if he had stopped in Venice. Lasso was now in middle age. He was no stick-in-the-mud, and his regular travels in Italy kept him in touch with the latest trends. Even so, his style had been formed over twenty years earlier and this began to show in the way that he differed from the new generation at the North Italian courts. For in spite of his progressiveness in his madrigals, he remained a contrapuntist, brought up in the modal system rather than the lighter diatonicism of the younger generation. His rhythms were built in the regular patterns derived from the French *chanson*; theirs worked towards a plasticity based on Italian speech.

[21] W. Boetticher, *Aus Orlando di Lassos Wirkungskreis* (Kassel, 1963).

His textures now seemed thick compared with the almost deliberate pursuit of 'effective' sounds in the new madrigal. The symbolism of his word-painting belonged essentially to the relatively unsophisticated methods of Zarlino, whose advocacy of scales for the expression of the ideas of ascent and descent, dissonance for harshness 'but never so strong as to offend', was also now over twenty years old.

All these traits are found to some extent in the Bavarian composers. The madrigals of the brothers Guami typify the school: less than vivid in their musical imagery, stolid in rhythm, and opaque in texture. When the Bavarians used chromaticism it was in the wildly experimental manner of the early inventors of the device, unlike such later composers as Marenzio who took it into their repertoire of resources for use *in extremis*:

Giuseppe Guami

It was secular music that was making advances in technique in this part of the century, and so Bavarian church music does not seem so much out of line with events. Lasso is indeed in some ways in the forefront of stylistic change, for if the fathers of the Trent Council would have frowned on his use of French *chansons* as the basis of his parody masses of this period, they would surely have applauded his simple textures, which allow the words to be distinctly heard, and the attractively straightforward harmonies. The motets of Giuseppe Guami, collected in a volume dedicated to Wilhelm, Duke of Bavaria in 1585, though less progressive, show the virtues of the style. The smaller-scale pieces are very much in the Lasso motet manner, contrapuntally conceived in ample phrases, but with that incisiveness of imitative tags which makes for a crisp, attractive style. Like others of the Bavarian school, Guami lacks the suavity of Palestrina, preferring somewhat rougher, dynamic rhythms; and he is not afraid of a touch of drama, of personal involvement. One of his five-voiced motets is indeed startlingly expressive. 'In die tribulationis' opens with a chromatic scale which reminds us that he may have known the Ferrarese organist Luzzasco Luzzaschi, whose mannerist Dante madrigal 'Quivi sospiri'[22] opens in much the same way:

The altus and cantus enter with the same theme.

It is only as the motet proceeds that its difference from the modern madrigal becomes apparent. It breathes in larger phrases, works the chromatic scale into longer paragraphs; it lacks the succinctness of the madrigal precisely because Guami is concerned with unity rather than diversity, and does not aim to keep the tension continually high. The words are a liturgical entity, not *poesia per musica*. It is a problem with which Gabrieli was to be much concerned later in life, and it seems likely that he knew this motet, if not while he was in Bavaria, at least when he was in Venice, for Guami's volume is one of the few still surviving in the old library of St. Mark's. He is even more likely to have known Guami's large-scale motets, ceremonial pieces for up to ten or a dozen voices, not in the *cori spezzati* style of Venice, but elaborately contrapuntal:

[22] Modern edition, ed. A. Einstein, *The Golden Age of the Madrigal* (New York, 1942), p. 53.

Giovanni's early madrigals

Those of his madrigals which we can definitely assign to the Munich years show that Gabrieli was affected by his surroundings. The setting of Petrarch's sonnet 'Voi ch'ascoltate'—the choice of poet, one of Lasso's favourites, is significant—is a rather stiff piece in which the seams are not well concealed and the musical scale does not match that of the poem. Typically it is in the old-fashioned *misura di breve* and the rhythms are French, rather than springing from the Italian language (see Example 6).

The tone is serious, with a basic minor-key feeling, though, like Andrea, Giovanni tends to gravitate to the major whenever possible, and there is a noticeable harmonic rather than contrapuntal bias, with frequent cadential progressions. The real lack of modernity comes less in those technical devices than in the treatment of the poetic images. 'Sospiri' (sighs) is ignored almost completely, with nothing more than a rest before one repetition in a single part (a realistic effect advocated by Zarlino). 'Io piango' (I weep) is not given even a simple dissonance, and 'dolore'

(sorrow) only the most innocent of suspensions. All in all little depth of feeling seems to be inspired by one of Petrarch's most serious poems, and it is difficult to believe that this is more than a student's attempt at the madrigal style of the school of Lasso.

'Quand' io ero giovinetto'[23] is quite different, though probably Lasso's example was again strong; but the poem belongs more with his *chansons* and *villanelle*, or even with Andrea's commedia dell'arte sketches. The narrator is an old man, looking back on the days when he was one of the boys in the piazza. Now, alas, nobody wants to know him and he returns home a saddened man. Once more the *misura di breve* appears at the head of each part, but this time it is highly misleading. The note values denote swift movement, lively and much more natural rhythms. The actual sound of the piece is more up-to-date, too, with two sopranos giving an essential brightness to the disposition of the tutti, making for a pleasing fullness. The verbal imagery, being less emotional and more 'realistic', receives an adequate musical equivalent: triple time for the joys of youth; delicate suspensions for the 'chains from which his youth was free' (here simplicity is very appropriate, for strenuous dissonance would convey quite the wrong impression); more intense discords for the sadness of old age. His contrapuntal learning is shown in the *seconda parte*: the old man is represented by something like an inversion of the theme of the *prima parte*, the young man in recollection. The anthology contains, according to the title-page, music by the 'virtuosi' of the Bavarian court; and this certainly describes the young Giovanni Gabrieli here.

[23] ibid, p. 44.

Gabrieli's return to Venice

Gabrieli published no church music until he returned to Venice, and though there are one or two pieces included in later volumes which might be the work of his time in Munich, they seem mature enough, more like Andrea than Lasso, to be considered among the main corpus of his music for St. Mark's. They might, of course, belong to those shadowy years between his recorded presence in Bavaria in 1579 and in Venice in 1584. He probably left Munich in the early 1580s. Duke Albrecht, his patron, died in 1579 leaving considerable debts, to which his love of music had contributed. His successor, Duke Wilhelm, was by no means opposed to music, but he was one of the most enthusiastic supporters of the Counter-Reformation, who indeed introduced the Jesuits into Bavaria to combat any infiltration of Protestants. In place of the grand *intermezzi* of the court, with Lasso as one of the *comici*, there were now religious dramas acted by the boys of the chapel. Lasso was eventually affected by the new atmosphere; his last years were clouded by a religious melancholia, to the distress of his wife and friends. 1581 saw the beginnings of the reduction of the Munich *cappella* to half its former strength, and we may assume that Giovanni was one of those who departed.

It could be that he wandered further in southern Germany, in the service of one of his many patrons there, but the likeliest explanation for our lack of knowledge of those years is that he returned to Venice, where for a man of his talent and experience an organist's post cannot have been hard to come by. The archives of even the major churches of Venice have so far remained substantially unexplored, while of the lesser parish churches, which number over a hundred, we are even more ignorant. His return to the Republic is further indicated by the style of two of his pieces which were published in an anthology *De floridi virtuosi d'Italia il primo libro de madrigali a cinque voci* (1583).[24] Both show that Giovanni was being brought up to date perhaps by a renewed acquaintance with the latest work of his uncle. The verse is no longer either the severe Petrarch or the satire beloved of Lasso but the 'amorous baby-talk' (in Thurston Dart's happy phrase) which infects madrigalian verse at this time. Not much in the way of passion here, nor of the hard-packed concrete imagery which Marenzio was choosing for his new kind of madrigal and which the vogue for Tasso was shortly to encourage; which means that it was highly suitable for

[24] See A. Newcomb: 'The Three Anthologies for Laura Peverara', *Rivista Italiana di Musicologia* (1975).

musical (as opposed to musical-cum-literary) composers such as the Gabrielis.

'Donna leggiadra e bella' opens with a motif based on the favourite chanson rhythm:

but everything else is in the modern vein. The texture, with two soprano parts, is bright and the colours are always changing as lower and upper voices group and regroup; the rhythms of the various phrases are made exceedingly Italian by the use of frequent elisions whereby the placing of two syllables on a single note erodes the strictness of exact musical divisions of time; the occasional image is taken up, 'fuggon' with a quick semiquaver motif, 'sospiri' with the usual rest but with a naturalness that is very far from his Munich pieces. 'O ricco mio tesoro' is a trifle more staid, taking the *misura di breve* more seriously and repeating the opening section almost literally. Yet here again the easy adoption of the modern style is self-evident. The clarity of the harmony, the contrasts of the various groups of voices, the way a word such as 'morire' suggests a passing minor chord in an otherwise sunny major phrase, are all exactly the kind of trait we find in Andrea's later madrigals. These two madrigals by Giovanni have the same memorability of phrase and ease of singing, which typifies the Venetian madrigal at its best and which were to make it the model for Germans and Englishmen in the next few years.

Giovanni's appointment at St. Mark's

It surely passed through the minds of both uncle and nephew that the opportunity for Giovanni to succeed Andrea at St. Mark's might soon occur, for the latter must have been in his sixties at least, a ripe old age in a century where a man could not expect to live beyond his forties or fifties, although there was no official age of retirement in the *cappella*. In fact, they became colleagues for a short time. Merulo, the great organist, resigned after twenty-seven years in the Doge's service. This must have seemed surprising, and in a way was a portent, for he was tempted away to a court willing to pay more generously than was Venice, to become a musician at the Steccata Chapel at Parma. There had been no election of an organist at St. Mark's for nearly twenty years, and while the usual procedure was followed, the shrewd Andrea saw to it that his nephew had the opportunity to take Merulo's place on a day-to-day basis. The usual procedure took the best part of six weeks. First the Procurators agreed that the post should be filled by open competition (there were occasions when they invited a musician to the job). Then the notices were sent to be displayed not only at prominent places in Venice itself but also in the provinces, such as Verona, Vicenza, Padua, and Udine. Then came the day of the *prova*. It was a system which favoured those who were on the spot, since they would have the longest to prepare and would know exactly what would be expected. Moreover, it virtually cut out competition from abroad. Giovanni was in a particularly favourable position if he had been a success during the interregnum. The competition took place on 1 January 1585 (Venetian style 1584); Giovanni's rival was one Marc'Antonio Antonini, of whom nothing is known. The result was almost a foregone conclusion, for the Procurators proceeded to the tests at the end of a meeting largely concerned with more important matters, and one of them indeed wished to leave before they had arrived at this particular item on the agenda. Naturally they took the advice of their *maestro di cappella*, Zarlino.

> . . . it being necessary to elect a new organist, the Procurators of St. Mark's, meeting in the sacristy to make the said election, by the method of secret ballot, which when opened, showed a unanimous vote in favour of the said Zuane Gabrieli, who, on this decision being announced, came into the presence of the Illustrious *Signori*, thanking them deeply and promising to give every attention and care to his office . . .[25]

[25] A.S.V., Proc. de Supra, Registro 137, f. 27v. Original in Kenton, p. 44.

CHAPTER TWO

Service at St. Mark's

THE procedure for the competition which Gabrieli won on that January day is laid down in a civil service collection of notes and minutes, available for use each time an appointment had to be made. There was no question of an arbitrary decision as at other courts where a duke or prince could appoint whom he liked without any testing of a candidate or fair trial.[1] This civil service approach expressed the Venetian desire for stability. The temperamental musician who was not prepared to obey custom and the relevant authorities was frowned on at St. Mark's. Not long after Giovanni Gabrieli had entered its service a quarrel broke out between the *vice-maestro* of the *cappella*, Baldissare Donato, and the *maestro di coro*, the priest in charge of ceremonial, about whether the Vespers psalms should be sung on a certain day in a double-choir version (as the priest wanted), or in the simpler *falso bordone* chant (as the singers—perhaps out of laziness—would have preferred). The singers 'answered back the *maestro di coro* with many impertinent words, resulting in tumult and scandal'[2] and were promptly fined five ducats apiece—a swingeing penalty in the circumstances. Whether the singers had a case or not was less relevant than the establishment of discipline, and, in a way, this emphasis helps to explain the type of composer who found St. Mark's congenial. They were on the whole efficient yet conservative, fluent rather than enterprising.

In return, the Procurators offered security. An appointment was virtually made for life, and if age or illness produced a financial crisis, they would often give an indigent singer an advance of pay or even an outright present. They found it very difficult to imagine that any sensible musician would not see the advantages of their conditions of service. The very year

[1] See Monteverdi's letter of 13 March 1620, in which he says that his income in Venice is assured for life, unlike that at Mantua where it ceased with the Prince's death or displeasure. English translation in *The Monteverdi Companion* (London, 1968), ed. D. Arnold and N. Fortune, pp. 53–4.

[2] A.S.V., Proc. de Supra, Busta 91, Processo 208, f. 12–22, referring to an incident on 8 October 1589: '. . . rispondendo al maestro di coro molte parole impertinente con tumulto et scandolo . . .'

after Gabrieli's arrival they passed a minute to try to combat the loss of singers to other courts (at which presumably the pay was better). 'Since various salaried servants of our Procurators de Supra, both musicians and others, bound to the service of the church of St. Mark, have been encouraged by hopes of greater preferment [*utilità*] that they have been promised by other princes, to abandon the service of the said church to which they are bound, in spite of the security and the permanence of the contract that they must know they have enjoyed and for many years have received'[3] they decreed that such people would never be received back in the employ of the Procurators. This attitude had disadvantages; for it meant that the *cappella* inevitably had its passengers. But apparently the quality of the music making mattered less than its reliability; and if this seems no recipe for greatness, it is understandable enough if we examine their reasons for the employment of musicians on an increasing scale.

At first sight, St. Mark's might seem to have the obligations of any major church. Masses were sung daily; but it is difficult to find out whether this involved the choir and other musicians of the basilica very much. Monteverdi, *maestro di cappella* in the year after Gabrieli's death, claimed to be restoring an ancient custom when he instigated a daily fully sung mass, devoted to the music of Lasso, Palestrina, and other masters of the *stile antico*.[4] But there is comparatively little evidence for similar keenness in the previous century. Significantly there is no great corpus of masses by composers employed by St. Mark's. There are more by composers at other churches in the city, where a more modest choir would require music of this kind for feast days. While it is possible that successive *maestri* bought suitable music from the presses of Gardano, Scotto, and Vincenti, it seems more than likely that at St. Mark's the choir was only engaged on a few days each week. The organists indeed, may have attended less often. In 1564, when a reorganization of the *cappella* made necessary an overhaul of the musicians' regulations, a decree announced that 'Organists who are engaged to play the said organs for a salary of 100 ducats per annum each must attend personally to play, and each day they fail to come and perform their duties, both on festivals and on the vigils of such festivals, both at Mass and at Vespers, for every and each day that they shall not play, they shall be fined 2 ducats for each offence . . . and the fine shall be subtracted from their pay.'[5] The phrase of importance is here 'both on festivals and

[3] A.S.V. Proc. de Supra, Registro 137, entry under 9 December 1586, printed in R. Lenaerts, 'La Chapelle de St Marc à Venise sous A. Willaert', *Bulletin de l'Institut Historique belge de Rome* XIX (1938), p. 250.

[4] A.S.V. Proc. de Supra, Registro 141, f. 1 v, dated 6 April 1614.

[5] Printed in Lenaerts, op. cit.

the vigils of such festivals'. There is not a word about the daily observances of the basilica.

Ceremonies at St. Mark's

But there can be no doubt that the grand occasions of the church year were given their due. Indeed the rite used in St. Mark's was given to elaborations not allowed elsewhere. This rite was known variously as Gradese (its origins came from Grado, an ecclesiastical centre even before Venice assumed importance), Patriarchino, or Marcolino.[6] It had not, as is sometimes assumed, any real connection with the Eastern churches, but was a variant of Roman ceremonial, close enough for much Gregorian chant to be sung, and for music meant for other cathedrals to be performed. The main differences seem to be the result of local accretions which were not removed at times when the Roman Church tried to purify its liturgy.

The major festivals of the Church year were not greatly different, though there was a tendency for vestments to be more colourful, and the services to be more dramatic (as on Easter Day, when a regular liturgical drama, the so-called 'Quem queritis' trope was enacted). The greater differences came on certain feast days to which Venice apparently gave greater importance than was common elsewhere. There were about a score of these, on which Doge and Signory attended Mass or Vespers in state, usually with a solemn procession; and nearly every one, though given the name of a saint according to the Church calendar, had some political or historical significance for the Venetians. There were, naturally, the feasts of St. Mark, protector of the Republic. St. Isidore, martyr, was commemorated on 16 April—or could it be the fact that the Serenissima had been delivered from the plotting of its only disreputable Doge, Marino Faliero, on that day in 1355? Saints Vitus and Modestus hardly seem to merit a grand procession to the church of S. Vito followed by Mass in St. Mark's, until it is realized that in the year 1310 a conspiracy of Baiamonte Tiepolo to overthrow the Republic was discovered on 15 June.[7] The church of S. Marina was equally favoured on 17 July because Padua returned to the Venetian fold on that day in 1512,[8] and S. Giustina's day was awarded similar

[6] Full discussion of the differences between the rites of the Roman Church and those in use in St. Mark's is contained in G. Diclich, *Rito Veneto Antico* (Venice, 1823). For a summary which also contains some interesting detail of ceremonial see the chapter written by A. Pasini in *La Basilica di S. Marco in Venezia*, ed. C. Boito (Venice 1881–8; Eng. trans. 1889).

[7] Sansovino p. 502. [8] ibid, p. 503.

dignity in memory of the victory of Curzolari in the Turkish Wars in 1571.[9]

Ascension Day ceremonies

But the most gorgeous of days was that of the Ascension of Our Lord. In the days of the Grand Tour travellers went out of their way to be in Venice on this day. A description by an English gentleman tells us what happened in some detail.

I happened to be at *Venice* thrice, at the great *Sea Triumph*, or feast of the *Ascension*, which was performed thus. About our eight in the morneing, the *Senators* in their scarlat robes, meet at the *Doges Pallace*, and there taking him up, they walk with him processionaly unto the shoare, were [*sic*] the *Bucentoro* lyes waiting them; the *Popes Nuncio* being upon his right hand, and the *Patriarch of Venice*, on his left hand. Then ascending into the *Bucentoro*, by a hansome bridge throwne out to the shoare, the *Doge* takes his place, and the *Senators* sit round about the *Gallie* as they can, to the number of two, or three hundred. The *Senate* being placed, the *anchor* is weighed, and the *slaves* being warned by the *Capitains whistle* and the sound of trumpets, begin to strike all at once with their *oares*, and to make the *Bucentoro* march as gravely upon the water, as if she also went upon *cioppini*. Thus they steere for two miles upon the Laguna, while the musick plays, and sings *Epithalamiums* all the way long, and makes Neptune jealous to heare Hymen called upon in his dominions. Round about the Bucentoro flock a world of *Piottas* and *Gondolas*, richly covered overhead with somptuous *Canopies* of silks and rich stuffs, and rowed by *watermen* in rich liveryes, as well as the *Trumpeters*. Thus forrain *Embassadors*, divers *noblemen of the country*, and *strangers of condition* wait upon the *Doge's* gallie all the way long, both comeing and going. At last the *Doge* being arrived at the appointed place, throws a *Ring* into the *Sea*, without any other ceremony, than by saying '*Desponsamus te, Mare; in signum perpetui dominij: we espouse thee, ò Sea, in testimony of our perpetual dominion over thee:*' and so returnes to the *Church of S. Nicolas in Lio* (an *Iland* hard by) where he assists at high *Masse* with the *Senate*. This done, he returns home againe in the same state; and invites those that accompanyed him in his *Gally*, to dinner in his pallace.[10]

By the time Richard Lassels attended this occasion in the second half of the seventeenth century, it must have seemed somewhat out of touch with reality, the more especially to an Englishman. Venice was no longer the Queen of the Seas. A century earlier it was a very different matter. Venice was still a great power. She had lasted substantially intact longer than any

[9] ibid, p. 514. [10] R. Lassels, *The Voyage of Italy* (Paris, 1670), p. 412.

other state. Even the Papacy had at times to evacuate Rome, indeed had had at one time a titular rival. Venice, in contrast, had a constitution which seemed almost invulnerable, with virtually no upheavals over the succession, or disintegrating rivalries between families of rulers. In the festive occasions already mentioned the hero is not the saint whose day is being celebrated, still less any individual Venetian: it is Venice itself. The role of the Doge as guardian rather than ruler was emphasized at his election; he was taken to the place where the body of his predecessor had recently been lying in the church of SS. Giovanni e Paolo, and told that his body would lie there before long. The feasts of Venice thus reiterated many times a year a lesson which can scarcely have been lost on the populace at large; and care was taken to involve them in such a way that they too felt some stake in their Most Serene Republic.

Venetian processions

For the remarkable feature of the ceremonial life of Venice is the way various elements of the community were brought together. If the ceremonies took place in church, it was not the religious who took the principal place, but the laity. As Berenson has pointed out,[11] the Doge himself, though the symbol of the state, had on these occasions a semi-clerical role. The order of procession for each occasion sounds more like that of a quasi-secular coronation than of a purely religious occasion.

Elegantly dressed as at the coronation, the body which goes with the Doge as its head consists of many ranks of personages and the civil authorities. And they come in a fixed order as follows, with in the beginning the 8 standards which were presented by the Pope. Next follow the silver trumpets, held up in front on the shoulders of several youths. And two by two the heralds, called in the Latin *Praecones*; these clothed always in turquoise blue which is peculiar to their costume, with long cloaks, wearing on their heads the red *berretta* with a small gold medallion bearing on one side the impression of St. Mark.

Behind them come the players with trombones, clad in red, playing harmoniously all the way. These are followed by the Squires of the Doge, two by two, dressed in black velvet. Then six canons wearing priest's vestments, because it has always been our custom to accompany the temporal with the religious. Near them walk the Stewards of the Doge, then the Secretaries of the College, the Senate and the Council of Ten; and then come those two chancellors of the Doge called *inferiori* and *ducali* according to the greatness of their service to the Republic. And behind these comes the Grand Chancellor; and all

[11] B. Berenson, *The Italian Painters of the Renaissance* (1952 edition), p. 10.

these are dressed in purple with closed sleeves with the exception of the Grand Chancellor who is dressed as Senator. Immediately behind is the chaplain of the Prince [=Doge] with the bearer of the Ducal Cap who carries a candle, with the Doge's page. Next come the ceremonial Chair and Cushion, the one to the left, the other to the right with the umbrella. And nearby comes the Doge in person, with the ambassadors of foreign princes around him. And in triumph, he always wears the ermine cape. After these come the Councillors and Procurators of St. Mark's . . . two by two, the judges, the Council of Ten, the army council and the other senators and civil authorities, hand in hand after the law, all clad in crimson silk with the sleeves *alla Ducale* giving a magnificence and splendour which could never be surpassed.

'It has always been our custom to accompany the religious with the temporal':[12] the phrase sums up the whole Venetian attitude. Priests, Doge, Signory, and the incipient bourgeoisie of the confraternities, were all brought together to worship God—and the everlasting City Republic. It must have been as difficult not to take pride in being Venetian as it was once for an Englishman not to take pride in being a member of an Empire on which the sun never set.

Nor was such pomp merely an opiate of the people; it was an essential part of the process of impressing foreigners. The Venetians entertained the new King of France, with the music of Andrea Gabrieli figuring large in

[12] Sansovino, pp. 492–3.

'Conciosia che in quel tempo, il corpo, che accompagna il Principe come capo, consiste di diverse qualità di persone & di Magistrati. Et allora vanno per ordine, & nel principio, gli otto Stendardi che si hebbero dal Pontefice. Seguitano poi le trombe d'argento, sostenute dinanzi dalle spalle di alcuni fanciulli. Et à due à due i Comandatori, chiamati da Latini Praecones. Et questi vestiti sempre di Turchino, da quelli del Proprio in fuori, con habito lungo, portano in capo la berretta rossa, con una picciola medaglia d'oro dall'uno de lati con l'impronta di San Marco.

Dietro a costoro vengono i pifferi co'tromboni, vestiti di rosso, sonando tuttavia harmonicamente. A questi seguono gli Scudieri del Doge a due a due, vestiti di velluto nero. Indi sei Canonici co Piviali in dosso, perche fu sempre costume de nostri d'accōpagnar le cose temporali con la religione. Appresso costoro caminano i Castaldi del Doge, & poi i Secret. del Collegio, quei di Pregadi, & quelli del Consiglio de Dieci, & dopò vengono i due Cancellieri del Doge che si chiamano Inferiori, & Ducali, rispetto al Grande che è per servitio della Repub. Et dietro a questi segue il Cancellier Grande, & tutti costoro sono vestiti di pavonazzo, ma con le maniche chiuse, fuori che il Gran Cancelliero, che veste Senatoriamente. Et immediate è il Cappellano del Principe col zago, che porta il Cero, & col Ballottino del Doge. Poi vengono la Sedia, & il Guanciale, l'uno della destra & l'altro dalla sinistra, con l'Ombrella. Et poco presso compare la persona del Doge attorniato da gli Oratori de Principi esterni. Et in trionfo porta sempre il Bavero d'Armellini. Dopò costoro vengono i Consiglieri, & Procuratori di San Marco . . . à due à due, gli Avogadori, i Capi de Dieci, i Savi Grandi, i Savi della guerra, detti di terra ferma, & gli altri Senatori, & Magistrati di mano in mano secondo le leggi, tutti vestiti di seta di color cremisino con le maniche alla Ducale con tanta magnificenza & grandezza che nulla più.'

the celebrations; Andrea's music was probably called upon again in the fêting of some Japanese noblemen in 1585.[13] The whole of Italy seems to have been determined to show these oriental noblemen occidental hospitality at its most lavish. The Japanese arrived in Venice from Rome by way of Ferrara, and the Signory were not to be outdone by Pope or Estensi. Sansovino, or rather the reviser of his guide to Venice, tells us of the events of those well filled days in no less than ten closely packed pages.[14] Processions, ceremonial rides on the lagoon, displays of holy relics, a visit to the glass factory at Murano, all the entertainments which Venetians have offered to their guests over the ages were on the itinerary. And our chronicler does not neglect to mention music, for on 29 June 'The church of St. Mark was . . . so full of people that one could not move a step, and a new platform was built for the singers, adjoining which there was a portable organ; in addition to the two famous [organs] of the church; and the other instruments made the most excellent music, in which the best singers and players that can be found in this region took part. The Most Illustrious Signory came, without His Serene Highness, however, who because of old age remained resting in his Palace; then came the Japanese princes and thus the Mass began, sung by four choirs with all the solemnity that was possible'.[15]

Musical style appropriate to these ceremonies

This mention of the Mass for four choirs is of especial interest, since in Andrea Gabrieli's *Concerti* of 1587, Giovanni included just such a work, not surprisingly if it was composed for this grand and recent occasion on which he too must have been employed as organist, if not as composer. We may guess at the effect the mass must have had on the assembly of Venetian dignitaries and oriental princes; and again we can see the considerations which the Procurators had in mind when appointing Giovanni to their service. It was fluency, grandeur of tone, and reliability which they were after; subtlety, if it came, would be a bonus.

[13] E. Harich-Schneider, *A History of Japanese Music* (London, 1973), pp. 463–4.

[14] Sansovino, pp. 457–466.

[15] Sansovino, p. 457: 'La Chiesa di S. Marco era parimente da ogni canto ripiena di gente in modo, che non si poteva mover il passo, & vi si era fatto un palco novo per li cantori, & aggiunto un' organo portatile; accioche insieme con li due notabili di Chiesa, & gli altri stromenti musicali facesse più celebre la armonia, dove intervennero i primi Cantori, & Sonatori, che si ritrovino in queste parti. Venne la Illustrissima signoria senza però il serenissimo Prencipe, che dalla vecchiezza impedito se ne stava riposatamente nel suo Palazzo; vennevi anco i Signori Giapponesi, & così si diede principio alla Messa, cantata in quattro chori con quella solennità, che si ricerca, & che ben può V. S. imaginare.'

When Giovanni Gabrieli was appointed in 1585 they had need of a composer possessed of these qualities, for the *cappella* was an ageing one. Zarlino, their director of music, was now quite old. He had been in their service for some forty years and in charge of the establishment for twenty. He had never been much of a composer, but he was undoubtedly one of the most learned men of his time, a theologian as well as a musician, and such men commanded—and still command—respect in Italy. Looking through the registers of the Procurators, one senses that his period of office had been efficient and peaceful. The *cappella* had gradually become larger, some notable musicians had been recruited, yet there had been no great innovations and no disturbance. Zarlino also managed to solve the administrative problem that arose out of the increase in personnel. The *maestro di cappella* at St. Mark's, like that at most other major churches, had the responsibility of teaching the boys and young priests. In 1574 a formal arrangement for a *vice-maestro* to undertake those duties was passed by the Procurators[16] and in 1580 the details were tidied up to allow this *vice-maestro* adequate leave from his other work (he was also a singer in the choir) to take charge of this aspect of St. Mark's music completely.[17] Zarlino was obviously very much a Procurators' man, a sound administrator as well as an adornment to their service.

Giovanni's immediate predecessors at St. Mark's—Merulo

While Zarlino had two composers of the rank of Merulo and Andrea Gabrieli for his organists, he can have had few worries. Merulo, if not as fluent as his colleague, was a capable composer, and one of considerable versatility. His early publications were principally of organ music, but two books of motets printed in his middle years at St. Mark's show that he shouldered part of the burden of providing ceremonial music, and some of his works for *cori spezzati* which came out only after he had left Venice almost certainly belong to his time there. Though he never achieved the popularity of Andrea as a madrigalist, he was a substantial contributor to anthologies, and he was one of the composers of music for the *Tragedia* of Cornelio Frangipani, given for the visit of Henri III.[18] There may have been some feeling of rivalry between the two. Claudio Merulo made an impassioned (and successful) plea for parity when Andrea managed to gain

[16] A.S.V., Proc. de Supra, Registro 133, f. 20v.

[17] A.S.V. Proc. de Supra, Registro 135, f. 10v.

[18] A. Solerti, 'Le Rappresentazioni Musicali di Venezia, 1571–1605', *Rivista Musicale Italiana*, IX (1902), p. 503.

a rent-free house in addition to his salary in 1571 (the pay of each was raised by twenty ducats, and they were charged a rent of twenty ducats for the house).[19] Yet their musical characters are more complementary than similar. In keyboard music Merulo is the creator of the serious, virtuosic, even romantic toccata, Andrea the composer of delicious, tuneful, and unproblematic canzonas. Andrea's madrigals tend to be frivolous, and are at their best when lighthearted; Merulo is more intense and more in touch with the trend towards the homophonic, declaimed madrigal style of the 1580s. Perhaps the most vivid contrast is seen in the volumes of motets they published in the 1570s. Both Andrea's *Motetti a 4 voci* of 1576 and Merulo's *Motetti a 6 voci* of 1578 set out to provide works for most of the major feasts of the year. Yet what a difference there is between them! Andrea's pieces are small in scale, never very intense, and extremely singable. Short, memorable phrases and rhythmic clarity remind us of the madrigals, and the charming alleluja of 'Filiae Jerusalem' might well celebrate the success of Damon with Phyllis:

Merulo's works are much grander. This is not just a matter of using larger forces, which naturally results in greater sonority. The melody is more ecclesiastical, built in longer segments and with more solid rhythms. If Andrea's music might well have been bought by his successor as *maestro di*

[19] A. S. V., Proc. de Supra, Registro 132, f. 33; copy in Busta 91, [processo 207], f. 29.

cappella of the parish church of S. Geremia, Merulo's is the work of one who has never known anything less than a *cappella regia*:

Merulo's departure must have come as a blow to Zarlino, for they had been colleagues virtually all their lives. The reason may have been, as suggested earlier, the money offered by Parma; it may have been also a natural desire to return to his native soil. And perhaps he was made restless by the feeling that changes were imminent, for the month after young Gabrieli had arrived, Zarlino was inspired to appoint some new singers.

Several singers having departed from this life in recent months, notably Prè Puliazzo de Petris and Prè Luca Gotterio, and having need of basses and other voices, Their Excellencies the Procurators having listened to many who sang in the *cappella* [elected] Fra Agostin of the Minorite Order to sing bass at forty ducats per annum and Fra Hieronimo of the Carmini as a contralto at forty ducats per annum.[20]

[20] A.S.V., Proc. de Supra, Registro 137, f. 36v; entry for 25 February 1585 (Venetian style 1584): 'Essendo mancati di questa vita alquanti cantori alli mesi passati cioè Pre Puliazo

Other appointments followed in the next few months, and these changes brought some new talent into the *cappella*.

Bellavere

The next year, 1586, Andrea Gabrieli died. The usual competition followed, for which all the candidates were probably Venetian. The winner, Vincenzo Bellavere, was probably rather older than Giovanni Gabrieli, and he certainly did not lack experience, since he published low *giustiniane*, with his predecessor at St. Mark's, as long ago as 1571, but otherwise we know little about his career. He was quite popular with the madrigal anthologists, and his Venetian roots are confirmed by his contribution to *Corona di Dodici Sonetti di Gio. Battista Zuccarini* (1586), a collection in honour of that remarkable lady, Bianca Capello, married, after some vicissitudes, to the Grand Duke of Tuscany. The piece, not unlike that of Andrea Gabrieli in the same collection, ends with a splendid triple-time

de petris e pre Luca Gotterio et facendo bisogno de bassi et altre voce havendo uditi li clariss^mi^ SS. Pro^ri^ molti cħ cantarono in cappella . . . [they elect]
Fra Agostin de fra menori p̧ cantar basso 40d
Fra Hieronimo de i carmini p̧ contralto 40d.'

section which might well have come out of some Ascension Day motet to be performed on the Bucintoro. His second book of madrigals, published in 1575, contains several grand pieces in a similar vein. The opening piece indeed is equally suitable for open-air performance, this time, perhaps, at a wedding (see Example 3).

Very little of Bellavere's church music survives: just a setting of the Magnificat and a motet published in 1615, along with much other Venetian music, in the *Reliquiae Sacrorum Concentuum* of Hassler. The motet is another excellent piece, composed with an ear for the potentialities of the St. Mark's ensemble, the double choir and the depth of the *trombone doppio* being used most imaginatively. The refrain indeed is very like those of the young Gabrieli of this same period (see Example 4).

Bellavere died after being organist at St. Mark's only a few months. The Procurators thus had three vacancies in as many years. They were faced with a problem: the Venetian system of open competition tended to favour those on the spot, who would see the notices in Venice or the cities of the mainland. How were they to attract capable organists from elsewhere? In the event, the post was not immediately advertised, and one suspects that some persuasive letter-writing took place. The next mention of an appointment in the minute book records not a competition, but a decidedly irregular procedure.

> ... [the Procurators] having received a plea from Zambatista Bell'haver on behalf of Signor Francesco Sugana of Treviso, in support of Signor Iseppo Guammi of Lucca, dated 1 June 1588, upon which Their Serene Highnesses have already determined that information concerning the quality and efficiency of the said Guammi should be obtained; which [information] having been examined by Their Highnesses in accordance with the said minute, and having heard of the honourable and efficient conduct and quality of the said Guammi and considering the interests and benefits of the said Church [of St. Mark], have appointed the same Giosef Guammi as organist of the said Church with a salary of 120 ducats per annum.[21]

Giuseppe Guami

The very tortuousness of the minute indicates that the Procurators were going outside their usual habits; and a supporting paper on the files strengthens the impression of some wire-pulling. Was it coincidence, we may wonder, that Guami, an old Munich friend of Giovanni Gabrieli, happened at this time to give a private recital at the house of a nobleman,

[21] Quoted in Caffi, I, p. 190.

Signor Pier Antonio Diedo, and that the audience included most of the musicians of St. Mark's? And that Francesco Sugana was an old acquaintance of his and Zarlino's? And that Zarlino knew him to be 'eccellente compositore et sonator suavissimo'? Added to which we may wonder what Bellavere had to do with it at all. Was there some little arrangement, perhaps, to help a widow or family? Guami was a man of considerable experience, and since he was at the moment only in the service of a

Genoese nobleman, who surely could not compare with the Signory of Venice, it might be that he would stay awhile at St. Mark's. Alas, he was a man who stayed nowhere very long, and he left for his native Lucca three years later, in 1591. In the meantime, Guami provided the experience that the Procurators were continually looking for; and if there is little evidence of his involvement in the composition of motets for the grand occasions, the instrumental ensemble of the basilica probably benefited from his stay; and so did Giovanni Gabrieli, who learnt from the virtuosity of his older colleague.

Donato

Even so, his appointment shows the predilection of the Procurators for maturity rather than youth; and so does the most disappointing replacement of Zarlino in 1590. Zarlino had been ailing for some time, and his *vice-maestro* Baldassare Donato had been taking on more and more of the burden. In 1588 the Procurators are still speaking of his 'long and fruitful service',[22] and in 1590 we are given a glimpse of his busy life, singing in St. Mark's, teaching the priests at the Seminary and the boys at the song school.[23] Nevertheless, this latter minute shows that all is not well, for 'the boys of St. Mark's are not bearing that fruit which is desired', and there is a warning that Donato must attend to his duties each day, or he will be fined.

To find Donato appointed as Zarlino's successor is something of a surprise. In 1590, he can scarcely have been less than sixty, for his best work as a composer was contained in publications of the 1550s, where he appears as one of the bright young men writing *canzoni alla napolitana* and similar frivolities. In this field he had been an immense success, his songs having a pleasing melodiousness and straightforwardness of harmony (he is the true predecessor of Gastoldi, whose *balletti* of the 1580s did much to oust a decaying modal system and establish a modern attitude to tonality). Since then fashions in music had changed, and by the last decade of the century he was scarcely a figure of importance. Moreover, he had had his troubles with the Procurators. He seems to have been a kind of shop steward for the singers of St. Mark's. We have seen him once at loggerheads with authority; and when he had taken charge of the *cappella piccola* in the long-past days of Cipriano de Rore, he had not turned out a success from the point of view of discipline. Maybe the conditions of his appointment

[22] A.S.V., Proc. de Supra, Registro 137, f. 148v.
[23] A.S.V., Proc. de Supra, Registro 137, f. 203v.

reflect doubts, for the noticeable emphasis on dignity was not usually necessary in such circumstances.

In the days recently passed, the Reverend Giuseppe Zarlino, *maestro di cappella* in St. Mark's, has departed this life, and since it is the desire of The Most Excellent Signors Procurators to appoint a *maestro* who is not just experienced and well practised in music, but one who has been in charge of other musicians, [who] is also prudent and modest in fulfilling his office; and since Their Most Illustrious Signory has been well satisfied with the efficient, long, and assiduous service of M. Baldessare Donati [sic], they have elected him as *maestro* of the aforementioned *cappella* for five years, he having till now had the position of *vice-maestro* of the same; and at the end of these five years he may be confirmed [as *maestro*] by the usual ballot, and he shall have the salary and emoluments of his predecessor, that is to say, two hundred ducats per annum and the same house. He shall be obliged to teach *canto figurato*, counterpoint and *canto fermo* to the clerics of the Seminario, and he may not go to sing in places outside the *cappella* of the Church of St. Mark, and he must uphold completely the dignity of this most honourable office, and will be held personally responsible to the officers [of the church] for such service of the church, and in all things appertaining to good order.[24]

The choir at St. Mark's in the 1590s

The Procurators actually confirmed his appointment six years later and, in fact, he may well have given them reasonable service as an adminstrator. A document probably belonging to his early years as *maestro* suggests that St. Mark's had only a small choir—the result of Zarlino's lack of energy?

In most reverend obedience to the orders of Your Most Illustrious Signory to the mode and form that seems convenient

I say

[24] A.S.V., Proc. de Supra, Registro 138, entry dated 9 March 1590: 'Essendo mancato di questa vita li giorni passati il R^{do} Isepo Zerlino m^{to} di capella di S. Marco, et desiderando li Ecc^{mi} Sig^{ri} Proc^{ri} provedere d'uno maestro che sia non solam^{te} molto [?] et prattico della musica ma come quello che haver esser superiori alli altri musici sia anco prudente et modesto in far il suo officio havendo sue Sig^{ri} Ill^{mi} havuto optima satissfatt^{e} della sufficiente longa et assidua servitù di M. Bald^{ra} donati lo hanno elletto per maestro della sop^{to} capella per anni cinque il qual ha fin hora servito per Vice m^{ro} di quella potendo esser confirmato in capo delli detti anni cinque a boss. et batt^{y}, e cosi successivamente con il salario e emolum^{to} secondo che haver il q. suo pcessor delli duc^{ti} dusento all'anno et la casa solita; Il quale sia obligato insegnar canto figurato, contrapunto, et canto fermo all clerici del seminario. Non possendo esso maestro andar a cantar in loco al^{o} furi [=fuori] della detta Capella della Chiesa di S. Marco, et consegnar in tutto la dignità di cosi honorevol grado dovendosi attrovar semp personal^{te} alli lori deputati per il servitio della chiesa acciò le cose passino con quel buon ordine che si dee . . .'

That in the Capella of St. Mark's we find the undermentioned singers

Sopranos
Antonio Spagnol: a beautiful and good voice, but not too secure.
Guglielmo Francese: a secure and clear singer, but not a very delicate voice.

Contraltos
Padre Zuanne Chiozotto: a most efficient singer, and where he lacks the delicacy of voice, makes up for it by good singing.
Fra Hieronimo of the Carmini: not much of a voice.
Fra Bernardo of the Frari: not too bad a voice, but he hasn't ever learned how to use it.
Battista of S. Pantalon: a big voice and secure.

Tenors
Giovanni Antonio Fiammingo: he has always had a good voice and is a good singer, but old age is now causing its decline.
Fra Agostin Fasuol: good voice and a good singer.
Paolo Romano: not a bad voice and sings honestly enough.

Basses
Fra Fabritio of the Frari: good voice.
Fra Giacomo Antonio of the Crocieri: good voice.
Fra Sigismondo of SS Giovanni e Paolo: honest voice.
Fra Agostin of the Frari: honest voice lacking grace.[25]

[25] A.S.V., Proc. de Supra, Busta 91, Processo 208, f. 56:
'Per obedire riverẽtemente all'ordine impostomi da V.S. Illmo nel modo, et forma, che la è molto bene con sapevole.

Dico

Che nella Capella di S. Marco si ritrovano li infra^ti cantori.

Soprani

Antonio Spagnol: Bella, et buona voce, ma nõ troppo sicure
Guielmo francese: Sicuro et franco cãtor, ma nõ cosi delicata voce

Contralti

P Zuanne Chiozotto: Sufficientiss^o cantor, e dove manca la delicatezza della voce, supplise co'l bel cantar
Fra Hier^mo di Carmini: non e di molta voce
Fra Bernardo di Frari: nõ e la sua voce di cattivo metale ma nõ l'ha saputo mai accomodar
Batt^a da S. Pantalõ: ha gran voce, et honestamente sicuro

Tenori

Zuanne Ant. Fiamẽgo: e stato sempre di buona voce, un bel cantante, me p̲ la vechiezza comincia declinar
F̄ Agustin fasuol: buona voce, et buon cantor
Paulo Roman non ha cattivo metal di voce, et canta honestamente

Bassi

F̲ Fabritio di Frari: buona voce

This hardly sounds the choir of a great monarch's chapel. In the next years Donato kept adding singers: a letter even went out to the ambassadors abroad to look out for singers.[26] As poacher turned gamekeeper, Donato managed to keep the *cappella* free from the trouble which could happen under more distinguished masters. Yet he failed to continue the tradition of the Venetian school of composers. He published his own church music in 1599, a volume of motets of no great quality, written in a style which, if pleasing enough, seems to belong to a different world from that of Merulo or Andrea Gabrieli—as indeed it may well have done; for some of these motets probably date from the 1560s at the latest:

The Procurators' caution in their minute appointing Donato makes one wonder whether they were not expecting his time to be an interregnum. If this was so, they miscalculated, for Donato lived on to 1603, when he must have been well over seventy. But in a sense, the Procurators were right, for there were new young men appearing on their horizon who were to form a new Venetian school, worthy successors of the generation who disappeared in the 1580s.

F Giacomo antº di Crocieri: buona voce
F Sigismondo da S. Zanepolo: honesta voce
F Agostin di Frari: honesta voce mācanta polite.'

[26] Ā.S.V., Proc. de Supra, Registro 193 bis f. 4.

Bassano

One was the cornettist, Giovanni Bassano. His playing had attracted such attention in 1576 that he was added to the establishment of St. Mark's. He was probably quite young at this time (he lived until 1617)[27] and his modest salary of 25 ducats was obviously intended to recompense him only for the festival days of the basilica. But in 1582 his salary was increased by 5 ducats 'in respect of his devoted service to His Highness',[28] and when Donato was eventually relieved of his teaching duties in 1596 Bassano was given the job at the Seminary.[29] This showed a greater respect for his abilities on the part of the Procurators than might at first appear, since instrumentalists were considered both musically and socially inferior to the singers, and a senior member of the *cappella* would normally have been chosen. His manual on ornamentation[30] was clearly of great importance to instrumentalists and influenced Giovanni Gabrieli's instrumental style, while his *Fantasie a tre*[31] are charming pieces probably meant for his pupils. In the mid-1580s, when these works were published, Bassano seemed likely to develop into a composer of merit, for some of his canzonets were thought good enough by Thomas Morley to include in an anthology of Italian music. But for some reason, though his two books of motets produced near the turn of the century show him active in composing for the Venetian festivals, and more than one item is as attractive as works by his more famous contemporaries, this side of his gifts was never developed.

Giovanni Croce

The best known of these young men was in fact not Gabrieli, but one of the singers praised by Donato in his report to the Procurators: Zuanne Chiozotto, known to us as Giovanni Croce. He was a local boy from the same town as Zarlino, Chioggia, the fishing port across the lagoon. Zarlino found him singing in the cathedral there, and it is not quite clear when he came to Venice itself. His first book of madrigals, published in 1586 (Venetian style 1585), has a graceful dedication to Battista Morosini, one of the Procurators, in which Croce praises his *maestro* and fellow

[27] His successor as *Capo de' Concerti* was appointed 12 December; A.S.V., Proc. de Supra, Registro 141.
[28] A.S.V., Proc. de Supra, Registro 135, f. 61v.
[29] A.S.V., Proc. de Supra, Registro 138, entry 16 March.
[30] *Ricercate, Passaggi et Cadentie* (Venice, 1585).
[31] Modern edition ed. E. Kiwi, *Seven Trios* (Kassel and Basle, 1933).

Chiozotto (as the inhabitants of Chioggia are called) as 'the glorious Monument of Music, my most honoured and not fully appreciated master'. The title page tells us that Croce is a singer in St. Mark's, though the date of his appointment does not appear in the registers. His dedication seems to have reaped some reward, but it is noticeable that his annual salary, at 36 ducats, was low—and remained so even when raised to 50 in 1590. The fact that he was a priest may have had something to do with this, and since he was a few years later employed in some capacity by the church of S. Maria Formosa, his stipend from St. Mark's was not his sole source of income.[32]

Their family relationship tends to make us associate the two Gabrielis with one another, yet if a true successor to Andrea can be found, it is Croce. Both possessed the same splendid fluency: Croce's madrigal books came from the presses almost annually, and scarcely an anthology was complete without his contribution. Emotionally also there is a link. Croce belonged to a generation influenced by Marenzio, the generation to whom the union of words and music was relatively straightforward, the image of the verse being reflected in musical symbols without distorting the musical shape, the melodiousness, or the harmonic structure. He is the musician of perpetual May, gay and carefree, with scarcely a cloud to cast a shadow. No wonder he became the favourite of Thomas Morley who, even when his scholarly instincts were offended, could still write '. . . yea, Croce himself hath let five [consecutive] fifths together slip in one of his songs, and in many of them you shall find two (which with him is no fault as it should seem by his use of them), . . .[33] If imitation is the sincerest form of flattery, Morley flattered him indeed, for Morley is very much his English counterpart.[34] As a composer of light music, Croce was still more popular —and deservedly so. Canzonets are his métier, his melodiousness and his very lack of ambition in the expression of deep emotion being precisely what these smaller genres require. His humorous pieces are the best successors to Andrea Gabrieli's *giustiniane*, if broader in humour and with the characters less well defined; and his songs of fishermen come as well observed from a Chioggian as do the etchings of foreigners in his *Triaca musicale* (Venice 1595) from an inhabitant of a great trading city.

This fluency in writing secular music is matched by a similar approach

[32] Croce's exact position at this church has never been firmly established but according to A. Ragazzi, *Serie Cronologica de' Piovani della Chiesa di S. Maria Formosa di Venezia* (Biblioteca Marciana Misc. 132.21), he was not the parish priest.

[33] *A Plain and Easy Introduction to Practical Music* (modern edition ed. A. Harman, London, 1952), p. 254.

[34] D. Arnold, 'Croce and the English Madrigal', *Music and Letters* (1954), pp. 309–19.

to church music. Not for him a retrospective volume or two, summing up a lifetime's work in cathedral or *cappella regia.* Instead there is a considerable involvement in church music for all kind of occasions and places. His most popular publication was a book of motets for four voices designed for any parish church with just four singers. The uppermost lines are modest in their tessitura, rarely exceeding the range of an alto, the melodic tags, if somewhat more dignified than those of his madrigals, easy to remember and to read. Again there is a lack of passion. Many of the texts are sombre enough, and for the post-Marenzio composer might suggest various kinds of musical excitement. Yet even 'In die tribulationis', which had stimulated Giuseppe Guami to chromatic waywardness, is treated in a totally impersonal way, the only sign of emotion to be found in the dark colouring which comes from lack of soprano tone, a result of practical rather than expressive considerations:

'Alleluja' refrains seem more to Croce's taste, and a comparison of that which ends 'Virtute magna' with that from 'Filiae Jerusalem' (see Example 1, p. 26) reveals the family relationship at once:

It is much the same with the vast quantity of Croce's other church music which, though less popular than these motets, still found a ready market (it was nearly always reprinted) in the next twenty years. Lamentations for Holy Week are set with the same straightforward attitude. Magnificats full of interesting changes of texture and extremely singable melody are exciting without ever revealing the emotional contrasts inherent in the poem. Yet, as in his madrigals, Croce seems, in a sense, very modern. His harmony is built on a few very simple progressions. It modulates to nearly related keys and at reasonably regular intervals of time. If this music is more deliberately popular than Palestrina—as befits a successful madrigalist—it has also Palestrina's sense of balance. It is as if the extremism of the 1590s exemplified by Giaches de Wert and the later Marenzio had never existed.

In this Croce is very Venetian, so Venetian in fact that it is not difficult to see why he was eventually to lead the *cappella* at St. Mark's. If Zarlino was an administrator after the Procurators' hearts, Croce was their composer. Fluent and versatile, he more than any produced the music for festival after festival. Moreover, he was very much a layman's composer. His widespread publication throughout Europe—in England, Germany, the Low Countries—shows that his music was not written for a clique or even for connoisseurs. This is in some ways the key to an understanding of this new Venetian school. At a time when the future of music seemed to be in the hands of the 'academic' composers of the North Italian courts at Ferrara, Mantua, and Florence, the Venetian school went its own way.

The new order of composers were even more insular Venetians than before; the older men had at least a few colleagues such as Merulo who came from elsewhere, but the moderns are almost entirely indigenous—the foreigners such as Guami staying only briefly.

And yet if the younger Gabrieli and his generation were both conservative and apparently oblivious of the world outside, this did not harm their gifts. The battle does not always go to the progressives, still less the avant-garde. Internationalism can breed a lack of character, while individual circumstances can produce individualism in artistic endeavour. That is what we find in the younger Venetians.

CHAPTER THREE

The Organist

WHEN Giovanni Gabrieli thanked the Procurators for appointing him organist of St. Mark's, it was no empty gesture, nor just the result of relief at obtaining a permanent and reasonably well paid post. It was indeed an honour, such as few organists could aspire to. Their profession was not, in Italy at least, of great distinction. If we look through the records of cathedrals and other great churches,[1] we find that the organist was rarely the senior musician, both player of his instrument and *magister chori*, as we would expect today. This latter role, better paid and more respected, usually belonged to a promoted singer who had also mastered the art of composition. The skills of the keyboard player, which the necessities of continuo-playing made so desirable for the creative artist in the later baroque, were by no means a *sine qua non* at this epoch. Title pages of books of masses and motets reveal relatively few organists among their composers. The two skills were separate. This may account for the fact that, like most performers, their fame was transient. What is less easy to understand is why so little music for them was published throughout the sixteenth century. Admittedly there is always the consideration which affects publishers to this day: a choir needs several copies of a motet, an organist only one of a canzona. Thus manuscript copies were probably made by individual players, who in any case were capable of improvising pieces for their own needs. Even so organists were numerous, and some must have been looking for distinguished music to play.

But in Venice, and most especially in St. Mark's, organists were valued. There had been an organist in the basilica for more than a century before the *maestro di cappella*'s post had been established and as ever, tradition decreed the continuance of this post, at a decent salary, even when the vogue for the Netherlands composers had suggested surrender to the ways of other courts. Many of them had been men of distinction, and in

[1] As for example that at Udine; see G. Vale, 'La Cappella Musicale del Duomo di Udine dal sec. XIII al XIX', *Note d'Archivio*, VII (1930), p. 87, ff.

Giovanni's earliest years Venice had some extraordinarily good organists. Annibale Padovano, Andrea Gabrieli, and Claudio Merulo all left their mark as both players and composers. The last of these has some claim to be the father of a school which stretches well into the seventeenth century through the person of Girolamo Frescobaldi. Though eventually Merulo was tempted back to his native city, his pupils form a cohesive group which must be thought of as essentially Venetian. No wonder that the Venetians were proud of their organists. One guide-book to Venice goes out of its way to list them with words of high praise, not forgetting to mention 'Zuanne Gabrieli [who] was one of the most celebrated, the melody of whose playing was such that the virtuosi from the cities of Italy ran to hear him and to praise him'.[2]

The organs of St. Mark's

The instruments they played on have long since perished, though the larger of the organs at St. Mark's was in use well into the eighteenth century. Indeed, when Gabrieli played it, it was already a century old, dating from the late fifteenth century. Sansovino[3] describes its external appearance and the paintings on its shutters, and tells us that it had seven bellows and seven visible ranks of pipes. What he can not convey is its tone quality, though it is noticeable that Banchieri, a professional organist not likely to judge an instrument only on its external appearance, described those of St. Mark's as 'most perfect'.[4]

They were not large instruments. Mattheson, describing the larger in 1739,[5] marvels at the specification, which he gives as follows:

Sub-Principal Bass	24′
Principal	16′
Octava	8′
Decimanona	3′ (a 'quint')
Quintadecima	3′ (a 'superoctava')
Vicesimasecunda	2′ (an 'octave biscomposita')
Vicesimasesta	1½′ (a 'quintlein')
Vicesimanona	1′ (an 'octavater composita')
Flauto	8′

[2] N. Doglioni, *Le cose notabili et meravigliose della Città di Venetia* (1662 edition), p. 203.

[3] Sansovino, 1604 edition, pp. 28–31, quoted in S. Dalla Libera, *L'Arte degli organi a Venezia* (Venice, 1962).

[4] Dalla Libera, op. cit., p. 37. For another enthusiastic account of his playing see T. Antonicek, *Italienische Musikerlebnisse Ferdinands II. 1598* p. 97.

[5] *Das Vollkommene Capellmeister* (Hamburg, 1739); facsimile reprint, ed. M. Riemann (Kassel and Basle, 1954), p. 466.

'And that is all, and there is no other manual; except that the pedal is coupled fast (befestiget), and gives the same notes', says Mattheson, remarking also that this is quite normal throughout the whole of 'Welschland', or Italy. In spite of some rebuilding in the seventeenth century[6], this was essentially the instrument known to Gabrieli; this is made reasonably certain by the specifications in other organs in Venetian *terra firma* throughout the sixteenth century. The Chiesa Maggiore at Udine, commissioning a new organ from Maestro Bernardino of Vicenza in 1516, wanted one identical to that of St. Mark's, complete 'cum contrabassi' and nine stops.[7] A year earlier another builder offered an organ for the church of S. Maria in Vado 'of the size of that of St. Mark's in Venice' saying that 'this instrument will have nine stops separate each from one another. The first stop will be the contrabasso'; and then he proceeds to repeat the specification virtually as given by Mattheson.[8] Again this was a big instrument for the time and place, as specifications for other Venetian organs reveal. The famous maker, Vincenzo Colombo, who kept the St. Mark's organs in good order, when planning one for the church of S. Maria del Giglio wanted to build one of the size he had already installed in the churches of S. Gerolamo (a large monastic church, whose music was very good, as various descriptions testify),[9] S. Bartolomeo, S. Angelo, and S. Alvise. These had just seven stops: the specification proved too expensive for the authorities of S. Maria del Giglio so he made them a slightly smaller organ, of the dimensions of one at the monastery of the Gesuati.[10] But if St. Mark's organ was large by comparison with those in the parish churches and monasteries, it would have seemed much less impressive to many Northerners. The smaller of the organs in the Oude Kerk in Amsterdam where Sweelinck played, which dates from the mid-sixteenth century, was considerably more ample; the larger one would have dwarfed it.[11] There is no reason to suppose that these limitations were felt as such by the Venetian composers. Their style perfectly fits the nature of their instrument, as can be testified by anyone who has heard their music played on such an organ.[12] It is music which demands clarity of tone but no

[6] E. Selfridge-Field, *Venetian Instrumental Music* (Oxford, 1975), p. 9.
[7] G. Vale 'Contribuito alla storia dell'organo in Friuli', *Note d'Archivio* (1927), p. 80.
[8] Dalla Libera, op. cit., p. 38.
[9] *The Life and Letters of Sir Henry Wotton*, ed. Logan Pearsall Smith (Oxford 1907, reprinted 1966), I, p. 59.
[10] Dalla Libera, op. cit., p. 60.
[11] A. Curtis, *Sweelinck's Keyboard Music* (Leiden, 1969), p. 163.
[12] As in the excellent recording (CBS 72810) of various Venetian pieces by E. Power Biggs, on the organ of S. Carlo in Brescia, an instrument made by Antegnati.

sudden changes of tone colour, which relies on melodic line and counterpoint, and eschews the sectionalization of variation form beloved of Northern composers. It is noticeable also that the echo effect invented by the Venetians in ensemble music, motets and madrigals, is exploited by Sweelinck in his fantasias, but finds no place in Venetian keyboard works.

The technique of organ playing

The nature of the instruments in St. Mark's thus to some extent dictated Gabrieli's keyboard style. We gain further knowledge of how he might have played from a treatise by another member of the Venetian school, Girolamo Diruta, organist of Chioggia Cathedral in the 1590s. Diruta was a disciple, perhaps even a personal pupil, of Merulo, as Giovanni Gabrieli may have been. His book *Il Transilvano* first appeared, published by Vincenti, in 1593, and was popular enough to receive three further impressions, the last in 1625. He added a second volume of the same title in 1609. The two together offered some severely practical and very useful hints to both the beginner and the more ambitious student. Diruta was concerned with both the technique of the player and high general musicianship. In technique he looked for two distinct virtues: a real legato touch, and adequate manual dexterity. He was highly critical of harpsichordists who did not achieve real smoothness when they came to play the organ, for by 'raising the hand and beating the keys, they lose half the sound (armonia)'.[13] Only if they learned to arch the hand and fingers (la mano si verrà incoppare é le dita ad inarcare) would they acquire the right technique. The arm must guide the hand, which must itself move lightly and gently as though one were 'caressing a boy' (accarezzare un fanciullo). Thus could the organist achieve a skill equivalent to that of such players as Bassano and Girolamo Dalla Casa on the cornett or violin. Moreover, the organist must study the art of fingering, for there were strong fingers (the second or index finger and the fourth) and weak ones (the thumb, third and little fingers) and 'good and bad notes' which from his examples seems to refer to which are accentuated rather than their actual position on the keyboard. The aim must be to play 'good' notes with the stronger fingers, using the other fingers to cope with playing on the shorter 'black' keys. Although his examples are not always very clear in their instructions, there is no doubt that they imply an individual view of phrasing, for his principles do not always lead to the easiest method. The modern performer

[13] G. Diruta, *Il Transilvano* (Venice, 1593); modern facsimile reprint, ed. L. Cervelli (Bologna, 1969), I, p. 5v.

would choose a very different fingering for his examples of *note variate*; but we can see that Diruta requires another effect:[14]

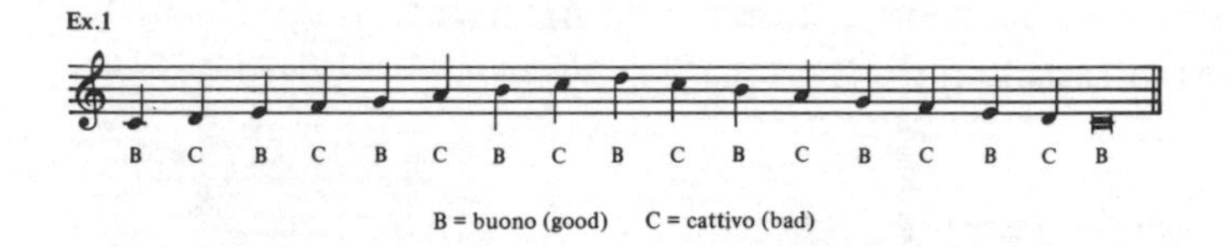

We expect this type of detailed instruction from modern primers. At the end of the sixteenth century it was still a quite new approach, and it explains the reputation of the Venetian organists who were practising in this way. They were virtuoso organists, concerned to impress their listeners. If the total *oeuvre* of Giovanni Gabrieli is rather small in comparison with that of some of his contemporaries such as Palestrina or Lasso, Croce or Marenzio, we must remember this part of his glory too, which has gone the way of all flesh, as has this side of the genius of Liszt or Busoni.

Score reading in the 16th century

Having taught the organist how to play rapid scales and figurations, Diruta then goes on to teach him both how to arrange his basic repertoire to suit his instrument and how to embellish this material. This basic repertoire was largely vocal music, most often French chansons for four voices, easily arranged by taking two voice parts in each hand. The chanson is frequently just the stuff for transcription. Its range is not too great to be accommodated under ten fingers, its counterpoint is not too complex. Yet it has strong rhythms and a general tunefulness, and does not lose too much of its meaning when divorced from its verse. Madrigals, because of their close relationship with the poetry in both rhythm and meaning, were by comparison ineffective.

Competence in score reading was tested at the *prova* in St. Mark's. Another requirement, improvisation over a *cantus firmus*, is Diruta's main concern in the second volume of *Il Transilvano*. Although this appeared only in the last years of Gabrieli's life, there can be little doubt that Diruta's teaching was common practice during the period of his career. It follows fairly closely the principles laid down by Zarlino, as Diruta ack-knowledges.[15] The pupil was made to construct the usual freely flowing

[14] ibid, p. 7. My fingering is derived from Diruta's instructions. [15] op. cit., II, p. 15.

parts over the long notes of the given melody, at first *a due voci*, then for three, and so on. He was given model cadences, then taught the tricks of invertible counterpoint, of imitation and canon. By the end, the organist would be a learned composer, as were the men whose ricercars Diruta included as examples: Gabrieli, Fattorini, Banchieri, and Diruta himself. These ricercars indeed fit the requirements of the St. Mark's competition extraordinarily well, for they take common figures of the sort easily developed from a book of plainchant and work them out briefly but with art. They are not very interesting music, but they show the same sort of solid craftsmanship that has been expected by colleges of organists from that day to this.

The art of ornamentation used by organists

The general musicianship indicated by Diruta's instructions is conservative. It is, however, very professional in its approach; and in this it echoes Gabrieli's musicianship, for he also is divorced from many of the latest fashions of his era, yet is the most professional of composers. Indeed, Diruta's teaching could seem very old-fashioned and academic if it were not for its other major topic, how to apply ornaments to these ensemble pieces. Venice was, as we shall see later, a centre of virtuosic embellishment; though, interestingly enough, it was not the organists who wrote the treatises on this topic, but the players of other instruments such as the cornett and violin. Diruta's methods, clearly derived from Merulo and Andrea Gabrieli, show that the organists preferred to apply ornaments in an orderly way, rather than merely display their dexterity. He is careful to show how scales used as decorative features must not confuse the harmony (a keyboard player having the whole score in front of him instead of the single line of a cornettist or singer can obviously be expected to show more awareness of such details). Fast-moving ornaments are in practice confined to trills, mordents, and turn-like figures (see Example 2).

All these conveniently fit under the fingers, as do their various extensions (culled largely from Merulo's music) especially if, as Diruta indicates, the thumb is brought into play when necessary. In this, the organists show that they have progressed beyond the standpoint of those colleagues whose embellishments are meant for 'all kinds of instruments', to quote Bassano's title page, regardless of their technical requirements. Diruta's is a down-to-earth attitude, with not a hint of the philosophy, or pseudo-philosophy, so common in Renaissance treatises. It seems to embody the very spirit of the Venetian organists, who are neither literary men nor particularly

interested in the wider issues that so intrigued their colleagues and rivals in Florence, Ferrara, or Mantua.

Genres of organ music

It is remarkable how much of Gabrieli's keyboard writing follows the pattern of Diruta's recommendations. Nonetheless, *Il Transilvano* concentrates on details of performance and musicianship. The genres within which Gabrieli composed he had evidently learned directly from his uncle Andrea and from Merulo. They can be divided into three main categories. One might be called 'improvisatory', for the toccata and *intonazione* are essentially pieces in which formal pattern is of little importance and the display of finger dexterity and the roving idea predominate. Another is the transcription and the imitation of transcriptions, usually called 'canzona'. The third is the 'learned' piece, entitled 'ricercar' or even 'fuga'. Not that the nomenclature is particularly consistent. A 'ricercar' can sometimes be a 'canzona' and vice versa; the improvisatory elements of the toccata occasionally turn up in both the other genres; while the 'toccata' is not always devoid of traits associated with the ricercar. If we look at the music rather than the titles, however, the basic classification will be clear.

Improvisation was perhaps more common in sixteenth-century music than playing from the written notes. The greater part of teaching was done by means of extempore invention, and every musician must have been well acquainted with it. However much modern scholars may study the instruction books and the models which teachers gave their pupils, we shall never know how well experienced musicians could practise the art. But the toccata of the Venetian organists is a sort of 'frozen improvisation', though even here the spontaneity of ideas must have been modified as the page was filled. Of Giovanni Gabrieli's teachers, Merulo had the most to teach him about such skills. He has the flair to seize on a short motif, be it a scale or other ornamental figure, and work out its implications in a memorable way. It may be a tiny *gruppetto* or trill which inspires him, but by incorporating it in different ways into the melodic pattern it no longer seems a trivial ornament, rather a gateway to the next section or paragraph. Merulo also had ideas on harmony. Since on an organ one cannot distinguish the part-writing clearly, especially when ornaments take attention from the contrapuntal nature of the music, it is possible to resolve dissonances irregularly, by the assumed (in practice unreal) crossing of parts. This led to a new kind of freedom, later to be exploited by Monteverdi in ensemble music, which gives a distinctly emotional, indeed 'romantic' tinge.

Andrea Gabrieli's toccatas

It will be easily understood why neither Gabrieli followed exactly in Merulo's path. Both undoubtedly learned much from him, but largely from his technique. The type of figuration which he developed is characteristic of their organ music also, as is the basic idea of the toccata as a piece which ranges from ricercar-like counterpoint to florid fingerwork. Spiritually, on the other hand, Merulo was not of their kind. Andrea's compositions in particular contain virtually no 'romantic' elements. He is at times a wit, usually an extrovert, and always a craftsman. The spontaneous, the unpredictable are rare in his music. In his madrigals the sentimental is equally uncommon, even though by the last decade of his life sentimentality was becoming the fashion (a fashion wich Merulo found attractive). For this reason, the elder Gabrieli is least happy in improvisatory genres. His few surviving toccatas are frankly dull. The passage work sprawls. Instead of working in short, pregnant *gruppetti*, mordents, or trills, he allows his *passaggi* to range for bars on end over two or more octaves without any attempt at giving rhythmic variety or unusual harmonic twists. Sequences or chords, and scalewise *passaggi*, are almost totally predictable; while the dissonances resemble those of Merulo (sevenths especially abound), their application is hardly ever so interesting. The music acquires personality, and the ornaments integrate into the piece, only when a contrapuntal episode works out a familiar theme, such as the chanson-esque middle section of the Toccata of the sixth tone[16] (see Example 3).

[16] Modern edition, ed. P. Pidoux, *Intonationen* (Kassel and Basle, 1967), p. 12.

Ex.3

Andrea's *intonazioni*, or improvisatory preludes lack even this substance; they have little distinction or distinctiveness. Andrea's genius lies elsewhere.

Giovanni Gabrieli's toccatas

Giovanni Gabrieli edited virtually all his uncle's keyboard music when it was published in the 1590s; and his organ works suggest that his own interests were not dissimilar, at least as far as these inspirational forms were concerned. As in Andrea's *oeuvre*, there are a set of preludes on all the useful 'tones'; there are also about a dozen toccatas—more than Andrea had written (or at least published), appreciably fewer than Merulo published. None of these is among his best work. The *intonazioni* have the virtue of brevity—great brevity, in fact, since they last only half a dozen bars each, about half the length of Andrea's comparable pieces. To the extent that the proportion of counterpoint to passage work is accordingly higher, they are marginally more interesting—indeed the opening of the 'Intonazione del 10⁰ Tono' is quite imaginative (see Example 4).

Beyond this there is little to be said.

The toccatas are of greater substance. This is not a matter of length. Gabrieli's toccatas are nearly all very much shorter than those of Merulo and often than his uncle's. Admittedly some have as little positive character

as Andrea's (the fifth Toccata in the Giordano collection at Turin[17] is a good example of faceless keyboard virtuosity); yet others of no greater duration have Merulo's sense of scale. Giovanni's talents here differ from Merulo's. He cannot invent a memorable fragment which will develop in numerous ways. The rhythms of his embellishments are almost as predictable as Andrea's, and the harmonies are often strings of perfect cadence-like progressions which any beginner could put together. But some of the detail seems to owe a debt to Merulo. Passing notes arriving from or departing to unexpected destinations add flavour to otherwise bland harmony:

There are ambiguities of tonality, where major becomes temporarily minor or the reverse. The eighth 'Giordano' Toccata, for example, opens with a simple reiteration of a G minor chord, intensified a little by an astringent passing note:

By the time the passage work has gathered strength, Gabrieli is ready to repeat this progression, but with important changes:

[17] Modern edition, ed. S. Dalla Libera, Vol. II (Milan, 1958), p. 62.

Ex.7

This is a real stroke of improvisatory genius, simple enough to come easily to mind, yet shaping the music so that a relationship between varying parts of the piece is established.

Most of the toccatas have merits of this sort, but still lack that distinction which makes Merulo outstanding in this genre. There are two exceptions, and both appear in a single source which was probably compiled after Gabrieli's death.[18] These seem more mature works, especially the second, which has ornamental figures of the kind extensively used in Gabrieli's later ensemble music. Whether this is correct or not, they are certainly better organized than those toccatas which can definitely be ascribed to the sixteenth century. The first of them is a bold piece in the seventh tone, a mode which Diruta states to be 'allegra e soave' and for which he suggests a bright registration of 'Ottava, Quintadecima e Vigesimaseconda'.[19] Its opening motif bounces gaily, with dotted rhythms worked out in imitative patterns between a notational four-voiced texture, until brilliant scales take over. These scales become organized into definite patterns, emphasizing outlines of chords, or suggesting mock counterpoint by transferring a motif from, say, a tenor to a bass register. There is something of Merulo's

Ex.8

[18] ibid, pp. 68 and 71. [19] Op. cit., IV, p. 22.

waywardness, too—here and there the semiquavers suddenly give way to slower motion, and the figuration in one hand can contradict the harmony of chords held by the other hand (see Example 8).

The Toccata in D, or first tone (for which Diruta suggests the use of Principale, with the Flauto or the Quintadecima) is even finer. Merulo's manner of using ornaments as short, pregnant figures here serves Gabrieli very well; and when the more usual *passaggi* occur later in the piece, they are broken up in an organized way, assisted by the use of the occasional rest to draw attention to tags passed from 'voice' to 'voice':

Ex.9

The harmony has many short cuts reminiscent of Monteverdi, and the irregularly resolved passing notes produce some pungent effects. Again there is a willingness to juxtapose new ideas; and towards the end, there is a most unusual moment when both hands play passage work, of which the harmonic aspect is daring:

Ex.10

The canzona

In spite of the excitements of these late toccatas, Giovanni's true genius as a composer of organ music is better seen in his canzonas. His uncle's canzonas contain some of the most attractive of sixteenth-century keyboard music, and show that virtuosity was not the only element of importance in keyboard composition. Andrea was one of the earliest composers in this genre. In the 1530s and 1540s, when he presumably learned his trade, the repertoire of organists and lutenists consisted mainly of arrangements of Parisian chansons. At Munich he found Lasso one of the greatest composers of French polyphonic songs. No wonder that he himself arranged chansons and imitated them in pieces for the keyboard. For Merulo, as for other Italian musicians of his generation, the chanson seems to have been less popular than the madrigal. Not surprisingly, the two are somewhat different in their approach to the genre, and since the young Giovanni must have known the canzonas of both well, it is instructive to see what these differences are.

Merulo's canzonas

Merulo found the chanson arrangement and the similarly conceived canzona were interesting mainly in so far as they could be freely embellished. We have only to look at the two versions of his canzona 'La Zambeccara' printed side by side by Ernest Ferand[20] to see how florid his keyboard style is. Though it is true that the four strands of the ensemble piece are preserved quite strictly in the organ arrangement, by the time the opening section is complete it is difficult for the ear (as opposed to the eye) to disentangle them. This is not just a question of the addition of notes; the

[20] E. T. Ferand, *Improvisation in Nine Centuries of Western Music* (Cologne, 1961).

tempo has necessarily changed from a clear-cut allegro measured in minims to something less speedy, in which the measure is at times the crotchet. Then, since the decoration is mainly applied to the uppermost and lowest strands, the inner parts tend to disappear. Thus Merulo's canzonas remain virtuoso pieces. The listener to 'Petit Jacquet'[21] might indeed think at the opening that he was to hear a toccata rather than a chanson arrangement, for its first bars develop Merulo's flourish rather than the song theme (see Example 11).

'La Gratiosa'[22] is still more toccata-like, some of its ornaments being rhythmically as complex as those in Merulo's improvisatory pieces.

Andrea Gabrieli's canzonas

By contrast Andrea Gabrieli's feeling for the genre is evident. Though there is no shortage of embellishment, there is also tunefulness in his canzonas. Crispness of rhythm, too, one of the most important characteristics of the chanson, is almost always preserved in his transcriptions. Nothing could be plainer than the opening of his version of Crequillon's 'Frais et Gailliard'[23] with its steady crotchet motion—unless it is the beginning of 'Pour ung plaisir'.[24] In both these pieces, *fioritura* eventually occurs, but it is kept in check, so that the essential nature of the chanson is always preserved. The closing section of the former, for example, has contrasts between the upper and lower voices in the well-worn tradition of early sixteenth-century polyphony. Merulo might have seen the rests in each

[21] Modern edition ed. P. Pidoux (Kassel and Basle, 1941), p. 35. [22] ibid, p. 12.
[23] Modern edition, ed. P. Pidoux, *Canzonen und Ricercari Ariosi* (Kassel and Basle, 1961), p. 9.
[24] ibid, p. 27.

part as blank spaces to be filled with ornamentation. Andrea, on the contrary, not only preserves the actual notes of the vocal original on his first announcement of the phrase: when it is repeated, his embellishments do no more than decorate. They do not fundamentally change its character (see Example 12).

This approach informs even the less brisk chanson transcriptions, such as his reworking of Lasso's 'Suzanne un jour'.[25] In spite of a very free use of *passaggi*, the outline of the song is in no way obscure, for the ornaments are never rhythmically complex, nor do they alter the basic harmonies. Often indeed they underline the structure by emphasizing important cadences with *gruppetti*, or by repeating small figures which decorate the repeated notes so prominent in many chansons.

When Andrea writes pieces in this style not based on vocal originals, he follows these principles just as closely. The *Ricercari ariosi*, especially, are very like canzonas. They belie the first word of their nomenclature by emphasizing the second: it is difficult to see any learnedness in them, while their airiness is very much in evidence. Catchy rhythms, engaging melody, diatonic harmonies are still more prominent than virtuoso elements. The first of these pieces uses a chanson motif that is extremely memorable, especially after it has been repeated several times in thoroughly worked out four-part counterpoint; it is made still more so when the section is repeated *in toto*—not to say by further development in the final section, based on an obvious variant. Even the fourth 'Ricercar arioso', a slightly less tuneful work, with a more filigree melodic style, still makes its climaxes not by decoration, as Merulo constantly does, but by strength of rhythm:

Such works are the epitome of Andrea Gabrieli's art: extrovert, pleasing, technically assured. They are the work of a man brought up in the tradition of writing counterpoint, even in a medium which does not necessarily demand or indeed encourage it. It is a consolidatory, not an innovative art, as Merulo's could claim to be. Andrea is musician first, virtuoso organist second.

[25] ibid, p. 6.

Giovanni Gabrieli's canzonas

Most of this also applies to Giovanni's music of this kind, though there are some notable differences between uncle and nephew. The first of these is obvious even from the titles of their organ pieces. Giovanni never once transcribes a French chanson. Only one secular work, the madrigal 'Labbra amorose e care', can be found in a keyboard version (the Gruber epithalamion in the Turin manuscript is taken from its religious contrafactum). The other transcriptions are all taken from his own sacred music. Evidently then Giovanni did not transcribe other men's works; and looking at the keyboard versions of his motets, we may wonder whether even these are his own arrangements or the work of the men who compiled the anthologies in which they are included. As far as the published volumes of the German organists Woltz and Schmid are concerned, we may be fairly sure that the transcriptions are theirs since Schmid says as much in his preface to the reader, which tells us that he has added his own embellishments and generally made the music suitable for the organist.[26] Those in the Turin manuscripts are near enough in style to make a similar assumption. While there is little doubt of their ascription to Giovanni Gabrieli, even when the vocal originals are lost ('Angelicos cives' especially has all the marks of the master), the decorations are not very close to his style. Those which transform 'Exaudi Domine' from the first book of *Sacrae Symphoniae*, for example, do not have that crispness which belongs to Gabrieli's other embellished music, nor indeed do they look Venetian after the manner of Dalla Casa or Bassano. Though the arrangement of 'Ego dixi', published first in the *Concerti* of 1587, is ingenious, the contrapuntal parts are so obscured by the ornamentation that it is difficult to believe that a sensitive composer would thus destroy the shape of his own music.

Where the figuration is the kind which Gabrieli uses in his instrumental ensemble pieces, it is still unsatisfactory in one way or another. Take 'O Doctor Optime', an organ version of the motet 'O Jesu Christe' from the *Reliquiae Sacrorum Concentuum*. In this, the decorative elements are largely confined to the cadences, and it does not lose a great deal by being separated from its text, since it has the strong musical shape of a rondo and the harmony is continuously interesting. Even so, it does not sound like organ music. The same applies to 'Domine Deus meus', from the same collection, which again has rondo elements and some fascinating chromati-

[26] B. Schmid, *Tabulatur Buch von Allerhand ausserlesenen* (Strasburg, 1607); modern facsimile edition, ed. G. Vecchi (Bologna, 1969).

cisms. The fact is that Gabrieli's motets are not suitable for organ transcription. They depend on the colours which a vocal and instrumental ensemble can provide, and which a keyboard instrument cannot. For the six or eight parts of the motets have to be substantially reduced to fit under the hands, in a way that is unnecessary in the four-voiced French chanson. There is no question of two parts per hand in this grand music. Nor is there that rhythmic life for which Andrea usually chose chansons for transcription. The long notes of the contrapuntal figures invite elaboration. In no time at all, the very shape of the music is changed, as it is not in 'Suzanne un jour' or 'Frais et Gailliard' when Andrea has added his *fioritura*. While the organ arrangements of the Turin manuscript remain an admirable way of discovering some of the qualities of Giovanni's motets, they are substitutes, as piano duets of nineteenth-century symphonies are substitutes, not authentic works in their own right.

This is totally untrue of the few real canzonas for keyboard which can be ascribed with certainty to the younger Gabrieli. True, they could all be written in partbooks for ensemble, and indeed there is usually a similarity to some of the canzonas in the 1597 *Sacrae Symphoniae*. Also, they follow the instructions of Diruta for keyboard reductions more exactly indeed than some of those by Merulo and Andrea, and the frequent decorative passages never obscure the basic four-part texture. But they represented a distinct advance away from the vocal arrangement towards an independence of idiom. The reason is that Giovanni has realized the necessity for using abstract formal patterns to replace the continuity provided by words in madrigal or chanson. The frequent recapitulation of opening material in the chanson was no doubt the starting point for the process; but he goes far beyond this, and all five canzonas of the Turin manuscript show some formal novelty.

The first is a good example. It opens, as does many a *canzona francese*, with a jaunty tune in evenly measured crotchets, decorated only at the end of the section, where a right-hand flourish marks off the structural division before the whole is repeated. The middle section takes a motif which is a kind of diminution of the canzona motto, and works it out at some length. It is interesting to see how the head of this motif, three quavers forming a strongly memorable unit, infiltrates the passage work so that ordinary scales and decorative figurations seem to have thematic significance. But the most obvious evidence of musical logic comes at the climax: here the canzona motto is stated three times with variations of register, ornamentation, and texture before its final notes lead into some tense harmonies:

Nor is the patterning process at an end. The canzona closes with a repetition of the middle section's theme, which occurs for the last time just before a flurry of scales leads to the plagal cadence.

The second canzona of the set is even more sophisticated in form. It bears some resemblance to that on the ninth tone in the first book of *Sacrae Symphoniae* (the fourth of the instrumental pieces in that collection). It is a rondo, the principal theme occurring five times and being separated by four episodes in triple metre. Again *fioritura* is used structurally, being applied only to the main theme's ultimate cadence on each repetition. This fairly ordinary pattern is developed with originality. The triple-time sections have subtle relationships of theme and harmony. The first is nine bars long, the second ten, the last two eleven; the first two rearrange the same theme, the last one presents it in inversion, the third is more independent (though there is a link here between subsidiary motifs of the third and fourth). Moreover the transitions from the triples back to the main theme show more imagination than is customary in similar circumstances in vocal music. The first link is as short as could be, a mere flourish in the bass; the second is longer and even develops this in its inverted form; so does the fourth, though it is no exact repetition. In other words, the element of unity is mixed with that of surprise, right through to the coda which uses the transitional material, suggesting, however faintly, that the rondo structure may not be complete.

It is this grasp of compositional technique which makes these canzonas worthy to stand by those for ensemble—which is as great a compliment as could be paid to them. Emotionally they have breadth and meaning. If the first and last of the 'Turin' canzonas are extrovert in the fashion of Andrea, the second and fourth are more typically pensive. That the second is in the ninth tone should make it 'allegra, soave e sonor' in Diruta's words; but in fact the dichotomy of major and minor is more strongly stressed than in other pieces in the mode, and we are never certain whether the piece is gay or serious. The fact that its first two chords are empty fifths allows the ambiguity that the classical writers of sonatas so much enjoyed, and the major of the third chord is compromised by the prominence of the minor sixth. Thus a bitter-sweet atmosphere which we shall find in much of Giovanni's larger-scale music is built up.

The fourth canzona is less ambiguous and full of the sadness and melancholy which Diruta ascribed to the second tone in which it is written (the registration should be for 'the principal alone with the tremulant'). Its main theme is close to that of the 'Canzon Primi Toni'[27] from the first book of *Sacrae Symphoniae*, and like that noble piece it seems to frustrate the expectation of cheerfulness by eschewing the major chord. Its opening bars virtually all consist of minor intervals, and when in the third bar a cadence on to the dominant of G appears inevitable, the entry of the bass averts this expectation (see Example 15).

The mood is maintained throughout. It is emphasized later by a string of suspensions, and no amount of dynamic rhythms (which are plentiful) or decoration in the closing stages can relieve it.

Historically speaking, it is surprising to find that the largest part of Giovanni's organ music is cast in the 'learned' form of the ricercar (or 'fuga' or 'fantasia' to give the alternative titles), for the popularity of the ricercar was, by the later years of the sixteenth century, distinctly on the wane compared with the canzona. This decline was no doubt due to the simple fact that serious quasi-religious contrapuntal music could scarcely hope to compete with the tuneful lightheartedness of secular songs. Two things may account for Giovanni's apparent preference against the odds.

[27] Number 7 of the collection.

The first is that he was a teacher, and like other teachers, he appreciated a genre which emphasized skill. Then, he was Andrea's pupil; and it was Andrea more than anyone who had helped to transform ricercars from 'grave chamber music' to something more in line with modern taste.

Andrea Gabrieli's ricercars

There are two main lessons which Andrea's ricercars taught his nephew. The first was the weight which may be attached to a single motif. In the four dozen bars of Andrea's 'Ricercar del Primo Tono',[28] to take an extreme example, only half a dozen cannot be directly connected with the major theme of the opening, and there is no subsidiary material of any great importance. The much longer 'Ricercar del Quinto Tono'[29] is not quite so austere. Its more than a hundred bars work out two tags; none-theless the second is related to the first, in rhythm and (by inversion) in general shape. Even a much freer piece, such as that on the third tone,[30] may treat the initial theme in one shape or another until half way through the work.

The second significant difference between Andrea's conception of the canzona and ricercar styles lies in the quality of the counterpoint. When there is no apparent attempt to work out all the implications of a single

[28] Modern edition, ed. P. Pidoux, *Ricercari II* (Kassel and Basle, 1970), p. 1.
[29] ibid, p. 10. [30] ibid, p. 26.

theme, as in these fugal pieces, there is still a greater elaboration of material. Thus Andrea makes a distinction between the two genres, even when he is using exactly the same themes. The chanson 'Martin Menoit' of Jannequin can become both. As a *canzona francese* it is a transcription with some rather simple *fioritura*. As a ricercar, it is almost a choral prelude, for the first 'line' of the chanson has been elaborated in a polyphonic web, not unlike those made from hymn tunes by Bach a century and a half later (see Example 16).

Learnedness can be dull. It is to Andrea's credit that in many of his ricercars it is not. Comparing some of his most extended works with the teaching pieces by the lesser men included in Diruta's *Il Transilvano*, we can see why Giovanni should take to the genre so readily.

Giovanni Gabrieli's ricercars

Of the sixteen surviving pieces in this genre by Giovanni Gabrieli, one or two look like exercises rather than accomplished music. The 'Fantasia del sesto tono' works out conventional points in a fairly mechanical way.[31] The 'Ricercar dell'ottavo tono' has more weight, but its exploration of the tag with which Arcadelt has brought his famous madrigal 'Il dolce e bianco cigno' to a close, almost a quarter of a century before Gabrieli was born, is too long and lacks variety. The sixth ricercar in the Giordano collection[32] is also too long, although it is a very scholarly piece after the manner of Andrea. But even here, interest is not entirely lacking, for in the coda a sudden burst of finger work disguises the fact that the theme is being brought back in a massive augmented version in the bass, contrasting with a diminished version which has gone immediately before.

All the remaining ricercars are satisfying pieces, and some are magnificent. Part of their secret is that they wear their learning lightly. Often, like Andrea's, they seem similar to canzonas, and all of them have subject matter which is in tune with the taste of their day. There are usually

31 This work may well not be by Giovanni Gabrieli. See W. Apel, *The History of Keyboard Music* (Bloomington, 1972), p. 411.

32 Modern edition, ed. S. Dalla Libera, *Composizioni per organo*, 3 vols (Milan, 1957–59). All subsequent references are to this edition.

several elements to the theme which are worked out at length. Firstly there is a reference to the canzona motto (a), to give some strength of rhythm. Then comes a keyboard motif (b) which lifts the music above mere academic counterpoint. Finally, there may be some method of securing the tonality of the subject although not in those themes which are already firmly tonal:

There is often some repetition within the theme, perhaps the sequential development of a short ornamental figure which will stick in the memory:

From such material, Giovanni constructs lengthy edifices which naturally take their emotional character from the balance of elements within the subject. The 'Ricercare del Settimo e Ottavo Tono'[33] just quoted is thus quite gay, since both the clarity of the major and the jaunty ornament of the last bar of the theme conspire to produce a brightness of sound. The obvious tonal version of the answer of the subject helps to preserve this, the more especially since when it occurs at the first display of all four 'voices', it acts as the bass in a splendidly full perfect cadence. The rhyth-

33 I, p. 41.

mic motif also suggests excitement when combined with a variant which fills in the points of comparative repose (if the quavers can be so described) with dashing semiquavers:

With the exception of the final two bars, which are a flourish over a plagal cadence, the whole of this ricercar is derived—and closely derived—from the theme. If this implies learnedness, a more detailed examination reveals less the kind of contrapuntal skill that we might expect than the capacity to provide varied accompaniment. This accompaniment is sometimes very thin: the ornamental figure is accorded a scale accompanying it in thirds when it first appears, and there is little of the cut-and-thrust of rhythm which the fugal composers of the late Baroque would apply. The outline of the ornamental figure is filled in, so to speak, thus producing a more ample sound without altering the harmony. Near the end, indeed, some cross rhythm does simulate counterpoint:

yet this is again a method of making the sound fuller, rather than of genuine polyphonic development.

So it is with the even more attractive 'Fuga del 9º Tono',[34] where again very little of the piece does not derive from the opening theme, or the counter-subject with which it continues. Subject and counter-subject remain largely intact, rarely receiving any substantial alteration, and since they appear within a very narrow range of tonalities—A or D predominating—it might seem that the ear would soon tire of their sprightliness, and demand some variety, some gravity, perhaps, caused by longer notes or dissonance. But Gabrieli's resource seems endless. The sketch of the opening statement:

[34] I, p. 52.

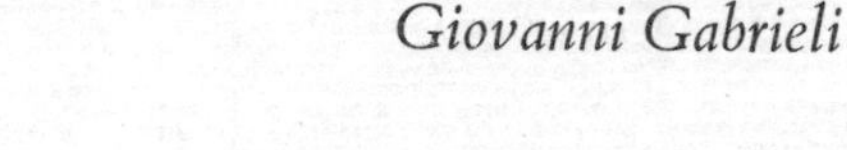

Ex.21

becomes a euphonious *faux bourdon* a couple of bars later:

Ex.22

Then there is a grand harmonization; a splendidly pompous display over a dominant pedal; a couple of statements which imply foreign keys (C and F—quickly to be frustrated as the basic A is re-established); and a final extension of the *faux bourdon* to make the most of the false relations implied from the start:

Ex.23

This technique of making the most of a theme without subjecting it to any sort of imitation is not the only thing to give the music its distinct power. The way the *gruppo*, or trill, is used at each cadence to underline a tonality which may or may not turn out to be more than transitory, and more especially the constant exploitation of the conflict between major and minor, so that in spite of the narrow range of tonality, there is always the possibility of surprise—these are elements which make for a sense of scale which belies the comparative shortness of the piece.

There are several other pieces in this vein. The first *fuga* in the Giordano collection,[35] of which the subject has been quoted above (see example 17f), is an equally noble work, its rhythms enlivened still further with occasional

[35] II, p. 28.

bursts of passage-work and its air of decisiveness increased by the harmonization of its crochet motif [b] which also acts as a splendid bass. The piece immediately following, also called *fuga*, is a lengthy work, its subject dominated by an expansive motif. Maybe it is a shade too long; the repetitiveness stemming from the chanson, where two upper voices frequently are contrasted with the two lower ones, is acceptable where the themes are short but causes a lack of momentum when they are not. Its climax is superb; the subject suggests some remarkable harmonies and the brief ornamental figures clinch the feeling of triumph by their conciseness being a variant of the *gruppo* rather than a *passaggio*:

Surely no Doge or Senator could be unappreciative of such music. Its charms and tunefulness, the gaiety mixed with a bitter-sweetness which arises because Gabrieli uses the minor for many of these pieces, gives them a special attractiveness, even if they do not offer the sheer excitement of Merulo's toccatas. Gabrieli does not always stick to this vein, and there are a few organ works in a more sombre mood. The 'Fantasia del 4º Tono'[36] looks at first sight like a ricercar in Andrea's austere manner. The white notes, sparse ornaments, the insistence on real counterpoint (it would transcribe quite well for four viols) all seem to belie the ascription to Giovanni. Playing it through reveals quite certainly that it is his work. It is a study in orderly dissonance, with the discords carefully prepared and

[36] I, p. 47.

resolved in a way that would hardly disturb Zarlino. It is the frequency of these chords which gives the emotional quality. At the beginning they seem incidental, a chain of suspensions leading to a cadence before the third 'voice' enters to enrich the sound. The second occurrence of dissonance indeed confirms this, a mere couple of discords of a very transitory nature preparing for the complete four-voiced texture. It is only when the original chain is repeated, then again, and again, until it has been heard in full half a dozen times, not taking into account other hints of its appearance that we realize that this, rather than the staid theme, is the real focus of the work. The other feature which colours it is its use of the minor tonality. The first third is a minor one, the minor sixth is frequently in evidence. For nine bars there is no firmly established major chord, and when, in the tenth bar, it finally arrives, it is a dominant chord leading straight into a minor tonic. Two bars later there is a hint of the major; it quickly passes, and thereafter does not recur. The concluding phrases in fact play on our expectation of the major, as a common cadential formula repeatedly invites a raised third. But each time we are disappointed, until at the last, the sixteenth-century proprieties insist on the *tierce de picardie*:

This is not popular music in any sense. Neither is the 'Ricercar a tre soggetti', as it is sometimes known,[37] though admittedly the material may

[37] I, p. 38.

seem a little more obvious than the 'Fantasia del 4⁰ Tono'. If we do not possess an entirely accurate version of it, since the original has apparently disappeared, there can be no doubt that it is Gabrieli's work, if only because of its strong resemblance to the marvellous 'Canzon fa sol la re', which will be discussed later. The 'three subjects' are not the constituents of a triple fugue but to all intents the three elements in Gabrieli's themes referred to above: the greatest is the third, the anchor which in four strong minims fixes the tonality. It is employed in *stretto*, it is played in upper and lower parts, acts as treble and bass, and its sledge-hammer blows have a power against which all else seems mere decoration. When the cadence it forms is given a major chord on which to end, all is serene; when the minor is preferred (as it is more often than not) serenity has vanished, though not the sense of struggle, emphasized towards the end by a string of dissonances of the same kind as in the 'Fantasia':

General assessment of Giovanni's organ music

Gabrieli's organ music is not his greatest achievement. The instrument he played in St. Mark's was not as capable of variety as the whole *cappella* of singers and players constantly at his disposal proved to be. Nonetheless, these last two pieces express the powerful, sombre side of his nature, while the best of the canzonas have the *joie de vivre* that informs his most triumphant works in praise of his native city. Historically this music seems to lead nowhere in particular; it is difficult, among Gabrieli's many pupils, to find anyone who was greatly influenced by it, and the school of native Venetian organists languished almost immediately after his death. Both the Northern Europeans and such Italians as Frescobaldi seem to pay more attention to the romantic style of Merulo than to the more classical approach of Gabrieli when they look towards Venice. Yet it is easy to see why Gabrieli's music was popular in its own day—or indeed throughout the first half of the seventeenth century (as its appearances in the German tablatures suggests). It was, after all, some of the first organ music to transfer effectively a sophisticated vocal idiom into true keyboard music.

While the ricercars of Andrea and the canzonas of Merulo could, without substantial damage, be translated back into vocal or quasi-vocal music (the 'voices' might have to be supplemented by instruments in the manner common at that time), the keyboard ricercars of Giovanni are conceived for the instrument. If they were written out in open score, the usual rubric on the title page, 'a quattro voci, per ogni sorte di stromenti', would still not be accurate: they are organ music. Yet the contrapuntal idiom is not abandoned, as it is at times in Merulo's toccatas. Giovanni Gabrieli's organ works, like Andrea's, are consolidatory rather than innovatory music, and they are a good starting point for the consideration of his more ambitious works precisely because this is so.

CHAPTER FOUR

The Early Music for Venetian Festivals

CEREMONIAL music was not new in the sixteenth century, least of all in Venice. Motets celebrating the visit of some great prince or a victory of arms can be found for at least a hundred and fifty years before Giovanni Gabrieli's birth. The first director of St. Mark's song school, Antonio Romano, provided a motet for the coronation of Tommaso Mocenigo in 1414 and yet another for that of Doge Foscari nine years later; and on this second occasion two other composers, Hugo de Lantins, a Fleming, and Christoforo de Monte from Feltre, a town in *Venezia terra ferma*, also contributed some music. The surviving series of account books of the Procuratia de Supra begins later than this, so we do not know whether grand forces were assembled for such celebrations; but Gentile Bellini's famous picture of a Corpus Domini procession of the 1490s shows clearly enough that numbers of singers and instrumentalists were employed at festivals. Motet texts from other cities tell us of musical celebrations for the accession of princes, weddings, peace treaties, and many other important events.[1] What was new in Venice in the later sixteenth century was the opportunity to practise this art continuously. In the motet books of Lasso, whose *cappella* we have seen to be most influential on the Venetians, out of over one thousand separate pieces there are scarcely twenty-five which fall into this category. Yet all but a handful of Giovanni Gabrieli's hundred surviving works for the church appear to have had this function, and so do about half the works of even a composer like Croce, who wrote for much more varied circumstances. The frequency of these events meant that composers had to become experts in the genre.

Whereas in other states the composer for some unique occasion could probably rely on large forces and some advance warning, the Venetian could not. Contrary to general belief, in Giovanni's early years the *cappella*

[1] A. Dunning, *Die Staatsmotette 1480–1555* (Utrecht, 1969).

of St. Mark's, even augmented for a festival, would have been quite small, consisting of about a dozen singers and ten instrumentalists, though later these resources were to be substantially increased. Rehearsal time was presumably always limited, at least at such festivals as Christmas and Easter when there was several days' music to prepare; on the other hand, the composers' burden was lightened by the fact that the performers too were highly experienced in this kind of music. No doubt, also, not all the music for each occasion was new. The Venetian liking for retrospective collections of a living or dead composer's work indicates that manuscripts were carefully preserved for decades. Thus the musicians of St. Mark's built up a corpus of experience which was unrivalled anywhere else.

The composers were fortunate that music was tending to become both simpler and more fluid in technique. Reading through the comprehensive pages of Zarlino's mid-century treatises or even the fin-de-siècle guide for English amateurs by Morley, and comparing their systematic explanations with the actual music of the time, it becomes obvious that whole ranges of musical device were in virtual disuse. Complexities of rhythm requiring a detailed knowledge of a large number of time signatures had almost gone, reduced to a few stock figures, of which the most complicated might be a two-against-three cross rhythm. Pupils were taught to write canons of varying degrees of difficulty, yet it is something of a rarity to find one in any but old-fashioned music by the end of the century. The vast apparatus of the modal system had gone too, broken completely by the frequent application of *musica ficta* to raise leading notes, turning a mode into something very like a modern key. Thus harmony also had become simpler, a trend encouraged by the popularity of diatonic light music, balletts and canzonettas by such people as Andrea Gabrieli, Donato, Gastoldi, and abroad, Morley and Hassler. All this made things much easier for composers whose audience, Doge and Senate, ambassadors, and gentry, had little interest in musical refinements.

Words and music in the late 16th century: the Council of Trent

The subtlety of late sixteenth-century music lay not in technical device but in basic philosophy. The evolution of musical imagery to match the words was highly advanced by this time: it was still of little use to the composer for St. Mark's, the more especially since much of this imagery demands that the music be seen. Zarlino's elementary symbolism of ascent by an 'ascending' scale assumes it; the sophisticated depiction of the eyes by two semibreves at the beginning of a Marenzio madrigal is incomprehensible without it; but this kind of expression would hardly be clear to an audience. More significant in this kind of music was the Reformation emphasis on verbal intelligibility, which affected Catholicism as well as Protestantism. The Roman Church had its reformers who, like Thomas Cranmer, insisted that in church music there should be as far as possible 'for every syllable a note'. In particular that most inventive and active Cardinal, Archbishop Borromeo of Milan, influenced a composer in his archdiocese, Vincenzo Ruffo, to try experiments with a simple kind of homophonic music, not very far from that of the Anglicans.[2] Ruffo's attempts at such a music and those of Kerll and a few others were short-lived. There was a vogue for music in a style 'approved by the Council of Trent' (the phrase used on the title pages of their publications) for perhaps a dozen years; by 1590, the movement was virtually over. But its influence went beyond the aims of the reformers. Church composers in general paid much more attention to the enunciation of the words. Their musical rhythms and phrases stem from verbal accentuation, even if the repetition of these phrases seems to break up the verbal text more than the reformers would have liked. And the normal texture is homophonic, with several if not all voices enunciating the same words at the same time, which further aids intelligibility; this is used at vital moments even in quite elaborately contrapuntal music.

Ruffo worked in Milan for some time, but most of his career was spent in Verona, where many of the Venetian composers were also well known. Nevertheless his style was taken up in Venice hardly at all. Croce composed a *missa brevis* which is indeed brief and homophonic, but it is very much the exception. It is not difficult to see why the style, at its strictest, never caught on. It was too restricted to allow for much emotional expression, which after all is a major purpose of music. Only when other resources were added to this simple style could the imagination of the composer be stimulated sufficiently; and naturally he sought for means that would provide more variety without destroying the basis of a simpler texture. So it was that colour—if we may thus call the concept of changing sonorities—became important. The most obvious sign of interest in new and greater sonorities throughout the sixteenth century is the tendency to use more voices with an increase in overall *tessitura*. Whereas in the mid-century, the motet and madrigal books contain a large number of compositions for four voices, twenty years later the norm is five and, for church music, the last decades see an increasing use of six voices.

With this went a tendency to write higher upper parts. In secular music,

[2] L. Lockwood, *The Counter-Reformation and the Masses of Vincenzo Ruffo* (Venice, 1970).

the new brightness was encouraged by the use of the female voice. Whereas the ensemble of the early madrigalist is for the most part strictly male, the madrigals of the 1580s imply the use of both sexes. Due largely to the fame of a trio of lady singers at the court of Ferrara, this broadening of the sound spectrum affected virtually the whole of secular music by the end of the century, when it was unusual for a male consort to sing the fashionable elegant pastoral music (though it might be found more appropriate for the bawdy songs of the madrigal comedies).

Adaptation of secular techniques for church music

In church, this had its corollary in the use of *castrati*. After the 1570s they became much sought throughout Europe. The Cappella Sistina had need of them; Lasso sent out his assistants in search of them in 1573;[3] and in the 1590s the Venetian Procurators, a trifle behind the times as usual, sent their letters to the Residents abroad to try and find them.[4] For in church music, at least in Italy, men, skilled in the art of ornamentation and with voices 'hoch und hell' (Lasso), were preferred to boys.

Another extension of range is in the use of instruments. There is no doubt that these had been used for generations, if not for centuries, in church music. Erasmus complained of them in the early years of the century;[5] the Council of Trent was exceedingly suspicious of them in 1562.[6] Yet in the 1560s the motet books frequently add to their title page 'Tum omnis generis instrumentis cantatu commodissimae', or, in its Italian equivalent 'accomodadi per cantar et sonar d'ogni sorte de istromenti'; but at this stage, there is nothing that a voice cannot sing, no conscious seeking after instrumental sounds. Even so, the fact that the composer could hope for a mixture of voices and instruments clearly stimulated his imagination.

Giovanni's early motets using a single choir

These characteristics—of relative simplicity, intelligibility of the text, and the extension of sonorities—are found in many of the early motets of the

[3] Boetticher, op. cit., p. 433.

[4] A.S.V., Proc. de Supra, Registro 193, bis, f. 4. This document is a letter to ambassadors and residents at Rome, Verona, and Munich searching for singers and 'in particolar soprani eunichi'.

[5] G. Reese, *Music in the Renaissance*, rev. ed. (New York, 1959), p. 448.

[6] K. G. Fellerer, 'Church Music and the Council of Trent', *Musical Quarterly* (1953), p. 576.

younger Gabrieli. These works are included in two volumes. The first is the *Concerti di Andrea e Giovanni Gabrieli*, the posthumous collection of his uncle's grandest music, published in 1587. There can be no doubt about the use of instruments here, and it is equally significant that nothing less than six voices will do for either composer. The second volume of ten years later, summing up Giovanni's own achievement to the age of about forty, begins with six-voiced pieces, with the familiar 'tam vocibus quam instrumentis' on the title page. Most of the works in these volumes, of course, require more than six voices; but even in the lesser pieces the air of spaciousness and sonority is at once evident. The pieces are mostly settings of psalms or parts of psalms with an exhortatory function. 'Inclina, Domine, aurem tuam, et exaudi me' begins Giovanni's very first published church music; and the opening, in long contrapuntal phrases which might come from any composer brought up in the old Netherlands tradition, inclines to the minor. Yet it is not long before the melodic phrases shorten, the harmony turns to the major, the texture becomes more homophonic, and the low notes of the basses give a richness of sound:

Ex.1

A companion piece, the 'Exaudi Domine' for six voices, from the *Sacrae Symphoniae*, reveals the same attitude. It is built in ampler proportions, a sign perhaps of greater maturity; and whereas 'Inclina Domine' has a cantus which could be sung by any fairly high counter-tenor, this needs a real soprano, supported perhaps by Giovanni Bassano's cornett. Here too there is imitative counterpoint at the opening, and the minor harmonies persist while the words 'deprecationem meam' are worked out at some length. But the climax of the motet comes appropriately at the cry 'non in labiis dolosis: laudabo te'. The voices group and re-group so that no one can miss its significance, and the shouts of praise inspire exciting rhythms reminiscent of Andrea and the composers of Munich:

Both these pieces could belong to Giovanni's years at Munich: there are others where, though the same traits appear, the interest in colour is so refined that they seem to come from a later period. 'Benedixisti', a setting of a prayer for Christmas Day, uses the same lively rhythms. Fragments of melody are worked out in imitation, though it is the eye rather than the ear which appreciates such subtlety. More important are the contrasts between the phrases which use the cantus part and those which do not. Since this is the main means of contrast, the work might well be performed as an aria for soprano or even counter-tenor with six accompanying instruments—trombones or viols. This form reveals to the full the expressiveness of the declamatory melody, narrow in range but shaped so that the meaning of the words 'peccata eorum' is delicately underlined:

This is a penitential motet, and yet the Venetian character of the music is brought out by the harmony. There is scarcely a minor third throughout the whole of the climax, and it is only at the conventionally plagal cadence that the self-confident major yields to something more devotional. The feeling of strength is underlined by the regularity with which the harmonic changes take place, usually at two or four beat intervals. There is nothing wayward, no sudden surge of passion in this kind of music.

We find the same steadiness, together with an even greater attention to a particular sonority, in the setting of 'Exaudi Deus' which follows 'Benedixisti' in the *Sacrae Symphoniae*. This is no aria, though it could be performed easily enough as a duet, the uppermost parts being tenor lines which neatly interlock with one another, supported by various groupings of lower voices. There is no doubt, though, about instrumental participation, since the lowest lines use the Cs and even a B flat below the stave. The whole motet is conceived for a range which scarcely exceeds two octaves.[7] The sonorities thus are sombre, but the tonality is so firmly vested in major triads that the mood is one of balance and trust, rather than of supplication. The way the following passage is based on a series of perfect cadences, with a touch of doubt only at the melismatic emphasis on the word 'iniquitates', is typical:

Yet it would be wrong to see the whole of Gabrieli's music in this light. In contrast with this confident manner, there is a more prayerful side to his nature which is revealed in a small number of motets for single choir in

[7] The pitch in use at St. Mark's is not known and the major authority on this subject, Arthur Mendel (see *Musical Quarterly*, 1948, and A. J. Ellis and A. Mendel, *Studies in the history of musical pitch*, Amsterdam, 1968) counsels caution about coming to any firm conclusions on 16th-century pitch in general. It can be said, however, that any major transposition, such as those advocated by Fellowes for English cathedral music, presents difficulties for the works of Giovanni Gabrieli.

the *Sacrae Symphoniae*. The most remarkable of these is a setting of another psalm, 'Miserere mei', for a balanced group of voices: soprano, two altos, two tenors, and bass; and the tessitura of each is such that the piece might be performed without instruments, as would be the case in Holy Week. This music shows clearly that Giovanni was a pupil of Lasso, that master of the art of expression. It uses chromaticism extraordinarily freely, as Gabrieli himself seems fully aware, since chromatic notes repeated several times are marked with apparently superfluous accidentals in the printed part books. Nothing is left to chance:

The chromatic changes are perhaps less dramatic than in Giuseppe Guami's semitonal scale at the opening of his setting of 'In die tribulationis' (see Example 4, Chapter 1); but they are better integrated into the harmonic scheme (see Example 6).

When, a little later, the chromatics turn to the use of flattened degrees of the scale for 'et peccatum meum contra me est semper', again the bass outlines conventional harmonic progressions, even though they use what were, for Gabrieli, unusual notes. But more significant than this daring is the subtle way he treats the words 'iniquitatem meam': without a single departure from his normal practice, and with little dissonance, the meaning of the phrase is brought out by the musical motif conflicting with the insistent minor sixth of the chord:

'Miserere mei' is unique among Gabrieli's early music, although significant when considering later works; but two Marian motets confirm the feeling that he was not merely an unemotional Venetian. 'Sancta Maria' at first sight looks like a typical piece for one of those festivals of the Blessed Virgin which the Republic celebrated with some pomp. The setting is for seven voices, with the usual depth of sound produced by divided basses and tenors, no doubt doubled by trombones. There is a triple-time section with the dancing vein and the repetitions which we shall see to be such a feature of the grander motets for such occasions. Yet the remainder of the motet is not quite so well balanced. The phrases are nervously short, and very rarely developed, though frequently simply repeated, especially for such emotive words as 'succurre' and 'intercede'. The harmony also changes irregularly, and the whole atmosphere is much more taut than in other motets for similar resources.

The other Marian motet, 'Beata es Virgo', is in a totally different style but also shows a breakaway from stately pomp. Its six voices are significantly divided in the madrigalian way, two sopranos and alto, tenor and two basses, and the opening phrase, scored for the three upper voices, is reminiscent in sound (though not in manner) of the Ferrara madrigals of Wert and Luzzaschi. The repetition of the phrase, scored for the lower trio, quickly removes this impression, and it is evident that when Gabrieli seeks the clarity of the higher voices, he is thinking in terms of dialogue. At the climax of the piece, the contrast effect is extremely beautiful, the decorative figures especially so as they cause pinpricks of dissonance:

Dissonance is more frequent than usual throughout the piece, though it is never astringent, and seldom more than a common suspension to underline the continual cadential harmonies; and the tendency to the minor is noticeable in its context in the *Sacrae Symphoniae*, though for other composers it would scarcely evoke comment. And while the actual layout of voices and the technique in exploiting sonorities is not far from that of Andrea's *Penitential Psalms* of 1583, the younger Gabrieli here seems more human, less public a figure, even if the piece was still probably meant for some festival of the Republic.

Motets for double choir by Gabrieli's predecessors

From this small-scale dialogue it is not difficult to see how Gabrieli's interests in grander concepts developed: and it is not a large step to his double-choir music—which constitutes the bulk of these two first publications. The vogue for double-choir music was established by his uncle, but that is no reason why it should almost monopolize Giovanni's ceremonial music, for other composers, including Andrea, found more varied ways of composing on a grand scale. Nor is it simply a question of Venetian tradition, for until we come to Giovanni's work, the tradition is quite tenuous. The roots of double-choir music are usually thought to lie in the psalm settings which Willaert published in 1550 under the title *Di Adriano et di Jachet: I salmi appertinenti alli Vesperi . . . a duoi chori*, though it is clear that the antiphonal singing of psalms was not new in the sixteenth century. Choir books containing antiphonal settings have been found dating from the fifteenth century[8] and at Treviso, not twenty miles from Venice, two composers, Francesco Santacroce and Giovanni Nasco, left music which shows some imagination in the use of a divided choir.[9] Willaert's settings seem less remarkable musically than historically, to judge by recent reconstructions[10] (the sources only provide an incomplete text). Their fame in their own time was probably because they provided a reasonably simple model of their kind, and solved some pressing problems.

The greatest problem from the point of view of the listener and theorist is caused by the fact that the division of the choir can obscure the presence of the bass. If one is nearer to the part of the choir which lacks the foundation notes, the harmony is bound to seem strange. The second great difficulty is simply that of ensemble. The further away from each other the performers are, the more difficult it is for them to keep together. Willaert's solutions to these problems were highly effective. The basses of the two choirs were essentially the same, though sometimes an octave apart, as we can see from a formula advocated by a Willaert pupil, Nicola Vicentino (see Example 9).

This, of course, effectively reduces an eight-part texture to seven parts and is indeed the first hint of a consciousness that doubling parts is needed at times to adjust balance—and thus can be said to contain the beginnings

[8] M. Bukofzer, *Studies in Mediaeval and Renaissance Music* (New York, 1950).

[9] G. D'Alessi, 'Precursors of Adriano Willaert in the practice of *coro spezzato*', *Journal of the American Musicological Association*, V (1950), p. 187.

[10] Modern editions, ed. H. Zenck and W. Gerstenberg (American Institute of Musicology, Rome, 1972), Vol. VIII, and 'Memento Domine David', ed. J. Long (Pennsylvania, 1969).

Ex.9

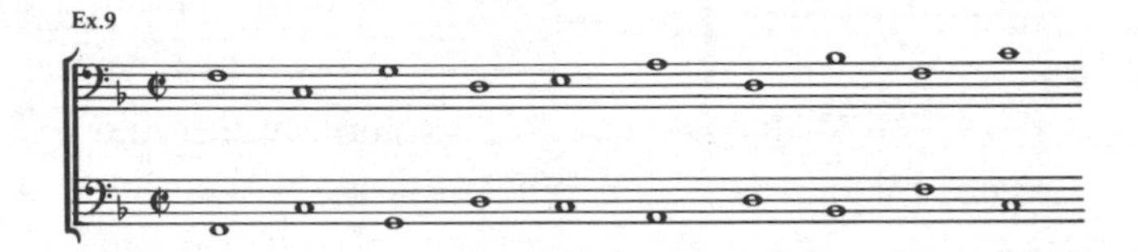

of the modern idea of orchestration. More than that, it points the way to the greater simplicity which is the solution of the problems of ensemble. Regular changes of harmony, already a trend in sixteenth-century music, here become a *sine qua non*. A few chords, which allow this octave formula to be effective, rather than the complex harmonies which are the result of true counterpoint, are equally essential.

The conditions in which Willaert was working must have helped in suggesting these solutions, for the problems of both the listener and the performer in St. Mark's derive from the fact that the organs are not on the floor of the church but in lofty galleries.[11] Admittedly the difficulties can be exaggerated, for the basilica is not as large as the great Gothic churches of northern countries, and its acoustical properties are therefore much more satisfactory. The choir galleries are not far apart, and they are well within sight of each other, so that a single conductor could control events. It seems likely also that in the earlier years of double-choir music in St. Mark's it was only these two galleries with organs that were used. Significantly, payments to musicians usually refer to them playing 'nelle organi'[12]—in the organ lofts—and there is little evidence that in St. Mark's they took to such excesses as later became fashionable in Germany, where groups of musicians were placed around the church, in the transepts, by the West Door, and anywhere else which might startle the unsuspecting audience. So Willaert's devices were quite feasible for the resources for which he was writing.

The popularity of his 1550 psalm settings, which achieved a second edition a few years after the first had appeared, has sometimes led to the belief that Willaert caused a new vogue. In fact very little music in the same style appeared in the next few years. The next most notable publication was a book of masses by Palestrina which appeared in 1572, over twenty years later. There are similar works by several minor composers in the next decade, including one or two within the Venetian orbit, and

[11] For a detailed discussion of the use of *cori spezzati* in St. Mark's see Witton E. Mason, 'The Architecture of St. Mark's Cathedral and the Venetian Polychoral style: a Clarification', *Studies in Musicology . . . in Memory of Glen Haydon* ed. James W. Pruett (Chapel Hill, 1969).

[12] For example, A.S.V., Proc de Supra, Cassier Chiesa Reg. 5, entry for 5 June 1598.

some of Lasso's grand motets probably date from this time. But this hardly constitutes a new fashion. As for the native Venetians, there is little evidence that they were following Willaert's example assiduously. Merulo's motets in the 1570s are not for double choir, nor are those of the minor figures such as Girolamo dalla Casa, published in the following decade. The only composer who we may reasonably be sure was constantly writing motets of this kind during the 1570s and 1580s was Andrea Gabrieli, and even he apparently did not think it worth while to publish his double-choir music at the time.

Influence of Andrea Gabrieli's 'Concerti' (1587)

When his nephew did publish it in 1587, the vogue began. The Bolognese composers of S. Petronio, minor Florentines, the German anthologists, all joined the trend during the next decade. Andrea's *Concerti* show why this happened, and show too that Giovanni was exceedingly fortunate to be there when this music was written. For the music is different in kind from that of Willaert and reveals a new imagination at work. This is partly because Andrea was little concerned with Willaert's 'rules', which he obeyed when it suited him and ignored when it did not. Thus the basses in parallel octaves are found quite frequently in his music, as are the basic simplicities of regular harmonic change and the few diatonic chords favoured by the older man; but there are occasions when both features are set aside. The influence of Lasso, in the strong rhythms which made possible the independence of many 'real' contrapuntal lines, never entirely disappears from these works, either, though in a sense it comes from belief in a technique which lacks relevance in this new music. These *Concerti*, however, create a new world of sound which no lively modern could henceforward ignore. The most obvious manifestation is the way Andrea marshals his forces. Some works merely divide the choir equally; many others do not.[13] An upper choir will be pitted against a lower one; if there are three choirs there may be one in the middle of these in range. The *coro superiore* often takes its uppermost part above the stave in the treble clef, while the *coro grave* often goes below the stave, so that the contrasts are obvious. It is for these parts that Andrea needed the trombones and cornetts of the new permanent ensemble at St. Mark's, and the violins and shawms of the part-timers. At times, there are even hints that a distinct orchestration is intended, since, if we follow the instructions for adding

[13] D. Arnold, 'Andrea Gabrieli und die Entwicklung der "cori-spezzati" Technik', *Die Musikforschung*, XII (1959), p. 258.

instruments of Michael Praetorius,[14] admittedly writing much later but with a thorough knowledge of Venetian techniques, we find signs of voice parts interlocking with one another to give duets while other parts are clearly meant to accompany them:

These are obvious manifestations of a new sound; more impressive still is Andrea's mastery of its implications. The divided choir naturally leads to a division of material. Instead of true counterpoint, in which parts mingle and cadences are frequently so obscured as to go by unnoticed, two

[14] Michael Praetorius, *Syntagma Musicum* III (Wittenberg, 1619); modern facsimile reprint, ed. W. Gurlitt (Kassel, 1959), pp. 152 ff.

choirs treated as distinct entities give rise to distinct phrases. These phrases can be welded together by an overlap of the choirs, they can be segregated, they can be lengthy and fully develop some thematic material or they can be short and pithy; they can initiate new ideas, or repeat those already stated; they can amplify a repeat with the ripieno of both choirs. It is in the realization of these potentialities that Andrea was a master. He also shows a new attitude to setting words. The structure of a sentence or paragraph in a psalm is here almost entirely irrelevant as it had never been for Willaert. Andrea's interests are in a musical structure in which the words are of secondary importance. Phrases are either long, which creates a solemn and relaxed atmosphere, or short to provide sheer excitement. There is no rule about the strict alternation of choirs; one choir may emerge from a tutti. Thus in place of a classical balance comes a chiaroscuro in which exaggeration has a place.

Giovanni's earliest motets for double choir

Giovanni also included three of his own double-choir motets in Andrea's *Concerti*. Each shows what he has learned. Closest to the manner of his uncle is the grand Christmas piece 'Angelus ad Pastores', massively written for two choirs, each of six voices. One is a *coro superiore*, with the uppermost part written in the treble clef, but it does not use the top notes implied by this very often, and the tessitura is not very different from those in the more modest works of Andrea. The *coro grave* has a bass line which frequently uses low Cs and needs instrumental support, though the words are still provided. Giovanni does not worry much about Willaert's rules: the lowest part of the upper choir is frequently not a real bass in the tuttis. Nevertheless, the major point of the style has been grasped. The harmonies are simple and change at convenient intervals. What counterpoint is left scarcely disturbs this textural simplicity, though Giovanni introduces a cadence which manages to maintain the independence of all the parts, providing a tinge of excitement in the way the suspended dissonance is clashed against its note of resolution (see Example 11).

But more than the actual technical details, it is the spirit of 'Angelus ad Pastores' that seems close to Andrea. The feeling of power at the climax, 'Gloria Patri', with its chords laid over three octaves and its repetition of the phrase to drive the message home, and the extension of both 'allelujas' so that they take up almost half the work, evoke Venice in its victorious post-Lepanto mood. This is naturally less true of 'Deus, Deus meus', a setting of a less optimistic psalm; though even here, it is power rather than

Ex.11

supplication which receives the musical emphasis. The disposition of the choirs and the general technique are much the same as in 'Angelus ad Pastores', and Andrea's interest in dialogue is also reflected, since the length of text makes Giovanni work in a more extensive way. The long segments for each choir in turn at the opening show how richly it is possible to work within simple harmonies, using such devices as the juxtaposition of major and minor versions of a chord and some elementary imitation of scales which lead to continual thirds. The quick-paced dialogue towards the end equally displays an understanding of its medium, even if the actual material is sometimes not very interesting.

But it is the work furthest away from Andrea's style which is the most appealing of these three. Superficially the Christmas motet, 'O magnum mysterium', has the hallmarks of the older man: the choirs are divided into high and low; the kaleidoscopic dialogue is in much the same manner; the 'alleluja' takes up a large proportion of the piece. It is the detail which begins to show a new personality. The most obvious divergence lies in the subtlety of the harmony. The very first phrase, in its ambiguous references to both major and minor, displays a highly sophisticated harmonic sense; and the repetitions of this phrase are quite magical, with the *coro grave* giving it an unexpected twist which leaves it on the dominant chord, and then the tutti enriching the harmonies by thick inner counterpoints:

Throughout the rest of the work there is a similar duality, based on the very ambiguity already stated, for with the *musica ficta* F sharps the tonality centres around G; without them, around B flat. The ease of moving from the one, with its minor implications, to the other, with its clear major overtones, keeps a harmonic interest which Andrea's music so often lacks. This infects even the 'alleluja', on which he manages to impose a gay dancing rhythm, more like that of a *balletto* of Gastoldi than the stolid regularity of most passages of this kind. Here the presence of the minor continues so that triumph becomes clouded by doubt, and noticeably the ending is a plagal cadence, rather than a forthright perfect cadence:

The double-choir works which Giovanni included in his *Sacrae Symphoniae* of 1597 reveal the differences between the two Gabrielis. For the *Concerti* created the vogue, but the *Sacrae Symphoniae* are in many ways much less like the model than are many of the works by other composers, inside and outside Venice, who were inspired by Andrea's achievement.

Giovanni's developing polychoral style

Like many other great composers, Giovanni based his technique on that of his immediate predecessor. There is little enough which cannot be found to have occurred in some form in the earlier man's work. Giovanni, for example, still accepts the convention of contrast between choirs, without too much change. Works such as 'Laudate nomen Domini', with its upper and lower groupings, are conventional enough, even if the *cantus* is kept rather high throughout the whole piece. Nor is the scoring of the eight-voiced setting of 'Jubilate Deo' very different, though here the two uppermost parts, written in treble clefs, are reminiscent of the soprano duets in many madrigals of the period, and contribute the same sort of brilliance. Indeed, considering that Giovanni had an expert instrumental group at his disposal, it is remarkable how little of this music cannot be performed by voices alone, though admittedly a mixed ensemble would sometimes make it easier and nearly always more effective. Willaert's rules concerning basses are not much in evidence, either, though very often the bass of an upper choir, though conceived as an inner part, does provide a reasonably satisfactory foundation for its group. Giovanni also can be more ingenious than his uncle in following these rules, as we may see in the following passage from 'Beati immaculati', where the flow of the parts conceals an almost perfect Willaertian situation:

Still, Andrea would have recognized the solid diatonicism of the following bars of the climax of the ten-part 'Quis est iste qui venit' (I add the figures as in a basso continuo part to make the harmonies clear). The resemblance to Andrea's music becomes more striking still when the words are considered:

Yet while Giovanni's harmonic range is derived from Andrea's, his harmonies and the way they derive from the texture begin to show the differences between them. We can see this in a motet like 'Laudate nomen Domini', especially since it is the sort of powerful text which Andrea enjoyed. The opening section is written in sound imitative counterpoint, using a conventional figure which strongly underlines the tonality of A

Ex.16

quo _ _ ni _ am Ja _ cob e _ le _ git
quo _ _ ni _ am Ja _ cob e _ le _ git
quo _ _ ni _ am Ja _ cob e _
quo _ _ ni _ am Ja _ cob e _ le _ git
quo _ ni _ am Ja _ cob
quo _ ni _ am Ja _ cob
quo _ ni _ am Ja _ cob
quo _ ni _ am Ja _ cob
si _ _ bi Do _ _ mi _ nus, Is _
si _ bi Do _ _ mi _ nus, Is _ ra _ el in _
_ le _ git si _ _ bi Do _ _ mi _ nus, Is _ ra _
si _ bi Do _ _ mi _ nus, Is _ ra _ el
e _ le _ git si _ _ bi Do _ _ mi _ nus,
e _ le _ git si _ _ bi Do _ _ mi _ nus, Is _ ra _
e _ le _ git si _ bi Do _ _ mi _ nus, Is _ ra _
e _ le _ git si _ _ bi Do _ mi _ nus, Is _ ra _
_ ra _ el in pos _ ses _ si _ o _ _ _ nem si _ bi:
_ pos _ ses _ si _ o _ nem, in pos _ ses _ si _ o _ _ _ nem si _ bi:
_ el in pos _ ses _ si _ o _ _ nem si _ _ _ bi:
in pos _ ses _ si _ o _ _ _ nem si _ _ _ bi:
Is _ ra _ el in pos _ ses _ si _ o _ _ _ nem si _ _ bi:
_ el in pos _ ses _ si _ o _ nem si _ _ bi:
_ el in pos _ ses _ si _ o _ _ nem si _ bi:
_ el in pos _ ses _ si _ o _ _ _ _ nem si _ bi:

minor. The dialogue which ensues is especially strong, primary triads predominating, until a triple-time section clinches the feeling of forcefulness with an assertion of the relative major key. All of this might come from Andrea, but the section which ensues is much more sophisticated, suggesting not only a tonic key but the subdominant and the relative major each time before the conclusive cadence of the tutti settles the matter (see Example 16).

Such a passage is remarkably supple. The words are enunciated clearly in a comparatively simple texture; the rhythms are not difficult for the performer; most remarkable is the way the harmonies change, so that acoustical overlap caused by counterpoint (as in the last three bars of this extract) causes no distress to the ear, for there are many linking notes between chords. Noticeably there is virtually no dissonance. Yet there is a feeling of scale, a continuous interest not restricted by the deliberately limited means. This is typical of many of these motets, which seem expansive and tautly organized at the same time.

Rhythm in Giovanni's motets

Giovanni Gabrieli organizes the rhythmic patterns of the idiom with equal skill. This presented more problems than might be thought. Certain resources were not open to him. For the true contrapuntist, the main consideration is the fitting in of one part against another, and thus divisions into regular units of time are taken for granted, even if this means

distorting syllables of the text or writing quite complex patterns. It was something which Giovanni had mastered as well as anyone, as the opening of 'Jam non dicam' shows, with its imitative entries and melismatic treatment of the words (see Example 17).

But the homophony of the *cori spezzati* style implies rhythms derived from verbal accent. The up-to-date madrigalist of the 1580s solved this quite often by following natural speech, which in Italian results in elisions, and by creating a melody which searches less for regularity in the divisions of time than a plasticity which gives the sense of speech. (This reached its most sensitive expression in the new recitative of the Florentines of the next generation.) It was necessarily a compromise, since a reasonably constant accentuation was felt necessary to control the harmony—and also to provide the composer with the resources of counterpoint when he felt it more expressive, as sixteenth-century composers often did. Still, the freedom which evolved in these circumstances can be gauged by following such a passage as this from one of Giaches de Wert's late madrigals:

This pliability of melody was essentially denied to the composer brought up in the Franco-Netherlandish traditions of which Lasso was one of the ultimate scions. For a composer whose major works were homophonic Latin settings (with no possibility of elisions) the problem was very real.

Two features of style came to his aid. The first was common to all music at the time of Gabrieli's education. As we have seen with his early madrigals, the debate whether to use the *misura di breve*, with the minim as the basic unit for both harmony and melody, or the crotchet-based *misura comune* was not yet over. In the madrigal, the question was settled by about 1580; in church music it was never really settled at all, since the *stile antico* uses the old note-values as late as the nineteenth century. Gabrieli's motets are all written in the conservative time values, but with remarkable flexibility. In example 19 the unit is a minim, against which there are syncopations; yet the syllables fall on minim and crotchet alike, and harmonies on crotchet beats are essential, not merely the result of passing notes. And the result is a masterstroke of declamation and flowing melody:

The syncopations of this passage are of a kind which is almost a Gabrieli fingerprint, and they are typical of a general liveliness of rhythm common in Venetian music.

In the dialogue of a double choir motet, one choir frequently resolves a cadence on the main accent of the bar, and the other choir takes up its argument on the next (weak) beat:

Or in a case where the crotchet is a syllabic unit:

Thus Gabrielian melody often implies an anacrusis—something of a rarity in sixteenth-century music (in secular music it comes in with the *balletti* of Gastoldi who constantly puts rests before his first note, so that the performer, lacking the aid of bar lines, will know where the accent comes). The effect is one of great excitement, adding a distinct drive to the rhythms, and since the entry of the choir inexorably draws attention to itself, the former weak beat is transformed into a point of tension which can be extraordinarily exhilarating. No doubt the young Gabrieli had studied the dynamic rhythms in the music of Lasso or Guami or his uncle, where they mainly derive from counterpoint. Here the *raison d'être* is to give variety to essentially simple music, since the rhythmic flexibility allows of the more or less accurate reproduction of speech rhythms:

The use of dialogue techniques

That choral dialogue inevitably influences other musical techniques is thus clear enough: it is also a resource in itself which Gabrieli mastered completely. His uncle, as we have seen, appreciated the possibility of making excitement out of different phrase lengths. Giovanni takes this aspect for granted. There are one or two conventional pieces, it is true, where the dialogue seems to be rather formalized. But in more exciting pieces, Gabrieli proves himself a great master in developing material.

For Giovanni this problem was more acute than it had been for Andrea, since he often worked with longer texts, where reliance on contrasts of colour and phrase length was certainly not enough. So, although the means were not unknown to his uncle, Giovanni makes them more subtle, capable of maintaining interest throughout a considerable piece. The eight-voiced 'Beati omnes' shows this new sophistication. As often, the opening statement is for one choir and at some length (eight bars); the other choir replies more briefly (three bars) and the section is concluded by a short tutti (three bars). At this point, the real dialogue begins. At first it seems conventional enough. The first choir sings 'Quia manducabis' to receive the reply 'beatus es', which is taken up by the first choir. But the reiterated 'beatus es' by choir two and its answer 'et bene tibi erit' are far from ordinary; and even more so the rejoinder 'beatus es' to its own statement of 'et bene . . .', as the phrase is extended by the tutti (see Example 23).

Throughout the remainder of the motet, there is scarcely a phrase which is not given something of this treatment, though not at such length. Most remarkable is the conclusion, a triple-time section on the words 'et videas

Ex.23

filios filiorum' which might easily have become a simple 'alleluja'-style statement of rejoicing with little in the way of development. In fact, the lower choir's response to the upper voice occurs no less than three times in exactly the same form, to receive three distinct answers: one a simple one-bar statement of 'et videas', the next one an extended phrase for the rest of the verbal text, and then a new statement of 'et videas' which causes a significant modulation, extending the music into a substantial paragraph.

Not every piece in the *Sacrae Symphoniae* is so closely argued, especially those setting very long texts, where such detailed treatment would extend the piece to unreasonable proportions. Still, there are few where these techniques are not exploited to some degree. Commonly, themes (which here amount to chordal blocks) are transferred more or less exactly from choir to choir, frequently at a distance of a fourth or fifth in the re-statement, and then given a new ending, either with a single choir or the tutti, or one choir will enter unexpectedly before the phrase ends. Occasionally there are suggestions of an overall shape evolving, as in 'Domine Dominus noster'. This is perhaps the least dialogue-like of these motets, a naturally large-scale psalm in which concision is required, and where thematic interplay enters only at a very late stage. But when, at the end, the opportunity for a variant comes in, he takes it, for the opening phrase, originally scored for one choir, is brought back with a tutti and with its last segment repeated.

Comparison of Gabrieli and Croce

A study of Gabrieli's techniques must precede any assessment of his music in general simply because the means were new and to discover what he was aiming at we must know what musical devices he had at his disposal. It is plain that he was breaking new ground almost all the time. There was nothing in the theoretical treatises to help him (later composers had Michael Praetorius' codification of *cori spezzati* devices) and not very much in the music of his contemporaries; though here it is instructive to compare his work with the motets published by his colleagues in St. Mark's during the 1590s, for he must have taken part in performing them, and have been able to examine their scores. They were dealing with liturgical texts which were often identical or similar to his own, and as one looks at their works, his peculiarly complex character emerges. His complexity is indeed the first feature which comparison elucidates, for in both technique and musical material he is more sophisticated. Giovanni Croce's setting of Psalm 47, 'Omnes gentes', and Gabrieli's 'Jubilate Deo', have much the same vein of Venetian rejoicing. Croce's piece exploits the mood; its solid block chords for both choirs immediately make an impression of strength, and the scale motif for the words 'Jubilate Deo', the mock trumpet calls of 'in voce tubae', the triple time for 'psallite', with its regular phrases, are all extremely effective. There is nothing in the harmony which provides any real tension; the rhythms of the 'alleluja' are ordered. It is the epitome of festive music. Giovanni Gabrieli's piece seems complicated in contrast. The long opening section in the minor—and in imitative counterpoint—and the sense of freedom in the harmony which explores the relative major and dominant, subdominant, and submediant, immediately broaden the whole scale of the piece. When we come to the triple time of 'laudate nomen ejus', it is obvious that, although the actual length is little different from Croce's similar section, the conception is much more far-reaching (see Example 24).

Ex.24a

Croce
Psal _ li _ te De _ o no _ stro psal _ li _ te
Psal _ li _ te Re _ gi no _ stro psal _ li _
Psal _ li _ te, psal _ li _ te, psal _ li _ te sa _ _ pi _ en _ _ ter
_ te Psal _ li _ te, psal _ li _ te, psal _ li te sa _ pi _ en _ ter

Ex.24b

Gabrieli
lau _ da _ te no _ _
lau _ da _ te no _ _
lau _ da _ te no _ _
lau _ da _ te no _ _ men e _ jus:
lau _ da _ te no _ _ _ men e _ jus:
lau _ da _ te no _ _ men e _ jus:

But Gabrieli is no less festive. In his motet, the final section, written in quite elaborate eight-voiced counterpoint, seems the more effective for succeeding more subtle passages. Moreover the extension and variation of material in itself gives a sense of grandeur unavailable to a composer

Ex.25

whose mastery is of the simple statement of ideas, however great and full of pomp these may be in themselves. In this respect, it is fascinating to see how these two diverse composers treat the word 'alleluja'. Croce enjoys the dance rhythms with the hemiolia at the cadence and the opportunity for close dialogue, and the solemn ritardando expressed by a return to duple metre. The second alleluja of his Marian motet 'Ave Virgo' shows him at his most forthright (see Example 25).

Gabrieli does produce similar settings, especially in motets for very large forces, where the 'alleluja' often acquires a structural function (see pp. 178 ff) but frequently provides something quite different. In the first 'alleluja'

of 'Jam non dicam' it is syncopation which generates excitement, while in the second a fragment of melody is worked out in sequence. In the Easter motet 'Angelus Domini' the words at first sight seem to have acquired a jog-trot music of no special interest—until the syncopations of the soprano part of the first choir are suddenly extended with an imitation from the second choir, and the whole broadens out until, typically, the momentum insists on a decoration of the final chord (see Example 26).

Giovanni's originality

Such comparisons reveal the differences in attitude between members of a school of composers often supposed to be homogeneous,[15] but Gabrieli's originality is at its height in a handful of double-choir pieces which are impossible to put side by side with other men's work, where there is no precise similarity of mood or technique to be found in music by Croce, Bassano, or Andrea Gabrieli. Significantly they are none of them settings of psalms or other lengthy texts and they all have a less stately and more human sense of prayerful supplication. And though they are still clearly for festive occasions, Gabrieli's music does not require vast forces to make its effect. Admittedly the top line of 'Beati immaculati' would be best projected by an instrument as well as the voice, and its high *tessitura* is needed to take away a hint of sombreness which might otherwise dominate the piece. The opening, an extended phrase for the *coro grave*, is sombre in feeling—and this is far from being just a matter of sonority. The second note of the uppermost part of the choir, a natural instead of the sharpened G which would brighten the whole atmosphere, is enough to give an unexpected intensity to the prayer; and the repetition of the first word with a firm A in place of that G leads to a brilliance totally unexpected (see Example 27).

So it is throughout the remainder of the work. There are moments of splendour which give the overall effect; yet the final cadence is plagal, the last chord a *tierce de picardie* rather than an affirmation of glory. 'O Domine Jesu Christe' is even less glorious, though it is not sombre either. It has a richness of harmony—that would not perhaps have been thought at all daring in 1590, or even thirty years earlier; yet in the passage where the vision of Christ on the cross is expressed, the way a common suspension can convey grief, especially when resolved unexpectedly on the minor degree of the scale, and the way minor and major vie throughout the piece

15 O. Ursprung, *Die Katholische Kirchenmusik* (Potsdam, 1931), p. 187.

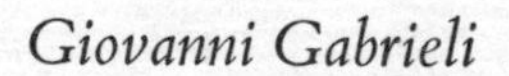

Ex.27

Be _ a _ _ ti im _ ma _ cu _ la _ _ ti in
Be _ a _ _ _ _ ti im _ ma _ cu _ la _ _ ti in
Be _ _ a _ ti im _ ma _ cu _ la _ ti in
Be _ a _ _ ti im _ ma _ cu _ la _ _ ti in

qui am _ bu _ lant in le _ ge Do _ _ _ mi _ ni:
qui am _ bu _ lant in le _ ge Do _ _ mi _ ni:
qui am _ _ bu _ lant in le _ ge Do _ _ mi _ ni:
qui am _ _ bu _ lant in le _ ge Do _ _ _ _ mi _ ni:
vi _ a; be _ _
vi _ a; be
vi _ a; be _
vi _ a; be _

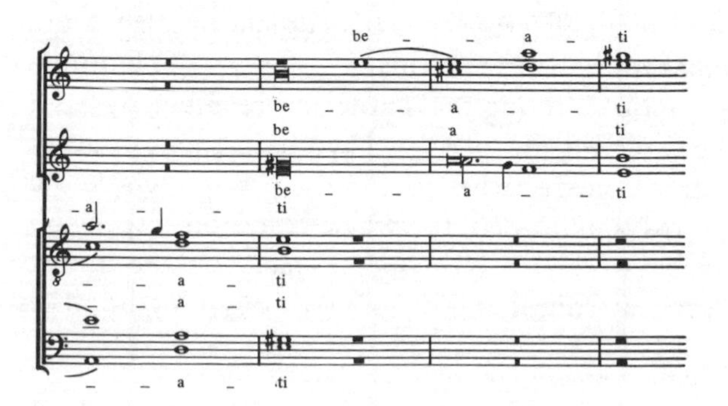
be _ _ a _ ti
be _ _ _ a _ _ ti
be a ti
be _ _ a _ _ ti
_ a _ _ ti
_ _ a _ ti
_ _ a _ ti
_ _ a _ ti

so that there is neither glory nor discontent, show the intensity of feeling of which Gabrieli is capable:

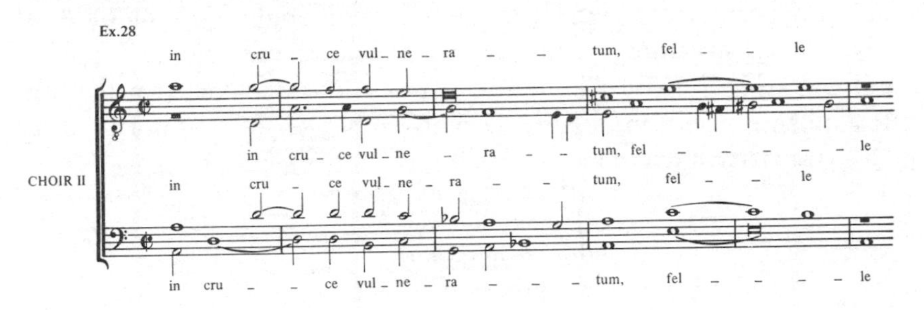

This passage is the culmination of twenty bars in which the indecision of tonality, the hints of dissonance have been constantly in evidence, and throughout the rest of the motet every idea is fully worked out. A forceful motif appears for the words 'ut vulnera'; the major-minor discrepancies are brought back at the phrase 'deprecor te'. The purpose of this uncertainty is revealed only in the final section where all the intervals suddenly turn to the major and for some seven bars there is hardly a minor chord to be heard, while the *altus* of the lower choir adds a flourish of ornamental melody:

The finest work in this vein, perhaps the finest motet in the whole *Sacrae Symphoniae*, sets a text to which Gabrieli returned later; it is not difficult to see why. 'O Jesu mi dulcissime' is a Christmas prayer, not unlike 'O magnum mysterium' in its invocation of the Christ child in the manger. Its text has features of which any composer of the later sixteenth century might have been glad, a high level of intensity, enough repetition of ideas to give formal structure (the first two phrases obviously run in parallel), a unifying overall mood. While for Gabrieli, the very fact that there is little explicit imagery must have been attractive, for he was not fond of madrigalisms in church music.

> O Jesu mi dulcissime,
> Adoro te in stabulo
> Commorantem;
> O puer dilectissime,
> Adoro te in praesepio
> Jacentem;
> O Christe, Rex piissime,
> Adoramus te in faeno
> Cubantem,
> In coelo fulgentem;
> O mira Dei pietas,
> O singularis caritas,
> Christus datus est,
> Jesus natus est,
> Datus est a patre,
> Natus est de virgine matre,
> O divina ergo proles,
> Te colimus hic homines,
> Ut veneremur coelites.

Gabrieli's setting is in some ways modest. A fully vocal performance is possible and indeed quite effective. The piece is no longer than most of the others in the collection. Yet the opening section is expansive: some fourteen bars for the *coro grave*, in which rich harmony is succeeded by a tense, closely imitative treatment of a figure for 'adoro te', and then in turn by the full sound of a series of passing notes. The scale is increased by the second phrase preserving the shape of the first, while altering the material so that the innocent melody of the opening becomes an emotive leap of a sixth. Such varied repetition is common throughout the piece, textures being filled out (the adoration motif comes back yet again in a version for full ensemble) or new contrapuntal elaboration given to a phrase which otherwise seems a simple re-statement. The climax, 'O divina ergo', for instance, seems to be an inflation of a chordal block at its second appearance, until at the end of the repetition one realizes that the decorative scale of the second choir's tenor has given a complete change of tonal direction. The approach to this climax, a sudden transformation from a G major chord to one of E flat, shows Gabrieli searching for new harmonic relationships: not, one notices, new chords such as the avant-garde composers enjoyed, but the juxtaposition of chords in unusual ways. And there is a rare touch of chromaticism for 'O mira Dei pietas':

Gabrieli's double choir motets up to 1597

The consideration of the motets for really large forces has been deferred until a later chapter since the obligatory participation of instruments necessarily caused the growth of St. Mark's orchestra, which must be discussed in detail. Nevertheless, although the obvious patriotic Venetian pieces have thus been excluded from this discussion, the most characteristically Gabrielian music lies in the double-choir music which forms the bulk of the *Sacrae Symphoniae*. It is music of great skill, the more so in view of its originality; more than that, it is music of great expressive power, with a wider range of emotion than appears on the surface. Its scale may preclude intimacy, but not personal feelings, which are frequently strong. It is not extravagant music, either, for although the very idea of *cori spezzati* suggests the kind of excesses characteristic of some nineteenth-century orchestrators, Gabrieli makes the techniques of the double choir an integral part of his conception and exploits them as economically as Berlioz manipulates his great orchestra. The tutti matter less than the dialogue in which all are involved, the ebullience less than the richness which can be wrung from eight different melodic strands. The other possible extravagance of the epoch is equally left unexploited. At a time when the words suggested strong contrast to a composer, Gabrieli remained surprisingly immune to the disease. A verbal image may suggest a musical figure, 'surrexit' a rising phrase or 'descendit' (as in 'Angelus Domini') a falling one: but it will be musical implications of the idea which will govern its working out.

This mixture of a sense of public ceremony and compositional skill at conveying personal emotion is less Venetian than Counter-Reformation. For the art of the resurgence of the Roman Church contains all these things. It is an art which speaks to the laity, yet without condescension, and it is based on the strongly held belief that there is one True Church. Gabrieli's music is certainly grand and impressive. But it speaks to an audience in a way that perhaps no previous church music had. The *missae breves*, even of Palestrina, express doctrines rather than personal emotion; the grandeur of Andrea Gabrieli is confined to less subtle propositions; the intensity of Lasso's *Penitential Psalms* belongs to the realm of *musica reservata* rather than of public music. The nearest approach to Gabrieli comes in some of the late works of Palestrina, such as the *Missa Assumpta est Maria*, where similar sonorities are both as colourful and as finely used. Even here, Gabrieli's range of both technique and emotion is wider. Above all, it is better tuned to an audience. Anyone not totally unmusical must have found it thrilling. There is never a need of technical appreciation to feel its purpose. Gabrieli's spacing of chords, especially those at the end of a piece, is blended to make an effect, not necessarily a bright one (though the end of 'Domine Dominus noster' shows that this can be done) but always satisfying to the ear. A price has been paid to achieve this. The individual melodic lines are no longer intricately wrought. Sometimes they are dull recitations of a few notes—though Gabrieli's penchant for counterpoint in his final sections can relieve this. But for Gabrieli it is the total effect which counts: church music is now a part of public life.

CHAPTER FIVE

The Madrigals

GABRIELI'S volume of *Sacrae Symphoniae* was the third massive retrospective collection of a Venetian composer's music. Its predecessors were Willaert's *Musica Nova* (1559) and Andrea's *Concerti*; and it differs from both in one very significant feature. They had been a mixture of secular and sacred, while Giovanni included only religious music. Maybe this was merely a matter of publisher's convenience, but on examining the role of the madrigal in his total *oeuvre* it is impossible not to feel that his preference lay in the main for the church. He admittedly had contributed to madrigalian anthologies since his youth, yet had taken no initiative in collecting this kind of piece into a single volume. And by 1597 his secular music had virtually dried up. There is no sign that he wrote any madrigals after he was in his mid-forties—and towards the end of these years, they became few and far between.

These facts are revealing. Lasso and Palestrina might at the end of their lives have repented of their earlier activities, but the publication of their madrigals and chansons (not to mention the former's bawdy lieder and villanelle) had done their reputations no harm in their younger years. As for the men of Giovanni's own generation, they were almost all concerned to achieve the fame that was only to be found away from the organ loft. Madrigal books dedicated to the right person were rewarded by money; and though this may not have represented a substantial form of income, the result might even be a post at court. Glory also rewarded the secular musician. The great names of the last two decades of the century were those of Marenzio and Vecchi. When Dowland visited Venice in 1595 he saw Croce, not Gabrieli, for Croce was a madrigalist of world-wide reputation. And when Thomas Morley wanted to be scathing about a cadence used by *vieux jeu* composers, he writes 'that is the trick of some old organist'[1]—and that in the very year when Gabrieli—some old

[1] T. Morley, *A Plain and Easy Introduction to Practical Music* (London, 1597); modern edition, ed. R. A. Harman (London, 1952), p. 272.

organist?—published his first magnum opus. Clearly success came to secular composers.

Gabrieli's large scale madrigals

Gabrieli could not avoid the composition of secular music altogether. From at least the mid-century, Venetian composers had written madrigals in praise of Venice, obviously for occasions when some spectacular processions outside St. Mark's needed, not a Latin motet with some liturgical connotation, but a frankly patriotic chorus to stir the populace. Indeed, the Ascension Day crossing of the Bucintoro to the Lido with the choir 'singing Epithalamiums all the way'[2] probably required something of this sort. Although no music of this kind by Giovanni Gabrieli has come down to us, there was one further occasion when official secular music was a *sine qua non*: the pastoral play given in the courtyard of the Doge's Palace several times a year. This seems to have been a whim of particular Doges, rather than a tradition, for the surviving corpus does not reveal a very extended run. There are some plays dating from the 1580s when Doges Da Ponte and Cicogna had a taste for them,[3] but the bulk came from Marino Grimani's reign, the decade from 1595; several times a year the courtyard of the Palazzo Ducale was the scene of such entertainments.[4]

The music for these pastorals was likely to be lost. Unlike motets, they could never be used again, since at the next festival there would be a completely new play. Nor was the verse of great quality, though admittedly clothed adequately with music, the plays might pass a pleasant hour or two. What may have been Gabrieli's first official secular work for his Doge survives[5] and is in fact part of the music for just such an entertainment, allowing us a glimpse of how the music fitted in. The final scene of the 'rappresentatione' given in front of Doge Pasqual Cicogna on the Day of St. Stephen (26 December) 1585 is a rather feeble poetic conversation between Apollo, Mercury, and the Muses. It begins

> O che felice giorno
> Quel fu mai lieto e dilettoso tanto
> Celebriamolo, o Muse, in festa e in canto.

[2] See excerpt from Lassels, Chapter II, p. 21.
[3] Museo Correr, Cicogna Op. P.D. 12594.
[4] Museo Correr, Cicogna Op. P.D. 11866–96. This is a collected edition made by Antonio Groppo in 1767. There are copies of individual items in the Biblioteca Marciana and also in the Raccolta Rolandi in the Fondazione Cini.
[5] The text is contained in 'Rappresentatione al Sereniss. Principe di Venetia . . . PASQUAL CICOGNA Il giorno di S. Stefano 1585', Biblioteca Marciana Misc. 179.9 p. 201.

Then after more dialogue the entertainment is drawn to a close with the same words. This time it is marked 'canto in liuti', and the implication is that it is a duet: a further marking says 'Qui segue una Musica di voci', and it may be that there was dancing also, for several of these Venetian spectacles end with morescas, as did Monteverdi's *L'Orfeo*.

Gabrieli's setting of an expanded version of the opening was included in an anthology put out by Gardano in 1590 called *Dialoghi musicali de diversi eccellentissimi autori*. Like most of the contents of the volume, it takes the form of a madrigal for double choir, and there is no attempt at a division of roles. But it is a much more tuneful piece than any of Giovanni's motets in ostensibly the same idiom. The soprano line of each choir is highly melodious and they work together quite effectively as a duet. We know that such dialogues were sung with lute or keyboard accompaniment, so this may be the 'canto in liuti':[6]

Certainly as a choral piece it would make an effective conclusion to the play. The writing is simpler than in the motets, with no intricate counterpoint (though there is an unobtrusive canon in the final bars) and no close dialogue work, which might be ineffective in the open air. In its place are some madrigalisms: a delightful melismatic motif that makes the phrases balance, a drone bass for the word 'sampogne' (pipes), strong rhythms of the kind attractive to the amateur singer, and plain diatonic harmony of no great sophistication. It is not really surprising that it was popular, though to find it as a 'Hodie Christus natus est' in the posthumous collec-

[6] In confirmation of this method of performance it is significant that the manuscript parts preserved in Kassel, in the Murhardsche und Landesbibliothek Mus. ms no. 57 N, contain two soprano parts, two bass parts, and two continuo parts.

tion, *Reliquiae Sacrorum Concentuum*, is a little more unexpected, for it has none of the grandeur which those words evoked from him for Christmas in St. Mark's, or the fervour of the more intimate religious music.

The verse of most of the other grand madrigals suggests that they were written in similar circumstances even though we cannot trace the precise occasions. Nearest in style to 'O che felice giorno' is a work from the same anthology, 'Dormiva dolcemente': Thyrsis is regarding the sleeping form of his shepherdess Cloris, while the cupids around her insist that, since time lost is never regained, it would be foolish to waste it. This is not a piece for large forces, and the upper voice of each choir is again flowing and melodious, though there is no reason to think that this also was sung as a duet. The difference between these two dialogues lies in the fact that 'Dormiva dolcemente' is more of a true madrigal, working out the images more closely. The 'sleep' motif in long 'white' notes; the turn for 'intorno' (around); the teasing decorative motif to show Thyrsis' foolishness, the lowering of the voices as he stoops over his beloved to kiss her; the kissing itself in a dancing triple measure; all these are exactly the sort of inventions which the Marenzians used for verbal illustration. The fine mastery of the idiom suggests a madrigalist of some fluency, and again we may wonder why Gabrieli did not develop further in this field.

Madrigal style as applied to works written for large forces

In the pieces for really large forces there is less scope for detail, though it is remarkable how madrigal techniques do prevail. The musical scale sometimes seems very expansive: 'A Dio dolce mia vita', for ten voices disposed in two equal choirs, outdoes even some of the grander motets simply because it hovers between the *misura di breve* (the official time signature) and the *misura comune* with its host of black notes. The latter eventually controls the tempo and sets the mood, a delightful anacreontic flirtation between Damon and Cloris. The poet suggests that since the shepherdess is so unaccommodating, death, in which their two bodies will be united, is the only solution; and although apparently the death image is not, for once, the veiled image of sexual fulfilment, Gabrieli's setting is far from tragic. There are, admittedly, dissonances for the image of death —but they are pinpricks; there are the minor intervals for the speeches of the young man, opposed to the rather flippant ripostes of his lady—but at the climax all voices sing mainly sonorous major chords. The verse has all the makings of the sensuous erotica of Giaches de Wert or the young Monteverdi. But though Gabrieli paints the somewhat detached, disdainful shepherdess well, more especially in her flighty rhythms, and makes the contrast with her more serious lover, there is little passion in the work. Long phrases inhibit the tensions of dialogue, the repetition of the final section gives size but takes away the drama. Gabrieli is more of a musician than a dramatist; the virtues of 'A Dio dolce mia vita' lie in its delightful music, not in its painting of a scene.

The same is true of an even grander work, 'Amor, dove mi guidi', a twelve-voiced, three-choir work built as solidly as the church music for similar forces. This time sonority is important, and the tutti is involved in nearly half the work, with a splendid peroration in the style of Andrea. In fact, its whole attitude is reminiscent of Giovanni's uncle. The verse has no pretensions to great passion. The lover asks why Venus is smiling. She replies that today he will win his beloved, his desires will be satisfied. Giovanni needs nothing more, for his contrasts come from the division of the choirs, not the divisions of mood. His 'beati tormenti' inspire a series of plain chords such as he might use for the 'Gloria Patri et Filio' of a psalm—and the phrase is repeated in exactly the same way as in his church music:

Ex.2

The passages for single choir which lead up to this are more obviously madrigalian, and since they have the firm harmonic framework customary in polychoral music, they take on something of the style of the canzonettas of the 1580s, especially in the working out of a melismatic 'smiling' motif for the word 'riso'. This is yet another sidelight on Gabrieli's nature, for here he reveals a lightness of touch unexpected in such a massive piece.

In fact, probably his most attractive dialogue madrigal is the one written for smallest forces. 'Dolce nemica mia' was published in the *Concerti*, which again suggests comparisons with Andrea, and its seven-voiced format puts one in mind of the latter's 'Tirsi morir volea' and of Baldissare Donato's similarly scored 'Ahi miserelle ahi sventurate noi'.[7] The protagonists are the inevitable boy and girl, he asking for her mercy to equal her beauty, she promising that the delights of love will all be the greater for a proper courtship; and they sing of their happiness together in the final lines. An absence of sexual innuendo in the verse probably suited Giovanni extremely well, for his interest is again less in the elements of dialogue than the opportunities it offers for varied sonorities. Thus he refuses the logic of representing the girl by upper voices and the man by lower voices, in favour of a texture in which a single voice of either choir can reinforce the other group, as needed to provide a fuller texture. The sense of the protagonists is not altogether lacking. The slightly sombre colour of the lower voices, their 'white' notes growing with increasing animation into crotchets and quavers, gives an idea of the male; the flirtatious, villanella-like cross-rhythms of the upper voices, the fragmentary, questioning motifs in which she offers (quite respectably) her eyes and lips, are the stuff of Arcadian shepherdesses. But when the two join together to give a full texture at the conclusion the music takes on a new depth, and the last half-dozen bars, with the dissonance, at first in brief crotchets, growing to more voluptuous minim suspensions when the piece broadens out, give a flavour of increased emotion (see Example 3).

Occasional music

These dialogues or double-choir madrigals indicate why Gabrieli became a favourite composer for wedding madrigals and pieces in homage of some great personage. There was a considerable demand for such works. Many madrigal books opened or closed with some such attempt to stir noble purse-strings; and a complete volume of madrigals could form a pleasant wedding present. It is more doubtful whether such works were always

[7] A. Einstein, *The Italian Madrigal* (Princeton, 1949), III, p. 155.

intended for performance; some may have been meant to delight the eye (for some homage books are very elegant in appearance) rather than destined for arduous rehearsals and performance; though it is a lack of archival material which suggests these doubts. For although private records of payments, receipts and so on seldom survive, the occasional description of a wedding does mention, among the grandeur of intermezzi and other scenic marvels, *tafelmusik* as a further delight for the guests.[8] As we have seen, visitors to Venice were honoured with lavish entertainments: serenades on the canals and concerts outside the palazzi in

[8] For a description of some of these occasions see H. M. Brown: 'A cook's tour of Ferrara in 1529', *Rivista Italiana di Musicologia* X (1975), p. 216.

the many squares of the city. The homage to the Fuggers, 'Sacri de Giove augei', which Giovanni included in the *Concerti* as a tribute to its dedicatee, looks very much as though it were meant for an occasion like this; its manner is very like that of Andrea's greeting to the Archduke Charles of Carinthia, 'Felici d'Adria',[9] Giovanni's has twelve voices in a single choir, and the material is subtly worked out. On closer examination the subtlety mainly consists in interesting groupings of the voices, rather than the passing of thematic material through the ensemble. Equal voices are normally paired so that they answer one another, and the inner parts frequently have little melodic significance. Still, there is considerable contrapuntal skill at the climaxes, combined with a simplicity and regularity of harmony which makes the piece quite capable of impressive execution.

Such works have been denied the name of madrigal by one commentator,[10] but this is true only if the range of the genre is narrowed to that of domestic chamber music; and there are many works in the sixteenth century which will not fit into that classification, such as the pair of madrigals 'In nobil sangue' and 'Amor s'è in lei', the first apparently by Andrea and the second by Giovanni, included in the *Concerti* (I say 'apparently' since mistakes happen on sixteenth-century contents pages, and it is just possible that both pieces were written by the same man). The *prima parte* of the pair is written in the old-fashioned counterpoint of the decade earlier, with steady 'white' notes throughout and a total lack of any kind of post-Rore expression. The *seconda parte* uses the *misura comune* (though a couple of the partbooks have a ₵ signature) and although the long note values still predominate, there is a moment of liveliness when the beloved's eyes are contemplated; and then, when it is claimed that their beauty turns night into day, a musical image is used which is reminiscent of a passage in one of Andrea's earlier madrigals, 'Quando penso a quel loco',[11] from the *Primo Libro de Madrigali* of 1566, complete with 'eye music' (the black notation) and tone painting of the most vivid sort (see Example 4).

The final section returns to minims and semibreves, but there are dissonances for the word 'amaro', a surprisingly passionate phrase involving unusual melodic qualities—the use of augmented thirds and diminished fourths—and a fine dominant pedal to bring the work to a superb ending.

[9] See Chapter One above.
[10] Kenton, p. 405.
[11] Modern edition, ed. D. Arnold, *Ten Madrigals* (London, 1970).

Ex.4

Madrigals written on a smaller scale

Other madrigals were commissioned from Gabrieli around this time, which indicates that he was in fact quite prolific in the genre in the late 1580s. Over a dozen of his madrigals were published during his first six years as organist at St. Mark's, no great number for a professional at this kind of music, but enough to show that he had developed a distinctive approach to its style. Surprisingly, the linked pair of *madrigali spirituali*, 'Signor le tue man sante' and 'Vergine il cui figliol', which he contributed to a fashionable collection called *Musica spirituale composta da diversi . . . a cinque voci* published by Gardano in 1586, are the least typical, and in some ways the least satisfactory. The long note-values throughout most of the piece belie the modern time-signature, and the same indecisiveness shows in other ways. There is plenty of word-painting: dissonance for 'weeping'; high notes for 'heaven'; a splendid melismatic figure for the glory of the ascension; and an equally imaginative touch in the slow descent of the Saviour to earth. There are chromaticisms, a 'sigh' motif for the plea of the penitent observer of these events. Yet it is impossible not to think how much better Gabrieli could shape these ideas in his motets, where he would develop the material rather than merely repeating it as he does at some length here. Admittedly he avoids the clever superficiality of Marenzio, whose spiritual madrigals of 1584 are much easier on the ear and mind, more modern and more effective—and noticeably deficient in passion.

Gabrieli is much more at home in another pair of madrigals published in 1586, 'Sacro tempio d'honor', with a second part 'Tal di vostra virtute'; perhaps these were wedding madrigals, or at least dedicated to a great lady. Gabrieli begins in his solemn manner with slow-moving block chords, leading to contrasts between upper and lower voices, the groups linked by quavers. But quavers soon bring in a lighter mood, and it remains lively, with a short triple-time section, in the best 'alleluja' tradition. The motet style is never far away: there is little attempt at word-painting; final chords are gently plagal; repetitions usually have some significant alteration. The motet feeling is reinforced by the fact that though the quavers are frequent, they never prevent the harmony from moving at a steady pace, for the figurations are constructed round triads instead of being freely moving melody from which the chords may evolve.

The influence of the modern madrigal style on Gabrieli

On first sight, these traces of the church musician disappear in the six madrigals which Giovanni included in his uncle's *Il terzo libro de madrigali a cinque voci*, printed in 1589. They were probably put in as a makeweight, for Andrea's music was clearly not left in convenient publishable packages, and nearly all the volumes edited by his nephew had to have an unusual form (for example, the volume of four-part madrigals is brought up to strength with some instrumental canzonas). Giovanni's contributions to the book were probably not all composed at the same time, since a couple of them are *misura di breve* works with older traits than those in the modern *misura comune*. Even so, they all suggest that Gabrieli was fully acquainted with the Marenzio fashion of the 1580s. The verse is admittedly not of the best. Still, it provides useful *poesia per musica*, light rather than deeply involved, and with enough imagery to give the composer a chance for some realistic touches. 'S'al discoprir' and 'Queste felici herbette' between them seem to contain all the vogue ideas of pastoral verse: flowers (to be set with a flourish or ornament), a touch of anguish (dissonances), birds (melismas), the extinguished light when the girl's eyes do not look at her lover (black notation), and so on. 'Dimmi ben mio' and 'Dolci care parole' neglect this aspect somewhat, but give a pleasant mood of none-too-serious lovemaking far from the solemnities of marriage, and this is reflected in the music. The bright colours of upper voices predominate in four madrigals out of the six. Indeed 'Queste felici herbette' might be written for the Ladies of Ferrara, for the uppermost parts need true sopranos and the middle voice demands a mezzo-soprano of the kind that Wert and Monteverdi wrote for.[12] The sprightly rhythms of this, and the others in the *misura comune*, are up-to-date, and when added to the dia-

[12] It is possible, however, that the piece was intended to be transposed, as the clefs fit the 'chiavette' criteria of various theorists. See G. Reese, *Music in the Renaissance* (New York, 1959), p. 530 for the clearest exposition of these theories.

tonic harmony the whole manner is typical of the later 1580s. In fact, they could well be the work of some minor—but highly competent—English madrigalist.

And it is precisely this which shows that Gabrieli is not really a Marenzian. These madrigals are the work of a church musician or organist—as were most of the English composers—not of an academician or courtier. The most obvious sign comes in the opening bars where in four out of six the favourite canzona rhythm 𝅗𝅥 ♩ ♩ or the derivative 𝅗𝅥. ♪♩ occurs. Einstein maintained that this was a composer's way of illustrating a narrative text, an observer's rather than a participant's point of view.[13] It might be true of 'S'al discoprir'; it is much more doubtful of 'Da quei begl'occhi' or 'Vagh'amorosi'. This very likely comes from the organist's custom of arranging French chansons for keyboard.[14] The first few bars of 'Vagh' amorosi' in fact would fit the disposition of the hand very conveniently:

'Da quei begl'occhi' has the more modern texture of upper voices but the same kind of thematic material, and the nature of Gabrieli's thinking is evident in the way that nearly all the motifs used for development are related to the chanson rhythm. The opening shows it in its pristine form; the repeated notes of 'Ch'amorzasse la fiamma' emphasize the similarity, the shape of the motif with its rise of a third maintaining the feeling of development; while 'fiamma ch'estinguer' is a clear rhythmic diminution (see Example 6).

As we have seen in Chapter Three, the chanson writers often repeat their opening section at the end, to give a neatly rounded formal pattern.

13 'Narrative rhythm in the madrigal', *Musical Quarterly*, 29 (1943).
14 See Chapter Three above.

Ex.6

a)

Da quei begl' oc – chi o ve s'ac – ce – – – se il fo – co,
Da quei begl' oc – chi o ve s'ac – ce – se il fo – – – – – co,
O – ve s'ac – ce – se il fo – co,

b)

ch'a – mor – zas – se la fiam – ma, ch'a mor – zas – se la
ch'a – mor – zas – se la fiam – ma, ch'a – mor – zas – se la fiam – –
ch'a – mor – zas – se la fiam – ma, ch'a – mor – zas – se la fiam – ma

fiam – ma,
– ma il no – – vo hu – mo – re,
il no – – vo hu – mo – re,
il no – – vo hu – mo – – re,

c)

Fiam – ma ch'es-
Fiam – ma ch'es – tin – – guer non po – trò più ma – – –
Fiam – ma ch'es – tin – – guer non po – trò più ma –
Fiam – ma ch'es – tin – guer non po – trò più ma –

– tin – guer non po – trò più ma – – i,
– i,
– i, non po – trò più ma – – i,
i,

Gabrieli does not quite do this, but he usually repeats, as in earlier pieces, the final section. In 'Dolce care parole' this repetition is exact. More often there is a subtler approach, as in 'Da quei begl' occhi', where a new ending is given to the phrase, or in 'S'al discoprir', where the very noticeable triple-time setting of 'ch'ascose il lume' leads to two totally different workings out of the succeeding material. Still more sophisticated is 'Dimmi ben mio', for although the concluding triple-time bars are exactly repeated, they are immediately preceded by the very opening of the whole madrigal, which vividly recalls the chanson style, except that chanson composers rarely thought of such an ingenious variation of their mechanical *da capo*.

It is not a coincidence that these madrigals appeared in a book of Andrea's works, for they are in many ways Giovanni's nearest approach to the style of his uncle. Andrea too uses repetitions, likes the same type of verse, has bright textures. Yet there is a difference. The older man is a member of the post-Rore generation, interested in the meaning of the words, even if he takes care never to choose verse which might drive him to extremes. Giovanni is much more the pure musician, whose first concern is with musical shape. A man who, in 1589, could set the words 'cruda' (cruel) and 'fera' (savage) to innocuous minor chords was scarcely aware of the way the genre was developing:

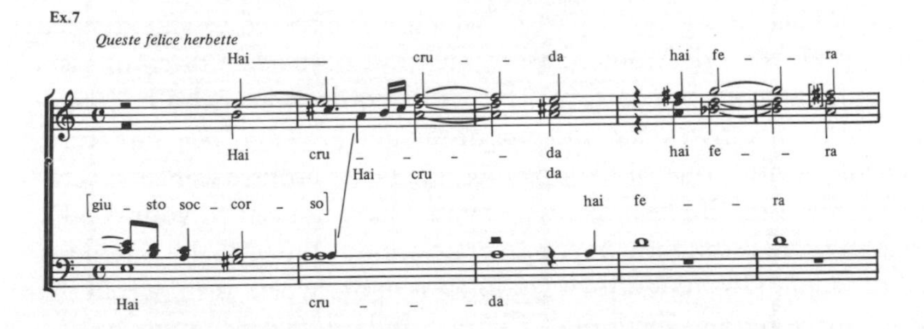

Again the analogy with the English comes to mind. Most of Gabrieli's preoccupations are to be found in the professional (as opposed to amateur) composers in England. They too are thorough in developing themes and shaping their madrigals into satisfactory entities which could stand apart from verbal considerations (hence on English title pages 'apt for voices and viols'). And so these mature madrigals of Gabrieli have English virtues. They are extremely pleasant to sing. Any irregularities of melody are smoothed away. The intervals which might cause difficulty, such as the minor sixth, are either avoided or carefully resolved. The complex syncopated rhythms which crop up in the work of Lasso's generation have been modified to pleasant little off-beat patterns which interrupt well-established metrical units. Decorative figures for verbal illustration or for purely musical delight are planned to emphasize main stresses, not to cause excitement by testing the singer's skill. Finally, there is no disturbing emotional exaggeration.

Gabrieli's declining output of madrigals

Gabrieli's production of madrigals diminished in the following decade. It was a decade of gloom for the serious composer. The favoured verses were now the laments from Guarini's *Il Pastor Fido*; the favoured musical style was mannerist. Experimentation was all the rage; no holds were barred in the exploitation of dissonance or angular melody and since 'progress' was so rapid, it is noticeable that the actual output of each composer diminishes. Monteverdi published virtually nothing for eleven years after *Il terzo libro de madrigali*, and even Marenzio, previously Schubertian in ease and productivity, slowed down to the pace of an ordinary mortal. If Gabrieli knew of the latest developments at this time (and he certainly did in later years), he might well have thought that the madrigal form was not for him. How far away he was from such things is shown in a six-voiced madrigal, 'S'io t'ho ferito', which he contributed in 1591 to a collection called *La Ruzina*, the greatest part of which was devoted to an extended sequence by Filippo di Monte, hardly the most up-to-date of composers at this time, with even a madrigal by Cipriano de Rore, who had been dead some twenty-five years. In spite of the old *misura di breve* signature, and the long white notes of the opening, the poem arouses some expectation of modernism. 'If I have wounded you, I have not caused your death'. Gabrieli's way of setting the poem gives no sense of the probably intended sexual meaning. His straightforward interest in the words is shown in the emphasis made by his repetitions of phrase. Indeed, Gabrieli must be one of the very few composers of his age actually to refuse dissonance for the word 'death'; at the cadence which concludes the first section, he manages to avoid the customary suspension (see Example 8).

It will surprise no one that he takes the opportunities offered by the repeated phrase. The canzona rhythm 𝅗𝅥 ♩ ♩ is stated in double note values; the chanson shape is even closer than usual, with a 'da capo' section (though characteristically varied) at the end; and in addition there is the middle-section ritornello, allowing for a sudden breaking away into new material. It is the organist at work again, and seen as a piece of abstract

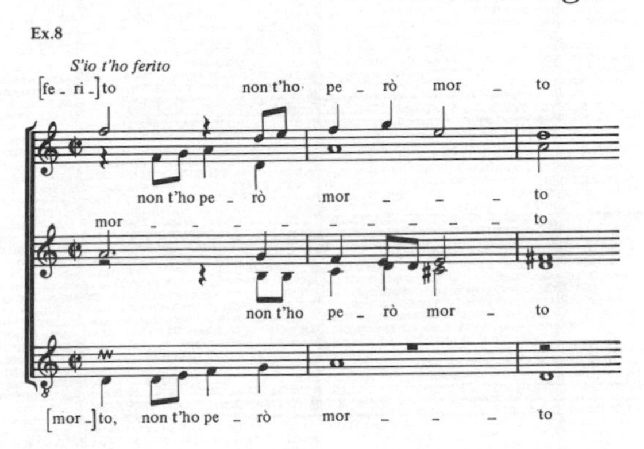

music it is a splendid work, using most effectively the sonorities suggested by the large ensemble.

Gabrieli and Marenzio: 'Il Trionfo di Dori'

Gabrieli's contribution to the famous collection *Il Trionfo di Dori* (1592), in honour of the bride of the Venetian nobleman Leonardo Sanuto, is another testament to Gabrieli's musicianship rather than his feeling for imagery, as can be seen by comparing 'Se cantano gl'augelli' with almost any contribution to the collection by other composers. The verse for all of them is full of strong visual images. The refrain 'Viva la bella Dori' is a gift to an 'instrumental' composer such as Gabrieli, but elsewhere he unexpectedly vies with Marenzio and the rest. The gambolling of the animals in this pastoral scene is expressed by the passage from one voice to another of a playful motif; Cupid's arrows are shot in a rapid canonic figure, and the fish in their deep pools are depicted by a descending scale. But compared with this Marenzio's own 'Leggiadre Ninfa' is even so a wonder of musical realism: black notation for the shady valleys, a flourish for 'fior', wreathing ornaments for 'ghirlandette', triple time for the dances of satyrs. Even the proportions of the setting of the refrain show the differences between them. In madrigals of much the same length (about seventy-five bars), Marenzio is content with some ten bars of coda, while Gabrieli has twenty-two; and his final eight bars show him writing a piece of solid counterpoint over a cantus firmus-like bass (see Example 9).

'Se cantano gl'augelli' was probably Gabrieli's most famous madrigal simply because *Il Trionfo di Dori* was the most famous collection to which he contributed. The anthology received a reprinting in Germany, complete with translations, and since it was the model for *The Triumphs of*

Oriana, Gabrieli's work must have been known in Britain also, though it is significant that it was Croce's madrigal in the volume which was translated into English, and probably inspired the emulation of Thomas Morley.[15]

Gabrieli's canzonettas

After this piece, there was a gap of three years before Gabrieli published any more madrigals, and it was a pupil, Francesco Stivori, who persuaded him to take up the genre once more for an anthology called *Vaghi e dilettevoli madrigali a quattro voci*. They might, however, be more accurately described as canzonettas, for all three works are really light music of the sort that Croce and, lately, Giovanni Bassano, had been producing. Thomas Morley described canzonets most aptly as '. . . little short songs (wherein little art can be showed, being made in strains, the beginning of which is some point lightly touched and every strain repeated except the

[15] J. Kerman, 'Morley and the Triumphs of Oriana', *Music and Letters*, 34 (1953).

middle) which is, in composition of the music, a counterfeit of the Madrigal'.[16] The melodic material certainly is just the same as in the grander genre, even to the separated 'sigh' motif to set the repeated exclamation 'Deh' in 'Labbra amorose e care', and the turn for 'canta' in 'Deh di me non ti caglia', which was a commonplace of madrigals at the time. The repetitions of the canzonetta are very much in evidence in them all too, for although they are not 'made in strains', that is, in separate phrases, the overlapping is never very sophisticated, and certainly never obscures the basic shape. But 'wherein little art can be shown' is certainly untrue. There is a great deal of technique in these pieces, just as in some of Morley's best work of this kind. In the middle of 'Ahi senza te', after the sombreness of G minor tonality, a chord of A major brightens the mood:

In 'Labbra amorose e care', the lover pleads to be allowed to live in peace in *faux bourdon* thirds and sixths:

The final section of 'Ahi senza te' broadens out by means of its ambiguous musical answer (setting the words 'la pena amara') to the previous propo-

[16] Morley, op. cit., p. 295.

sition 's'al mio cor vuoi scemar'. Such devices are far from the innocence of the lesser composers of light music, and show that a great master can reveal new potentialities in even the most apparently simple forms.

Gabrieli's final works in secular genres

The gap of silence now increases to five years. This time it is the wedding of a friend, and collaboration with another which spurs Gabrieli to secular music. In 1600 Georg Gruber of Nuremberg married Helen Joanna Kolmann, and music by Gabrieli and Hans Leo Hassler was printed by the famous Nuremberg publishing house of Kauffmann in their honour. We do not now even possess the originals of the wedding songs they wrote, for although Winterfeld transcribed from them nearly a century and a half ago, they have since disappeared and we are left only with his nineteenth-century score, which, for all its utility as a record, poses problems which only the prime source might settle. That, and a *contrafactum*—that is, a version with religious words—which Gruber included in Gabrieli's and Hassler's posthumous *Reliquiae Sacrorum Concentuum*, are all that survive of 'Scherza Amarilli', Gabrieli's contribution to the celebrations. Seen out of context, this is a very curious piece, more a motet than a madrigal, for although there are madrigalian figures, it begins with a typical 'Alleluja' refrain (which is what it becomes in the *contrafactum*), and the sonorities which one associates with the *cappella* of St. Mark's. Yet there is nothing quite like it in his religious *oeuvre*, for the rhythms and the short-breathed counterpoint of the madrigalian sections are secular enough. But if difficult to classify, it is certainly a brilliant piece, grand enough for the most sumptuous of nuptials.

It may be that in this same year the most magnificent of all Gabrieli's secular pieces was composed, for the text of the dialogue 'Udite chiari e generosi figli' refers quite clearly, as Egon Kenton has pointed out,[17] to the arrival of a new century, though his suggestion that it was written for 1 January 1600 must be approached with caution, since the Venetian year began in March. In fact, a more probable occasion would seem to have been at the end of the entertainment given on St. Stephen's Day, 26 December 1600. It was the usual rather feeble poetic affair, called *Le Nozze di Hadriana*,[18] and would hardly be worth attention if it had not a chorus of the Sea Gods, the 'Dei Marini'. The words for some of the items are given; others are not. 'What sweet sounds, what new sound is this?', says Curtio Romano, to which Plavio Pastorello replies 'It is the sound of the

[17] Kenton, p. 360. [18] Museo Correr, Cicogna Op. P.D. 11866–96.

shells, the shells of the Tritons . . .'—which is where Gabrieli's music comes in. It is preserved only in a set of manuscript partbooks in the 'Schütz collection' in Kassel.[19] It is written for two massive choirs, one marked 'Sirens', the other 'Tritons'; and these are surely the 'Dei Marini' of the poet. In the opening bars the Tritons call to one another as in a

19 Mus ms. no. 57 H.

normal dialogue.[20] But an altogether larger scale is soon apparent, and the grandeur of sound even before the second choir enters is quite astonishing. The manuscript parts tell us that the uppermost line of the first choir is

[20] Kenton aptly suggests (pp. 360–1) that these cries might come from a fisherman greeting a friend sailing some highly coloured Chioggian barque in the heart of the lagoon.

meant for a *cornetto muto* and that the other fourteen parts (excluding the organ) are for voices, but it is not impossible that Gabrieli assembled all the Bassano players, and those led by Laudis, and indeed any others who could be found, to add to the effect. The sheer sound of so many separate strands is what is so impressive. The entry of the tutti 'Su dunque ardit' altera nobilissima schiera' is typical Gabrieli; it might almost be the beginning of a grand doxology by the musician of the Lepanto victory; though this is still grander, and with its chromatic change richer harmonically (see Example 12). Giovanni was to write splendid motets in his remaining years; he never wrote anything more superbly sonorous. It is a piece without shadows, full of major chords and perfect cadences, dynamic syncopation and dancing triple time.

We do not possess another note of secular music which we can date to Gabrieli's later years, not even occasional pieces with Latin words which could be ascribed to ceremonial outside the church.[21] The pastorals in the courtyard of the Palazzo Ducale continued until at least 1605, yet there is no sign of Gabrieli's music in them.

We shall probably never know why he wrote no more secular music. He could easily have been a master of the madrigal, as he was of the motet, even if his secular works would not have followed the trends current at the turn of the century. Certainly his thirty-three madrigals contain some delightful music. Against the trend, they remain Venetian in their musicality and singability. They are not a major contribution to the genre compared with those of other composers in Italy; but in England or Germany or any other country which did not produce such overwhelming riches they would be treasured.

[21] Einstein thought we had lost a corpus of concertante madrigals, but there is no evidence for this, rather the reverse, for as we shall see, his pupils were not encouraged to follow those particular paths.

CHAPTER SIX

The Early Instrumental Music

IT was probably Andrea Gabrieli's experience of the excellent group of players at Munich that caused St. Mark's to found its own permanent instrumental ensemble, for it was within two or three years of his return, about 1565, that the new venture began.[1] Venice was late in making such arrangements: many other cities employed instrumentalists in their civic churches during the sixteenth century.[2] The reason for the delay probably lies with the organization of Venetian institutions. Six silver trumpets had for many years accompanied the Doge on his processional visits throughout the city. They appear in pictures dating back to the late fifteenth century. The Doge paid for these out of his own pocket, as we learn from documents concerning Doge Venier, who tried to divest himself of this responsibility in 1583. The Procurators reminded him that this tradition dated back to 1462 and that he must contribute 180 ducats each year for this purpose.[3] These silver trumpets fulfilled one of the functions of the *piffari* in other towns where public show demanded them as symbols of authority rather than for any musical purpose. They were there when distinguished visitors arrived[4] and attended at state ceremonial. And in many places, they went into church with their masters, presumably changed instruments (for the players were extremely versatile) and took part in the music of the Mass or Vespers. Several cities in *Venezia terra firma* maintained this practice. At Bergamo, the players were often employed in S. Maria Maggiore;[5] at Udine, the regulations licensing the *piffari* in 1493 specifically say that they were to play 'on the special days when solemn processions take place . . . to the Glory of God and of Our

[1] See Chapter One above.
[2] D. Arnold, 'Instruments in Church: some facts and figures', *Monthly Musical Record*, 85 (1955).
[3] They won the case after a commission of enquiry. See A.S.V., Proc. de Supra Busta 67, Processo 148.
[4] Mantua Archivio Gonzaga Busta 402.
[5] C. G. Anthon, *Music and Musicians in Northern Italy during the Sixteenth Century* (Harvard thesis, 1943), p. 240.

Most Serene Prince and Master of Venice'.[6] It was the persuading of the Procurators of St. Mark's which must have been Andrea Gabrieli's task in 1568; and it is not surprising that the initiative came from players from Udine.

Ser. Hieronimo of Udine having made the offer to provide, at his own expense, with wind instruments and with two of his brothers and other musicians, the *concerti* in the organ lofts which usually take place each year to the honour of the church of St. Mark, when the Most Serene Signory come to church at the time of the solemn festivals of Christmas and Easter, and other festivals throughout the year, as will seem best to the Most Excellent Procurators, and as the said Hieronimo will recall; which things being considered by the Procurators at their meeting in the room of His Highness, having consulted His Serenity on 16 December last year and having heard of the efficiency of the said Ser. Hieronimo and how good he is in his profession and work, with the said two brothers; Their Excellencies, having voted, determined that the said Ser. Hieronimo should have the position to provide the *concerti* completely at his expense, as said above, for which he shall be given each year from church funds 75 ducats, payable in four-monthly instalments of 25 ducats.'[7]

Two things are significant in this agreement. Firstly, the stipend was not very large compared with the singers'. This partly reflects the social status of the *piffari*, which was not to be compared with that of employees of the church; and partly it must have been due to the fact that they were not expected to attend so frequently. The singers were supposed—though they often did not—to sing daily. But for the number of times the players were called upon each year, twenty-five ducats still does not seem over-generous. The minute recording the original appointment of the brothers from Udine is not specific on this point, relying on Girolamo's memory and the Procurator's reasonableness; but an entry in the main paybook for 1599 [Venetian style 1598] gives us the details for one musician which probably reflect the custom of the previous twenty years or more.

'... to Battista of Udine, the violinist, who has served in St. Mark's Church since the death of Michael the violinist, on nineteen occasions at half a scudo per occasion as usual, on the following days. The day of the Madonna at mass and vespers; the day of St. Isidore at mass; the vigil of St. Mark at vespers and mass; Easter Sunday at mass; the vigil of Ascension Day at vespers; the feast of Corpus Christi at mass; the day of the Apparition of St. Mark at mass; the day of cele-

[6] G. Vale, 'La Cappella Musicale del Duomo di Udine dal sec. XIII al XIX', *Note d'Archivio'* VII (1930), p. 106.
[7] IMAMI I, p. lxvii.

bration for the peace,[8] the feast of the Nativity of Our Lady; All Saints Day at mass; Christmas Eve at vespers and the midnight mass; Christmas Day at mass; the day of Circumcision at mass; the feast of the Epiphany at mass; the day of Purification at mass . . . in all nineteen occasions at $\frac{1}{2}$ scudo, in all $9\frac{1}{2}$ scudi, on the orders of S. Zuanne Gabrieli, the organist, as entered in the file on 15 February, since [Battista] was not paid with the others'.[9]

The second matter of some moment in the Procurator's agreement is that Girolamo da Udine was left to find other players to make up the ensemble. How often he did this, and whom he co-opted is not therefore revealed by the official documents, but it seems unlikely that the ensemble consisted of more than three or four during the 1570s. The payment of several musicians by the Procurators in 1576[10] seems to indicate that anything larger was beyond Girolamo's means and he must have been relieved at the appointment of Giovanni Bassano as cornettist in the same year, to make up a decently complete unit of instrumentalists without involving him in further expense.

The role of instrumental music in church

It is fairly certain that the main purpose of these players was to swell the sound in the sung parts of mass and vespers. Instrumental support always reduces the problems of intonation and even of balance inherent in *a cappella* performance. So these musicians took part not just in the grand *Concerti* of Andrea Gabrieli, but in many smaller works too. Whether they played independently of the choir, and if so what they played, is a little more uncertain. The descriptions of the ceremonial at St. Mark's in the official records kept by the *maestro del coro* and in the more generalized

[8] See Chapter Seven.

[9] A.S.V., Proc. de Supra, Registro 5, entry under 27 February 1599 [Venetian style 1598]. '. . . a Battista da Udene dal Violin, qual ha servito in Chiesa di S. Marco dopo la morte di Michiel dal Violin, cioè officij n° 19 a S^{do} $\frac{1}{2}$ p officio giusta l'ordinario, nell' infrascritti giorni, cioè in giorno dell^{a} Mad^{na} à messa et à vesp^{ro} offij n° 2: il giorno di S. Isidoro à messa officio uno; la Vigilia di S. Marco à Vesp^{o} et à messa officij 2; et il giorno di Pasqua di maggio [?] off^{o} uno; La Vigilia dell'Ascension à Vesp^{o} off^{o} uno. Il giorno dl. Corpus Dom^{ni} à messa off^{o} uno, Il giorno dell'apparition di S. Marco à messa off^{o} uno; Il giorno che si fece la procession della pace off^{o} uno, Il giorno dlla Natività della Madonna, officio uno, Il giorno di tutti santi à messa officio uno; La Vigilia di Nadal à Vesp^{o} et à messa la notte, et il giorno à messa in tutt^{o} officij N° 3. Il giorno della circoncision à messa officio uno; il giorno dell' epifania à messa officio uno, Il giorno della purification à messa off^{o} 1. In tutto officij n° 19 à S^{di} $\frac{1}{2}$ p officio sono s^{di} $9\frac{1}{2}$ appar p polizza de S. Zuanne Gabrieli Organista di 15 Febraro posta in filza, quali non donatilà pagati alli suoi tempi come li altri . . .'

[10] A.S.V., Proc. de Supra, Registro 3, entry for 31 December.

accounts by such observers as Sansovino do not go into such details, telling us merely that instruments were used. Moreover, though there is a wealth of information about the practice of the seventeenth century in this matter,[11] it is not certain how far this can be applied to a previous era. Nevertheless, a book of church music published in 1622 by Carlo Milanuzzi, who was for a time the organist at Giovanni Gabrieli's own Venetian parish church of S. Stefano, makes clear the possibilities open to the musician:

Concerto for 5 voices for the Introit
Mass [on the madrigal] 'Liquide perle Amor' for 5 voices
Canzona for 5 instruments, entitled 'La Zorzi', for the epistle
Concerto for 5 voices for the Offertory
Concerto for 2 voices for the Elevation of the Host
Canzona for 5 instruments, entitled 'La Riatelli', for the Post Communion
Canzona for 2 instruments [for the viole bastarde?] for the Deo Gratias.[12]

There were thus three pieces for instruments during the Mass, and this in a church whose music could scarcely compare with that in St. Mark's. Something of the same kind could well have been heard in the basilica, though in the 1570s probably not on quite this scale.

The surviving repertory of such music is surprisingly small. The Venetian publishing houses were, it is true, printing music for instrumental ensemble in some quantity from about 1550 onwards, yet a great deal of it, such as the *bicinia* which fill several volumes, the *Fantasie et Recerchari* of G. Tiburtino (1549), and even the *Fantasie, Recercari Contrapunti* (1559) containing works by various composers within the Venetian orbit, seems teaching material rather than music for public pomp. Nor do the works of the musicians of St. Mark's, Jacques Buus and Annibale Padavano, fit into this category; their ricercars look and sound more like chamber music for viols or at least more subtle instruments than those deployed in the Doge's chapel. The dance music which was the staple fare of the *piffari* most certainly could not be considered suitable, and it is likely that vocal music of various kinds was performed. It is significant that Girolamo Dalla Casa's book of instructions on how to embellish melodies, *Il vero modo di diminuir, con tutte le sorti di stromenti*, includes such works as Rore's 'Ancor che col partire', Palestrina's 'Vestiva i colli', and Andrea Gabrieli's 'Amor mi strugge il cor'.

11 S. Bonta, 'The uses of the sonata da chiesa', *Journal of the American Musicological Society* (1969), p. 54.
12 C. Sartori, *Bibliografia della Musica Strumentale Italiana* (Florence, 1952), p. 282.

Andrea Gabrieli's instrumental music

The only volume by a Venetian which contains original instrumental works apparently suitable for the ensemble of the 1570s is by Andrea Gabrieli, the *Ricercari e Madrigali* collected by Giovanni and published in 1589. The madrigals can be traced back to the 1570s, for some of them were performed at the Lepanto celebrations, and the instrumental pieces may date from the same period. There are seven of them, all entitled 'ricercar', though, as in the organ works the terminology is not exact and at least a couple of them are what later composers—including Giovanni—would certainly have called canzonas. All the pieces are for four instruments and thus ideal for the St. Mark's ensemble of the Bassano Dalla Casa period, but even here a distinction between chamber and extra-liturgical church music suggests itself. The 'Ricercar del Secondo Tuono',[13] for example, is a learned piece, written for viols and thus for the domestic enjoyment of the player. The musical language is based on that of the motet. There is very little which could not be sung, for the ranges of the individual parts are clearly defined within those of the soprano, alto, tenor, and bass. There are no awkwardnesses of pitch or melodic intervals, no harmonies which might cause a lapse of intonation, and no ornaments to trouble a less than agile throat. The phrases are admittedly long, but not more so than those in the music of the older Netherlanders on which the style is based. Against this must be set two features which suggest that if it is an instrumental motet, at least it was not meant for church use. One is that it has the flavour of an academic exercise, for the first theme is worked out throughout the whole of the piece, sometimes in its original form, giving variety by new counterpoints, sometimes in augmentation, and in one passage translated into triple time. This might have interested the player: the listener inevitably finds it less appealing. Another feature also suggests domestic performance: there is no attempt to exploit the actual sound of the ensemble. The carefully balanced sonority usual in Andrea's quasi-homophonic passages, where the upper notes of voices or instruments may add brilliance, or the deeper registers may convey sombreness, is totally absent in this neutral piece of polyphony. Further, it is a very long work; yet apart from the triple-time section, it has virtually no variety of texture or mood. The ricercar 'del Primo Tono'[14] is equally academic; here two linked motifs are worked out in the greatest detail and at considerable length. But in this work we see Andrea beginning to move away from the purely learned atmosphere into one of extrovert enjoyment for the listener.

[13] IMAMI I, p. 64. [14] IMAMI I, p. 45.

The time signature is the *misura comune*, but the long notes of the opening indicate a basic minim unit which persists for about two-thirds of the piece. Then a seemingly scholarly thought transforms it: an augmentation is pitted against a diminution. But the result is so lively that Andrea is even forced to use rather awkward octave leaps to maintain the rhythm, and a gay, almost madrigalian atmosphere is achieved:

This final section, though, shows an attempt at a more sympathetic style, and there are two pieces in the set which seem to extend this to the whole of their no less careful construction, though both are somewhat shorter than the ricercars. They are really canzonas, with the familiar chanson rhythm, the repetitions of opening and closing sections, and the lively gait of secular music. The 'Ricercar del Sesto Tono'[15] soon reveals how well it is written for wind instruments by using phrases developed from the chanson motif to show off their powers of articulation. Most of the figures are shaped from scales and motifs which seem essentially instrumental in idiom. It is, however, in purely musical terms that it gains over the more learned music of the true ricercars. The popular flavour of the jaunty opening theme may seem rather light for the working out it receives, but at the climax, counterpoint is put aside and a homophonic phrase, with a single instrument at odds with its fellows and thus underlining their rhythmic power by its cross accents, seems almost military in its fanfare-like strength (see Example 2).

It is in a popular style and it is not difficult to imagine it used to escort the Signory from St. Mark's into the Square, though the actual sound is not particularly brilliant. The piece does have a fullness derived from the fact

[15] IMAMI I, p. 74.

Ex.2

that the whole ensemble is constantly deployed; the brightness which could come from the frequent use of the upper notes of instruments is, on the other hand, not to be found. Again, its tessituras are those of voices. The 'Ricercar del Duodecimo Tono'[16] is quite the opposite and perhaps this is why it is the most popular of Andrea's pieces among brass ensembles of our own day. The way it begins the cantus on a top G is totally unvocal, and indeed demands skill in an instrumentalist. The repeated notes of the canzona motif again dominate the piece, and there is much power in the rhythmic drive of the climax. Its formal pattern is still more organized than that of the 'Ricercar del Sesto Tono', for not only does it repeat its opening section and the central triple-time passage, but it brings back the opening as a *da capo*. Still, it is its very brilliance of sound that makes the predominating impression of grandeur.

Giovanni's earliest instrumental music

Giovanni edited his uncle's ricercars, and the link is evident in the four similar pieces which he wrote for an ensemble *a quattro*.[17] They were not published until 1608, when they appeared in an anthology edited by Alessandro Raverii, but they were probably early works; on stylistic grounds, they seem to belong to the years when Gabrieli was busy writing madrigals in a similar idiom.[18] 'Canzona' was by 1608 the most fashionable title for an instrumental piece, but for these pieces by Giovanni it is no mere convention. The chanson motif dominates them all; all have some characteristic repetition of a whole section, with, in three out of the four, a *da capo* of some dimensions. The spirit of the chanson is here too, for the mood is lively, and even the one in the minor key lives up to its name 'La Spiritata'. The hallmarks of Andrea's canzonas are stamped on these pieces in various ways. Though 'La Spiritata' is not a learned piece,

[16] IMAMI I, p. 86. This is the ricercar printed in Davison and Apel, *Historical Anthology of Music* (Harvard, 1946), I, p. 147.

[17] Ed. A. Einstein, *Vier Canzoni per sonar* (Mainz, 1932).

[18] The latest possible date for 'La spiritata' is 1593, when it appeared in a keyboard version in Diruta's *Il Transilvano*, and stylistically the other three belong to the same period.

most of its material can be traced from the opening rhythm; there are the contrasts between the upper and lower pairs of instruments restating the same material. The fourth canzona begins its cantus on the top G in the same way as in Andrea's 'Ricercar del Duodecimo Tono'. Above all, the idea of a climax in which a homophonic or quasi-homophonic texture is used to emphasize a rhythm appeals to Giovanni, who uses it in each piece:

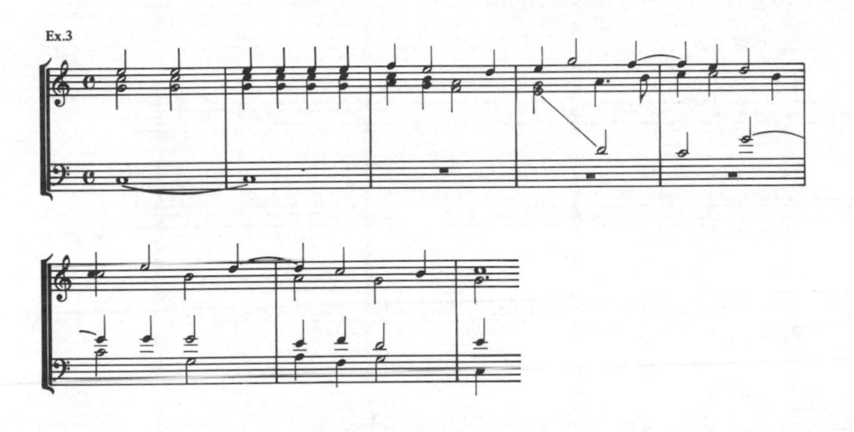

All these pieces are much more suitable for the ceremonial of St. Mark's than those of the elder Gabrieli. The fact that they are all true *misura comune* works, with the gaiety that goes with the 'black' notes, makes them more immediately attractive, and the nature of the counterpoint shows that the freedom of the modern madrigal has helped to create this atmosphere. There is little real polyphony as in Andrea's more learned ricercars. When, in the second canzona Giovanni begins the second main section with imitative entries in the older manner, it sounds quite foreign to the style, and he soon reverts to his normal, essentially harmonic texture. The chordal nature of his music governs the nature of his melodic material. The bass entry of the opening theme of this canzona, virtually unchanged from its original version in the cantus, shows exactly how each metric unit, however full of quavers it may be, outlines a chord:

Ex.4

This means that instead of the highly dense counterpoint which makes Andrea's pieces ineffective for the listener, however interesting they may be to the player, Giovanni can deploy one instrument at a time, while the other three support it, to give a fullness of sound which the ear can readily appreciate. It is difficult to imagine a richer sound for four instruments than the central section of the second canzona. The sustained dominant pedal resolving on to a tonic chord, the substantial bass minims leading to a new key centre, the way the crotchet theme comes mainly in one part at a time while the others 'harmonize' it in an almost chorale-like manner, all result in a climax of considerable power:

These canzonas have, too, instrumental freedom in agility and tessitura. Giovanni Bassano's skill as a cornettist has evidently allowed Gabrieli to write florid and un-vocal cantus parts. These do not as yet contain the virtuoso passage work which he later exploited; but such passages as this clearly lie well under the player's hand:

The most obvious exploitation of instrumental tessitura is to be seen in the uppermost parts, which maintain an altitude that would hardly have been expected even from the most skilled of castrati. But it is equally interesting to find that in the inner parts, Gabrieli exploits low and high notes. The soprano clef of the altus in the fourth canzona, for example, implies a range at least up to E, and at the climax, the upper register is required, as it is also for the tenor. The experienced madrigalist would avoid the introduction of important thematic entries in the lower part of the range; yet Gabrieli goes below the stave in the announcement of the 'chanson' motif, and insists on fast-moving passage work in the same register. The ensuing brilliance points the way ahead, for though these works are still modest and do not materially depart from the canons of sixteenth-century instrumental music, they show quite unusual understanding of the idiom. This is already ceremonial music, albeit on a small scale.

St. Mark's in Giovanni's early years there

In the years just before Giovanni's appointment to the basilica the ensemble was expanded—perhaps in response to just such music. In 1581, the Procurators took an opportunity which came their way:

> . . . it being convenient for the service of the church of St. Mark to have at its disposal the musicians who are needed for the occasions when music is required, and if the occasion presents itself, to be able to obtain the best and principal [musicians], it is a good thing to prepare for such occasions, as was prudently done in the case of the agreement with Sig. Gerolamo of Udine; and since at the present time Sig. Francesco da Mosto is in the city, a man who has been heard in the *concerti* given in the organ lofts last Christmas Night to universal satisfaction, and since Their Excellencies the Procurators wish to come to an agreement with this man so that he does not depart from this city and that he shall be available for the aforesaid occasions: Thus Their Excellencies the Procurators, all seven being met together in the Procuratoria, have voted unanimously that the said Francesco da Mosto shall be appointed, at a salary of 30 ducats per annum, on condition that he takes part together with the aforesaid Gerolamo of Udine, or in the chapel with [Giovanni] Bassano in the aforesaid music, and to continue in this service as shall be required, and as shall be ordered from time to time by the *Maestro di Cappella*.[19]

[19] A.S.V., Proc. de Supra, Registro 135, f. 28, entry for 24 February 1581 (Venetian style 1580): '. . . essendo conveniente che per servicio della chiesa de S. Marco nelle occorrentie delle musiche si habbia pronti quelli musici che in quelle fano bisogno, et quando si offerisce occonē di poterne haver de i primarij, o principali, sia buona cosa fermarli per tal occorrentie sicome fù prudentam^{te} fatto nel fermar S. Gerolamo da Udene, et rittrovandosi al p̃nte in questa citta S. Francesco da Mosto, il quale con tanta universal sattisfatt^{e} fu udito nelli concerti delli organi la notte di natale pros^{e} passata, Volendo i c^{lmi} SS^{ri} Proc^{ri} fermar quest' homo acciò nō parta da questa città et si possa havendo nelle occorrentie sop^{te} Pero li Cl^{mi} SS^{ri} Proc^{ri} tutti sette in n^{o} ridotti in Proc^{a} hanno a bossy. et batty. con tutte sette batty. de si condutto S. Franc^{o} da Mosto pred^{to} alquale sia dato duc^{ti} trenta all'anno con obligo a lui di dover intervenir insieme col sop^{to} Gerolamo da Udene, overo in capella con il Bassano nelle Musiche sop^{te} et continuar in tal servicio adoperandosi sicome occorrerà et sicome dal Maestro di Capella de tempo in tempo li sara imposto.'

Francesco da Mosto was, it may be noted, one of the exiles from Munich, after the death of Duke Albrecht had chilled the musical climate there. He might well have known Giovanni Gabrieli and influence might have been brought to bear on the Procurators through Andrea. But in any case, they seem to have been in a generous mood. The following year[20] they increased Bassano's salary by 5 ducats and a month later they agreed on an innovation which was to be decisive in the creation of a permanent ensemble of great distinction. 'Their Excellencies, the Procurators, seeing the success that the instrumentalists of St. Mark's Church have had, in playing with the *cappella* [i.e. the singers] on wind instruments, to preserve this custom as it is observed up to the present, have decreed that the Treasurer be allowed from time to time to use that number of players which appears necessary for the service of the said *cappella*, and to play at those times when His Highness the Prince goes to church'.[21] Thus the Treasurer was no longer required to justify his expenditure in detail to the full committee of Procurators. This was a decision which obviously increased the flexibility of the *cappella*, so that the composer of the ceremonial music could find the ensemble that he desired. Another minute of the same day's meeting tells us more about the use of instrumentalists.

Their Excellencies the Procurators, having seen how well it worked originally to introduce just three players in the said *cappella*, and finding by experience that this number was inadequate and therefore having increased this number to six, of whom only those originally appointed have hitherto been paid; and this state of affairs no longer being satisfactory, thus, so that they shall continue to be of greater ornament [to our Church] Their Excellencies have decided that the players shall be given 15 ducats to show the satisfaction that they have given to the present time.[22]

Clearly the instrumentalists are now considered of some importance. The method of organizing the ensemble is also plain: there are to be six players

[20] ibid, 1 January 1582 (Venetian style 1581).

[21] A.S.V., Proc. de Supra, Registro 135, f. 66, entry for 5 February 1582 (Venetian style 1581): 'Li cl^{mi} SS^{ri} Proc^{ri} vedendo la reuscità che fanno li sonadori della giesia de S Marco ch sonano con la capella e intrumen^{ti} de fiato per conservar l'instituto sinhora osservato hanno ter^{to} che sia in libertà del C^{mo} Cass^{r} che per tempora si trovarà tal quel N^{o} de sonadori che le parera ricercar il bisogno per il servicio de essa capella, e per ie sonar al tempo che il Sereniss^{o} Princ. entra in chiesa de volta in volta'.

[22] ibid 66v 'Li oltras^{ti} claris^{i} SS^{ri} Proc^{ri} havendo veduto che se bene fo al principio introdotti tre soli sonadori con essa capella, e per esperientia conosciuto che tal numero era imperfetto et però essendo sta acresciutto al nõ de sei de qual non sono sta pagati se nõ quei primi, e questi adoperati di più nõ hanno havto satisfatt^{e} alcuna però accio che habbino causa de continuare con maggior ornam^{to} Sue Sig^{rie} Clar^{me} hanno terminato che le siano dati du^{ti} quindeci per sodisfat^{e} di quanto sin'hora hanno operato.'

on the permanent staff, in addition to which the Treasurer is allowed to co-opt others as occasion warrants. Thus grew an inner fixed number of players supported by a group whose number was variable.

The Treasurer's paybooks over the next thirty years, although not quite complete (the years immediately preceding 1586 are missing) and occasionally not itemizing individual festivals so as to show which musician played on a certain day, do give the main payments for the major festivals in one form and another. As far as the extra musicians are concerned, it seems that one of the organists or the *maestro di cappella* would engage a man to bring his own group of players, personally telling him what was required. Around 1586, the main 'fixer' was one Piero from Oderzo. Oderzo is a small town to the north of Venice, perhaps possessing its own *piffari* at this time, which would account for the appearance of its players here. They were quite busy in St. Mark's during 1586 '5th May . . . to Piero from Oderzo and his company of musicians for the undermentioned music, given in the chapel at 2 scudi per occasion. Thus on the vigil of St. Mark's Day at Vespers, St Mark's Day at both Mass and Vespers, and the day of St. Isidore, in total 8 scudi'.[23] A month later '10 scudi to Piero from Oderzo and his company for five *concerti* given in the chapel at 2 scudi per occasion, viz: the Vigil of Ascension Day at Vespers, Ascension Day at Vespers, Easter Day, Corpus Christi, and the Day of the Apparition of St. Mark'.[24] Even August found them receiving payment from the Treasurer 'To Piero from Oderzo, and company, for the concerti given in church on the Day of the Madonna, and the name day of His Highness [= the Doge] at 2 scudi per occasion, 4 scudi'.[25] In September they were paid for their help on the Day of Our Lady;[26] in November it was for All Saints' Day;[27] and an entry in the following January shows that they were employed on Christmas Eve, Christmas Day, the Day of the Circumcision, and Epiphany.[28] Thus these men were in St. Mark's quite regularly throughout the year.

[23] A.S.V., Proc. de Supra Registro 4; entry under date: '. . . a Piero da Oderzo et compagni Musici per li sottoscritti musiche, fatte in cappella à scudi doi per volta, cioè la vigilia di S. Marco à Vespro, il giorno di S. Marco à Messa, et à Vespro, et il giorno di S. Isidoro sono scudi otto.'

[24] ibid 28 June 1586 '. . . fatti in Capella, à scudi doi l'uno la vigilia dell'ascension à Vespro, il giorno dell'ascension à vespro. Il giorno di pasqua di Marzo, il giorno del corpus Domini, il giorno dell'apparition di S. Marco.'

[25] ibid, 28 August: '. . . à cassa ducati . . . à Piero da Uderzo, et comp$^{\underline{i}}$ p li concerti, fatti in chiesa il giorno della Madonna, et il giorno dell'annual di sua S$^{\underline{te}}$ à scudi doi per volta, scudi quattro.'

[26] ibid, 23 September. [27] ibid, 5 November.

[28] ibid, 13 January 1587 (Venetian style 1586).

The paybooks, it may be noted, do not tell us how many were in Piero's company, though since the usual rate for other similar players was half a scudo for each performance, it was probably just a group of four. But this does not mean that only these musicians were employed on grand occasions. In August, we read: '10 ducats paid to Zuane Gabrieli, organist, to pay [the musicians for] the *concerti* given in the organ lofts on the Vigil of Ascension Day, with twelve instruments, both organ lofts being used, and the platform specially made near the pulpit to accommodate these musicians'.[29] Similarly at Christmas 'Paid to Sig. Francesco and Sig. Marco Laudis, to Nicolò Mosto, Sig. Ventura violinist and Sig. Steffano Scotto for the music given in the organ lofts on Christmas Eve and the morning of Christmas Day at Mass, at 2 scudi for each [person], in all 10 scudi, on the order of Zuane di Gabrieli, organist.[30] These players were superior to the others, and the brothers Laudis and Nicolò Mosto were especially well known around Venice for the next decade or more. In February of 1587 the Treasurer made a payment 'to Sig. Giacomo Casseller, violinist, who played in the great organ loft in the music given on Christmas Eve and the morning of Christmas Day, the same being missed out when the rest were paid on the 13th January last.'[31] From these entries, we can obtain a good idea of how these festivals were celebrated. Although Piero's group appears to be of four musicians, on Ascension Day and its Vigil there were probably twenty-two players in St. Mark's (Piero's company, Gabrieli's group, and the six salaried players); at the Christmas Masses, there were at least sixteen, possibly more, since a payment to one Michael Bonfante on 18 December entered in the same register, for *concerti extraordinarii*, mentions the occasions of *Natale presente*, which could be interpreted as an advance.[32]

[29] ibid, 19 August 1586: '. . . . cont^{i} a Zuane Gabriel Horganista p pagar li concerti fatti in horgano la vigilia della Sensa, con dodeci instrumenti, cosi nelli horgani tutti doi, come nel palco fatto far appresso il pergolo dell' evangelio per causa di tal musiche . . .'

[30] ibid, 13 January 1587 (Venetian style 1586); second entry: '. . . a S. Franc^{o} et S. Marco Laudis, S. Nicolo Mosto, S Ventura dal violin, et S Steffano Scotto per la musica fatta nelli organi la notte, et la mattina de Nadal alle messe à scudi dui per uno sono scudi diese portoli di Zuanne di Gabrieli Horgan^{a}.'

[31] ibid, 23 February 1587 (Venetian style 1586): '. . . a S Giacomo Casseller dal Violin sono [=suono] nell'Horgano grande nelle musica fatta la notte, et la mattina di nadal, il qual non ve^{nne} a fuor detto suo pagamento adì 13 zenaro pass^{i} quando furono pagati li altri Musici . . .'

[32] ibid, 18 December 1586.

Andrea's music for the increased ensemble

These players obviously were employed in the 'vocal' music of the Mass and Vespers. Music specially written for them alone, by contrast, is very rare, as is any music for such a grand scale ensemble written in the sixteenth century. There is music for the intermezzi performed at the wedding celebrations in Florence in 1539 and 1587,[33] but this is hardly relevant here. Among Venetian publications, there are only a couple of pieces by Andrea which really show what this ensemble might have played. One is a very strange work, a *battaglia*. This is an offshoot of the vogue for Jannequin's famous *La Bataille de Marignan*, a piece of primitive realism, full of the imitation of swords clashing, horses galloping, fanfares and so on. It had a quite extraordinary popularity throughout the whole sixteenth century. Andrea must have known it both at first hand and in the imitation by his former colleague, Annibale Padovano, who had composed an instrumental battle piece for the wedding of the later Duke Wilhelm of Bavaria in March 1567, when it was played by cornetts and

[33] Fully described in Howard Brown: *Sixteenth-Century Instrumentation: The Music for the Florentine Intermedii* (American Institute of Musicology, 1973).

trombones.[34] Andrea's *battaglia* is very similar, though more realistic still, with obvious fanfares and a triple-time section which suggests galloping cavalry. It is hardly a distinguished work, but because it borrows fanfares for wind, it is really idiomatic in its use of the instruments in a way that adaptations of vocal music could never be (see Example 7).

His other work for large ensemble is entitled 'Ricercar per sonar à otto', which was included in the 1587 *Concerti*. It is in fact a canzona, built on the usual motif and with a *da capo*, the return of which is distinguished by an extremely skilful overlap of counterpoint. The density of the counterpoint makes the work less effective than the scale of the ensemble might suggest, and the extremes of the instrumental ranges are ignored. Even so, there is a crispness about the rhythms which adds power, and the climax is reminiscent of the *battaglia*:

Giovanni's music for the increased ensemble—the earliest works

The origins of Giovanni Gabrieli's grand instrumental manner lie elsewhere than in these few pieces. In the 'secular' section of the *Concerti* there are three pieces which are important links in the chain. These are apparently madrigals, each, however, bearing the direction *per sonar*, or in the case of 'Lieto godea' *per cantar et sonar*. They do not seem to be music for dramatic entertainments, and domestic music-making was hardly on this scale, as a rule. Though true double-choir pieces, they are quite different in style from the *spezzato* motets which Giovanni had so far published. Nor are they madrigals in any conventional sense, though they use madrigalian symbolism skilfully. In 'Lieto godea' the word *fugge*, as the lover flies from Cupid's arrows, provides a canon between various parts, the soprano of each choir predominating so that the point can hardly be missed. The same concept dictates the opening dialogue of 'Fuggi pur se

[34] Boetticher, op. cit., p. 340.

sai', and the *rai*, rays from the beloved's eyes, are expressed by quaver scales. Her descent from heaven in 'Chiar'angioletta' naturally has a Marenzian downward scale[35] and if the cries of *Ohimé* lack the *sospiro* rest, their division between the opposing choirs is effective. But these pieces are not really madrigals; they are true *canzone alla francese*, nearly all the stylistic features being French. Each begins with the canzona motif; two out of three have a *da capo*, all have that measured rhythm which seems foreign to Italian pronunciation, 'Lieto godea' especially having few of the elisions normal in madrigals of the period. This is one reason why these pieces are so attractive, for the regularity of accent gives a dance-like flavour which Giovanni maintains throughout. The other popular feature is the prominence of soprano melody in both choirs rather than counterpoint. 'Chiar'angioletta' begins with an imitative phrase, but within a few bars homophony reigns; the other two works could be easily performed by two melodic instruments accompanied by two organs or harpsichords, for the quavers occur in the top line, the underlying parts being given 'white' notes:

Every phrase is stated at least twice, once by each choir, and sequences are frequently used (see Example 10).

[35] It is rather reminiscent of that master's wedding madrigal 'Scendi dal paradiso', published three years before.

Ex.10

The latter are foreign to Giovanni's madrigals and to a lesser extent to his motets. The only other piece of this period to use sequence, the dialogue 'O che felice giorno' may have been used as a duet,[36] and the nature of these *arie di sonar* (the title given to 'Chiar' angioletta' in the *Concerti*) suggests that something similar might be intended here. These pieces, in spite of their tunefulness and straightforward textures, are not just gaily extrovert. 'Lieto godea' especially, though full of strong major chord progressions and even those *battaglia* rhythms, nevertheless maintains a tinge of melancholy with a modal progression in its repeated opening phrase (see Example 11).

Most instrumental ensemble music was hybrid in character at the time when these works were published, and so this aspect of their nature is not surprising. The use of sequence and the *battaglia* rhythms indeed shows that Giovanni was gradually achieving a specifically instrumental style.

Instrumental techniques known to Gabrieli through his colleagues

Giovanni's incentive to develop in this way must have been powerfully increased by his close relationship with the Venetian players, especially Giovanni Bassano and Girolamo Dalla Casa. In the 1580s, both of these virtuosi produced manuals, not to teach methods of playing their instruments (though Dalla Casa does give some useful hints on tongueing) but to instruct on the art of embellishment. Their books belong to a genre of which there were many examples in the sixteenth century, but they were probably among the best known.[37] Certainly Giovanni Gabrieli was in-

[36] See Chapter Five pp. 108 ff. above.
[37] Howard Brown: *Embellishing Sixteenth Century Music* (London, 1976).

fluenced by their methods of applying 'divisions' to a melodic line, and all his written-out ornaments can be derived from their treatises. We can see also some of their methods frequently at work in his instrumental music. The natural tendency to embellish a scale results in sequences; the use of constant semiquaver patterns gives a regularity and order in rhythms. Perhaps more significant still is the embellishment of a single line throughout a piece rather than sharing the ornamentation out equally among the parts. How far their methods were generally accepted is impossible to say; but it is fairly safe to imagine that where there was a virtuoso player, he was given his head to some extent, with a resulting texture of main part plus accompanist. And since the cornett was the most agile of wind instruments, and certainly more so than the trombones with which it was associated, it is probable that the tendency towards a prominent upper part, accompanied by somewhat slower movement in the lower voices, was strengthened. This is precisely what we have seen in Giovanni's double choir madrigal-cum-canzonas; and is even more obvious in a number of Giuseppe Guami's instrumental pieces,[38] as in the following passage from his canzona 'La Novellina', which at times seems a duet between a very fluent cornettist and a skilful but necessarily less fluent trombonist (perhaps Giuseppe's brother Francesco):

Giovanni's mature large scale instrumental works

Guami was, of course, Giovanni's colleague from 1588 to 1591; brother Francesco was in Venice even longer; and Francesco was only one of the virtuosi in St. Mark's *cappella* in the vital ten years between the publication of the *Concerti* of 1587 and the *Sacrae Symphoniae*; vital years indeed for

[38] Modern edition, ed. I. Fuser and O. Mischiati (Florence, 1968).

Ex.13

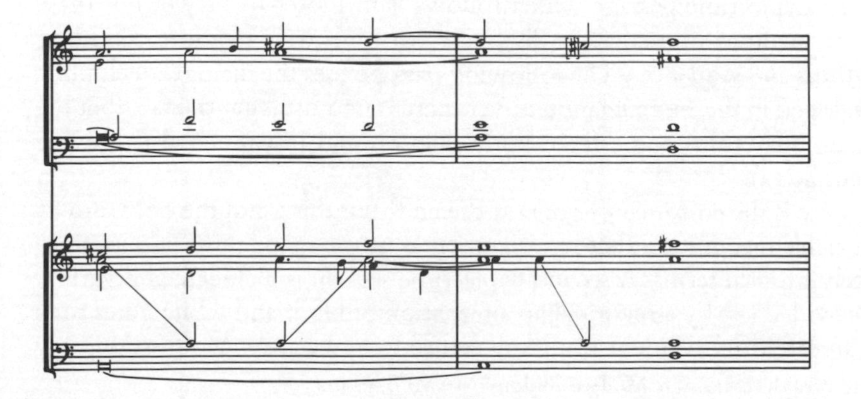

Venetian instrumental music, and perhaps for that of all Europe. The sixteen instrumental pieces included in the latter publication are not only the finest ensemble music of the sixteenth century, but the beginning of a distinctive style for the composer and his many followers over the next twenty years; they are the earliest of their kind to equal the best music of madrigal and motet genres, and indeed they mark a turning-point in the history of instrumental music. Comparing them with similar music of the same epoch, such as Guami's *Canzonette alla Francese* of 1601, or the occasional pieces of Viadana and Banchieri, it is evident that they belong to a different class of mastery, for although these lesser composers write both attractively and competently, they have neither the emotional range nor the compositional virtuosity (not at all the same thing as instrumental virtuosity) of Gabrieli. There are gay works, brilliant works, melancholy works, emotional works among these sixteen pieces; and from the point of view of technique, there is a complete command of instrumental resources, coupled with the mature vision of a composer at home in the most sophisticated harmonic and contrapuntal usages of large-scale church music.

The canzonas

Even in the most apparently innocent of canzonas the integration of means is complete. The 'Canzon Septimi Toni'[39] for two four-part choirs fizzes like champagne from the start with the canzona motif given a simple diatonic harmonization and some skipping dotted notes leading to *battaglia* rhythms. The repetition of the material by each choir ensures memorability and balance; and yet the motet-like counterpoint of the final two bars of the section avoids the obvious (see Example 13).

The triple-time passage which follows is in motet-like style; but these motet qualities immediately disappear, to give way to more sparkling rhythms and sequences. The following passage uses the dialogue technique developed in the *spezzato* motets, yet there is no mistaking the fact that the dynamic rhythms come from both chanson and instrumental usage (see Example 14).

There is the customary *da capo* at the end; but this is not the only sign of Gabrieli's recognition that in instrumental music shape must be sought in purely musical terms. A second triple-time section is included, and variety is provided less by a madrigalian alternation of black and white notes than by an ease of movement from key centre to key centre. Modulation may

[39] No. 3 of the collection. Modern edition, IMAMI II, p. 30.

be too strong a word for these, but the way a cadence will suggest a movement to the supertonic, or a touch of a flat third will cast doubt on the permanence of that centre, or sequential progressions seem to tumble through key after key because they are based on chords a fourth apart, captures and sustains the interest throughout.

There is not a single note in this work which could not be sung by voices, any more than there was in 'Lieto godea', yet it is unmistakably designed for playing. The same is true of a number of these canzonas, though the balance between vocal and instrumental writing varies in each of them. The other canzona 'Of the seventh mode'[40] begins with a chanson motif integrated with a flowing line and worked out in imitative counterpoint. By the end of the first section, a motif which outlines the interval of a third appears. It is only when this is developed at a later stage as the basis of an extended sequential pattern that we realize how the ornaments of Bassano and Girolamo Dalla Casa have sunk into Gabrieli's consciousness (see Example 15).

[40] No. 2 of the collection. Modern edition, IMAMI II, p. 14.

The opening theme has a short quaver figure based on a turn, not at all uncommon in madrigals; but its reappearance, again worked out in sequence, in a section quite widely separated from the opening, is quite unmadrigalian. The continual reminder of the chanson rhythm also subtly unifies the whole piece. Shape is obviously uppermost in Gabrieli's mind, for it is in fact a kind of rondo, with a triple-time section acting as the refrain, as in the rondo motets, with their 'alleluja' refrains. Whereas triple time in such motets is usually joyfully extrovert, however, here it acts as a slight cloud on the horizon. The vitality of the duple-time sections now seems stronger than the dancing measure. It is mainly the minor chord at the end of the third bar which gives this impression, through its persistence in repetition, and the eventual cadence on *A* rather than on the tonic note seems to be a *tierce de picardie* of this minor chord, rather than an affirmation of the major (see Example 16).

In fact, completely sunny works are a rarity in this collection. Even a canzona obviously destined for a joyful festival, such as that in ten parts on the twelfth mode,[41] has its moments where a chain of dissonances upsets a succession of major chords. But the main purpose of these is to give more impact to the rhythms, as do the very short motifs deployed in madrigalian manner from time to time, and the canon at half a beat's interval between a couple of upper parts. Again there is nothing beyond the range of the voice; but by using the upper notes of two treble instruments in his *coro acuto*, and keeping the bass line of the *coro grave* in its lower register the impression is given that the forces employed are larger than, in fact, they are. Such means make these instrumental compositions even more impressive than many of the motets. The 'Canzona Primi Toni'[42] for ten parts is an example of how to make a small group of players sound like a veritable orchestra. The upper four lines have treble clefs, while the middle parts have soprano, mezzo-soprano, and alto ranges. The ten separate strands are treated independently instead of in double choir, so that the four treble parts are not used simply as an upper

[41] No. 10 of the collection. Modern edition, IMAMI II, p. 158.
[42] No. 7 of the collection. Modern edition, IMAMI II, p. 75.

group, which would give a light rather than a solemn sound, but can be used almost continuously. The total effect is thus extraordinarily brilliant, especially at the grand climax where the involvement of all the uppermost parts, bandying a short motif above the stave one to another, keeps up the splendour for bar after bar. Yet even here there are deeper touches which stem essentially from the musician interested in moulding the shape of themes and harmonies. This same sustained climax achieves part of its tension because, after a succession of perfect cadence progressions, what seems to be a clear move towards a cadence in C minor is interrupted by a D major chord which pulls it unexpectedly back to G. The ensuing brightness is superb:

Virtuosity in the canzonas

In other pieces the techniques of decoration begin to influence the nature of the music more strongly. This does not necessarily imply that virtuosity is used merely for the glory of the individual player. Indeed it is fascinating to see how nearly Gabrieli can approach great concertante writing without any feeling of display for its own sake. Perhaps the most attractive for the listener of all the canzonas of this kind is the very first one in the *Sacrae Symphoniae*,[43] an eight-voiced work for two groups of players; although

[43] No. 1 of the collection. Modern edition, IMAMI II, p. 1.

he does not specify the instruments to be used, the inspiration was very likely the cornett playing of Giovanni Bassano and Francesco da Mosto, for the prominent parts of both choirs are the uppermost ones, flowing along in quavers to the accompaniment of trombonists with supporting harmonies. The first four-bar phrase might have come out of Girolamo Dalla Casa's treatise, for the quaver figuration is developed from one of his examples of how to ascend the scale between minims:

Girolamo himself, however, would not have repeated it without variation. Yet it is precisely the regularity of the sequence which gives this tune its attractive gait. The second group repeats the tune, develops it, then hands it back to group 1 to start the whole process once again, giving a total of four statements in the first twenty-four bars (the way the phrases fall into balanced patterns is also significant in maintaining the popular flavour). This very tunefulness distracts our attention from the skill of the player, which becomes a prerequisite of the performance rather than an object of admiration. This assumption means that when later Gabrieli wants to gain a climactic feeling from the melody, he uses ornaments which really do draw attention to the player, and some rapid fire of motifs requiring dexterity of finger and tongue between the two virtuosi in the concluding stages of the piece reveals the inspiration given by these excellent players. The influence of Girolamo Dalla Casa here seems at its strongest, not just because of the ornaments themselves, but because their application reveals a casual approach to the harmony which reflects the position of the player without a detailed knowledge of what is happening in the other parts. The ornaments do not quite fit the chords: a figure outlining G and E flat will first come in a chord of C minor, but immediately after, it occurs when the other parts are holding a chord of G, so that the E flat seems out of place. The speed at which the ornament is taken means that the resulting dissonance is hardly very significant; yet, remembering the defence by Monteverdi of similar procedures—quite deliberately chosen for expressive purposes—in his *Fifth Book of Madrigals*, only eight years later, we would be wise to reserve judgement, the more so since it is the use of decorative figures in such contexts that makes some of Gabrieli's later music so powerful. And for all its apparent gaiety, the joy in this piece, as so often in Giovanni's music, is not unmixed. The opening phrase has its proportion of minor chords; the triple-time section too centres around the minor; and the very end emphasizes the plagal cadence of G minor with a prolonged display of E flats.

Concerto-like elements in canzonas

The very texture of this canzona, with its emphasis on the upper parts, tends to make it feel like a duet. When the two parts imitate themes closely, descend by scales in thirds, pass motifs one to another, the inevitable concentration on them destroys the true counterpoint between the total ensemble. It is not a far step to reducing the larger grouping to a lesser plane in the development of material and giving the virtuosi most of the interest. No imaginative composer could resist exploiting the skill of these virtuosi to the full, and one work can only be seen as such a display piece, an ensemble piece equivalent to the toccatas of Merulo whose frank avowal of this attitude had, after all, been known to Gabrieli since childhood. The piece, the 'Canzona Duodecimi Toni'[44] for ten parts, is seen even from the list of contents of the *Sacrae Symphoniae* to be quite out of the ordinary, since it is given in two versions. The first has the conventional format of a double-choir canzona, though unusually the instruments are named—and what an incredible ensemble it seems today, with four cornetts in each group, together with a trombone to add the bass, making eight cornetts and two trombones in all; and the trombone is simply a second best of a suitably ranged bass cornett, for clearly Gabrieli has imagined a homogeneous colour, the upper four 'voices' of each group extending over the range from the lowest notes of an alto to the higher notes of the soprano. The second version is entitled 'the same canzona arranged for playing with the organ'; in fact this consists in cutting out certain passages in all but the cantus parts of each group, so that only the two uppermost cornetts play throughout (to save space Gardano does not reprint them in the original partbooks, merely noting that they can be used for each version). But they are not to be left without harmonic support, for Gabrieli's intention is obviously that these passages should be given with organ accompaniment. No parts for the two organists are supplied, which makes one suspect that an organ *partitura*, as such parts were called, is missing from the surviving sets of partbooks. Such things

[44] No. 11 of the collection. IMAMI II, p. 180.

were already known in Venice,[45] for Giovanni Croce had provided one for his *Motetti à otto voci libro primo* published by Vincenti in 1594; and so had the Bolognese composer Banchieri, whose work was extremely well known in Northern Italy, for his *Concerti Ecclesiastici* appeared in the next year (the publisher was again Vincenti). Still, organists were probably expected to make their own scores of such music, so it may be that Gardano did not bother to provide a *basso seguente* at additional expense. One further feature is unusual for Gabrieli: both versions are 'echo' pieces; this is not, however, unusual for almost any other Venetian, Donato, Croce and many others had written such pieces, yet it represents an interest in effect rather than in solid musical values that was unique in Gabrieli's music up to this time. Clearly, this work lies outside his normal development.

Nevertheless, one could hardly tell this from the first version, which seems very little different from several other canzonas in the volume. There is an unexpectedly massive tutti at the beginning, whereas Gabrieli often prefers to build up to his sonorous climax a little later; and the *cantus* parts are more florid than the others, with much passage-work. Yet even here, it is noticeable that since he has four 'equal' partners (the cornetts) in each choir he passes the material around as a good contrapuntist should. The echo effects are perhaps slightly inhibiting to his normal development of the phrase, and this may account for an unusual lack of melodiousness; the development of motifs in sequence, so typical of the instrumental music of this volume, is not permitted by the quick interchange between the groups. But here also, the Gabrielian flair is at work, for sometimes his echo choir refuses to take second place, and initiates material which is then mirrored by the principal group. At the climaxes, the relationship of choir and echo breaks down completely, and Gabrieli treats them exactly as he would do in any other double-choir work.

It is when we turn to the second version that the novelty of the piece emerges, in texture, in basic planning, and in attitude. The stress on the two upper parts, now revealed in their true glory, and their contrast against the tutti, reduces the significance of the echo effects, which seem no more than incidental. Instead, it is the broader concertante features which assume importance. The main feature is the contrast between tutti and *concertino*. There are five passages for the tutti. They are of such varying length that they do not seem to be seen as pillars of the structure, yet since each begins with a strong statement of the canzona rhythm, they contribute a major and unmistakable sense of unity. The four solo

[45] F. T. Arnold, *The Art of Accompaniment from a Thoroughbass* (London, 1931).

sections which come in between also begin with this motif, but soon depart from it, involved in the interplay of ornamental motifs. The difference between tutti and solo, however, lies less in the nature of the melodic material than in harmonic attitude. The tutti is slower-moving, with solid diatonic bass notes underlining irregular changes of harmony:

The solo is more often like the top line of contrapuntal interplay, with less predictable harmonic changes, and a melody whose phrasing is also often unexpected:

This is not, however, a concerto movement of the Vivaldian type.[46] The Baroque concerto depends on an understanding of tonality which was not possible to Gabrieli. This is still a canzona on the twelfth mode. Most tuttis begin on its tonic and though several times they move to a new key to allow the solo sections some variety when they take over the canzona motif, there does not seem to be an overall tonal plan. Nor would it be correct to assume that the solo passages are for virtuoso display, the tuttis for simply structural importance. The decorative cornetto parts are continued into each tutti, so that there is no real distinction—indeed the ornaments are more florid in the tuttis, perhaps because the fuller sound requires them if the cornetts are to be heard clearly. And the final tutti, which should sum up the movement with a re-statement of the opening, in fact simply confirms the tonal centre and brings the piece to a triumphant conclusion with some closely argued dialogue between the double choir groups. Many canzonas do have a da capo ending; the absence of one here indicates that Gabrieli was still thinking in terms of *cori spezzati* rather than anything else.

Influence of the St. Mark's ensemble on Gabrieli's canzonas

This highly original work reveals how alive Gabrieli was to the means at his disposal. Such a piece could not have been written except in the Venice of the later 1580s and 1590s. It is an obvious reflection of the structure of the ensemble led by Girolamo Dalla Casa, with its virtuoso *salariati*, in particular the superb cornettists, augmented by the freelance players whose employment was so liberally encouraged.[47] And that Gabrieli was thinking seriously about St. Mark's resources and that this 'canzona in echo' was no flash in the pan, is indicated by yet another 'Canzona Duodecimi Toni' for ten players.[48] Here the division between the virtuosi and the rest is much more marked. The tutti announces its solid material at the outset, with a four-bar phrase ending in the clearest of cadences. When it returns, this phrase is maintained almost exactly, neither altering its tonality nor being extended so that it leads into the solo material which follows. This gives a sense of symmetry, but the solos provide the neces-

[46] There are tenuous links between early and late baroque developments in ritornello form, notably in a work by Gabrieli's pupil G. B. Grillo. See A. Einstein 'Ein Concerto Grosso von 1619' in *Festschrift Hermann Kretzschmar zum 70 Geburtstag* (Leipzig, 1917).

[47] See p. 138 above [fn 21].

[48] No. 9 in the collection. IMAMI II, p. 118.

sary imbalance. Here the two cornetts[49] are conceived as an entity, tossing fragments of melody one to another, vying with each other in displaying the dexterity of scales and ornaments. The first solo section begins with a canzona motif but ends its six bars with dashing scales leading to a cadence in the dominant; the second is longer, semiquavers again giving the sense of climax; the third is over twice the length of the first, the duet interplay more complex, the ornaments developed in sequences; and in the two later episodes *gruppetti* (trills beginning on the upper note) and scales are fashioned into balanced entities by duet interplay. There is imbalance also in the accompaniment, the early solos being supported by a trombone or two, gradually needing more instruments to fill out the harmony until all are employed in the final section—though it is not too difficult to distinguish the 'concertino' ensemble since six of the ten parts are more involved than the remainder. This piece does have a concerto structure, and it would not be hard to make an arrangement which deployed all the forces assembled for Ascension Day in 1587, with the ripieni playing in the refrain and the *salariati* only employed in the episodes.

Uncharacteristically serious canzonas

Such forward-looking works as these concertante canzonas do not necessarily represent the most rewarding of Gabrieli's instrumental music. This is to be found in pieces which are not markedly different, stylistically, from his motets; for example, the 'Canzona Noni Toni' for two four-voiced groups, in which the instruments are unspecified. The glories of this canzona are in its play on tonality. The piece opens sadly, and not until the tenth bar do a conventional *tierce de picardie* and some block chords suggest the return of Venetian self-confidence after the bleak divisive counterpoint. But this is only fleeting. The triple-time section opens with what must be the gloomiest of allelujas (the gloom is indeed strengthened by the associations such passages normally have) (see Example 21).

Gabrieli's black mood is made still more pronounced by the way that this phrase, which the first time it comes gives way to some more brilliant, major harmonies, is in the concluding bars bereft of such cheer; and a quotation of those strange modal harmonies of 'Lieto godea' (see Example 11 above) does nothing to remove the bitter taste.

[49] No instruments are indicated, but the range and nature of the passage work makes this likely, although it would also be interesting to try a performance with violins as soloists.

Ex.21

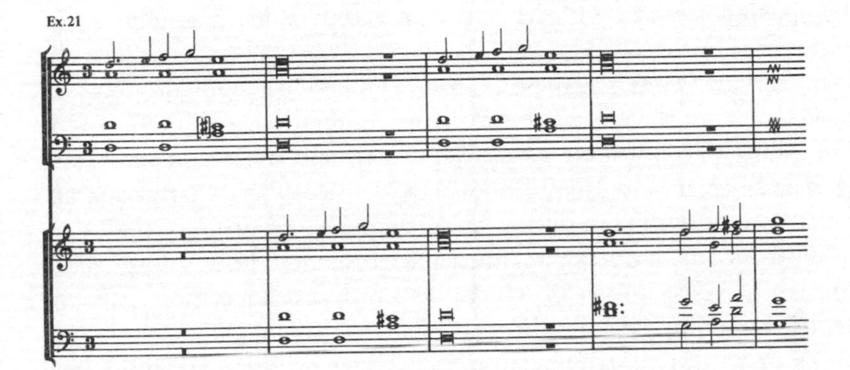

The sonatas

Least forward-looking of all are the sonatas, of which there are three in the *Sacrae Symphoniae* (the last canzona, the piece for fifteen instruments, really belongs to this category from every stylistic point of view). The title seems almost a contradiction in terms, for of all the instrumental works of the collection, these are the nearest approach to vocal music, and apart from some low parts designed for trombones they could almost be taken directly from motets. To all intents, they are the successors of the ricercar, the older, rather than the newer, learned type; they are just as much studies in sonority as are the grandest of the ceremonial motets. But all these pieces are sombre rather than brilliant, as though the white notes of the *misura di breve* must imply solemnity. There are no ornaments, no sequences—or rather they are such long-breathed sequences that they are scarcely noticed as such—no gay repeated notes derived from either the canzona motif or the *battaglia*. In their place are solid chords, close-knit counterpoint developed so that independent strands ensure sonority in spite of simple harmony and regular rhythms. The instrumentation demanded, in the two pieces where it is indicated, stresses trombones rather than the lighter cornetts: six are needed for the 'Sonata pian e forte', no fewer than twelve for the 'Canzon à 15'. The higher notes of the *violino*—which in range seems more like a viola—and cornett are not in evidence.

Yet these works are anything but unexciting. The most modest of them is the 'Sonata pian e forte', which requires just two four-part 'choirs'. The clefs denote a conception not far from that most moving of Giovanni's early motets, the meditation on the mystery rather than the feasting of Christmas, 'O magnum mysterium'; and the first section is very like the opening of that piece, in its sustained chords and steady tread. The length of the opening section, with its refusal to accept modern tonality in its cadences; the almost equal length of its answer from the second choir; the excitement which comes as these lengthy segments are gradually replaced by rapid dialogue; the ending in eight-part counterpoint; all these are the stuff of Gabrieli's most noble motets for Christmas Day and Easter. Other things help to create a unique emotional experience. The dynamic anacrusic rhythms which emerge during the dialogue more strongly than they do in most motets, are less integrated into a melodic flow, more baldly stated than in vocal music, in which the words are uppermost; and the occasional skipping, dancing phrase in the later part of the piece also reminds us that this is instrumental music. Above all there are those new markings 'pian' and 'forte' which have perhaps unjustifiably[50] given the work its fame in all the histories. At first, they seem no more than a device for obtaining balance between the two groups, and indeed they are necessary in one or two places for this purpose. Deeper acquaintance with the music shows that they also have an emotional function, for they occur so irregularly that the listener is never certain when he will be overwhelmed with sound, or when he must strain his ears for some more subdued phrase. Far from being the showpiece for orchestral brass which it has become in modern times, the 'Sonata pian e forte' is mainly dark in tone, a sign that in its Venetian ambience, human doubt also had its place.

The larger forces of the other two sonatas do not mean a bigger sound, except perhaps at the climax of that in fifteen parts, where the very number of the instruments means that the chords have to be spread over the complete range. This is exceptional, for in fact tuttis are comparatively rare in these pieces. Both open with extended sections for single choirs in which the interest lies in the development of melody, as simple motifs grow into long-breathed strands, and close imitation between the parts cuts across the cadences. The harmonies at first sight seem simple, successions of dominants and tonics on a very few key centres, deployed with a steady regularity. This simplicity is only apparent; a turn to the minor, a cluster of notes which means that a suspended dissonance is heard at the same time as its note of resolution, or even against an astringent passing note, confirm the emotionalism of the sombre instrumental colouring. The longer-ranging aspects of harmony are significant also, as exemplified

[50] Priority belongs to Banchieri, who used them in an echo canzona published just a year before Gabrieli's publication—*Canzoni alla francese a quattro voci per sonar Dentrovi un echo, & in fine una Battaglia a Otto, & a dui Concerti fatti sopra Lieto godea* (Venice, 1596). But the parodies of 'Lieto godea' show that Banchieri was well acquainted with the early music of Giovanni Gabrieli, so it may be that he did obtain the idea of piano and forte from the Venetian after all.

Plate 1 The hall of the Scuola Grande di S. Rocco where the annual celebrations of its patron saint took place. (*Mansell Collection, London*)

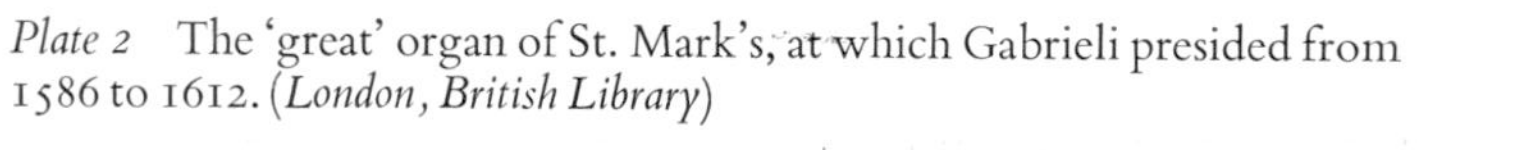

Plate 2 The 'great' organ of St. Mark's, at which Gabrieli presided from 1586 to 1612. (*London, British Library*)

Plate 3 Gabrieli's patron, Doge Marino Grimani. (*Museo Correr, Venice*)

by the way in the 'Sonata Octavi Toni', a firm declaration of G major at the end of a firmly 'white-noted' passage is denied by a sudden move to the tonal centre of its supertonic, a change exciting enough to prepare for dynamic rhythms with *note nere*:

These are all devices that we have seen in the church music, and there is indeed very little that indicates this is instrumental music in style. We shall find that the layout of the groups in the 'Canzon à 15', with its *coro semi-acuto*, *coro grave*, and an intermediate group differs little from the grandest of the church music which will be considered in Chapter Seven. There is no formal pattern as in most of the canzonas, no feeling of the dance as in the strong rhythms designed for tongued instruments. Yet in these magnificent works for instrumental ensemble, Gabrieli's music reaches maturity, for the sign of maturity is emotional balance.

CHAPTER SEVEN

The Grand Ceremonial Music

THE Doge was unable to change the fabric of Venetian life, but he could affect its colour. Although the committee structure restricted his political action the ceremonial occasions could be influenced by his personal tastes. Giovanni Gabrieli served three Doges (a fourth was elected only a few days before Giovanni's death). Of these it seems that Pasquale Cicogna, who came to the throne in 1585, was of no particular significance to his musicians; nor indeed was Leonardo Donato, Prince for the last six years of Giovanni's life. But Marin Grimani, who ruled from 1595 to 1605, had a profound influence which must be mentioned in any account of Gabrieli's work, for he was apparently musical—and without doubt, fond of ceremonial. His first act on election was to distribute alms among the poor, and to see that there was rejoicing throughout the city. It was a costly business. He paid out 1,413 ducats in fees, while the wine cost 163 ducats and the food 843 ducats—all out of his own pocket. The musical profession also benefited.

– To the Flemish *trombetti*	4 Scudi
– To 5 players from Padua, headed by Angelo of Padua	Lire 15
– To a group of players	6 Grossi
– To a group of players who were sent away	4 Grossi
– To S. Giovanni Bassano and his company of players as a present from His Highness, as usual	8 Ducats
– To Nicolò, *trombetta*, and his company [of 8 musicians] for having played 3 days at 1 Scudo per man per day	24 Scudi
– To Giacomo Boscardo, drummer, and his company of 7, for having played 3 days at 1 Scudo per man per day	21 Scudi
– To Giovanni Giacomo Bustin for 6 violinists who played 3 days at 1 Scudo per man per day	18 Scudi
– To Piero Ponentin and company of violinists for having played 3 days at 1 Scudo per man per day	18 Scudi
– To Pasqualin Savioni and his company of 6 wind players [piffari] for having played 3 days at 1 Scudo per man per day	20 Ducats, 2 Grossi

– To Messer Francesco dalla Bataglia 230 Lire, 4 Scudi to dispense to players and others	37 Ducats, 16 Piccoli
– To Messer Francesco Tiepolo for having paid players on the first evening at the Cà Grimani	5 Ducats, 4 Grossi
– To Messer Giuseppe, player at the banquet at St. Mark's	4 Ducats, 5 Grossi
– To Ser Giovanni [dalla Casa] of Udine and company of wind players of His Highness for their fanfares [*signali*]	25 Ducats
– To Messer Giuseppe, player	38 Lire[1]

Sansovino's guide book tells us

He was created Doge with the greatest joy and jubilation throughout the city which was demonstrated especially by the people, who did not cease for many days to acclaim the name and family of the new Doge with incessant voices, making bonfires of the wood that had been in the Square to make the stalls for the Ascension Day Fair, and as a new kind of demonstration [applauso] the benches of the Magistrates were put outside the Palazzo and burned in the Piazza [S. Marco].[2]

During the rest of his reign, extraordinary festivals and ceremonials abounded. There was the splendid reception of the Duke and Duchess of Mantua in 1596;[3] the totally superfluous coronation of his wife as Dogaressa in 1597;[4] the celebration of the peace between France and Spain in 1598, a treaty which hardly affected Venice, but which Grimani nevertheless used as an excuse for grand processions, in which the musicians of the confraternities took an essential part, and for a Mass in St. Mark's 'that was most solemn, full of diverse concerti, of instrumental and vocal music that was most noble.'[5] The pastoral plays in the Palazzo Ducale flourished as never

[1] G. Giomo, 'Le Spese del Nobil Uomo Marino Grimani nella sua elezione a Doge di Venezia', *Archivio Veneto*, Vol. 33 (1887), pp. 443–54.

[2] Sansovino, p. 629: 'Fù creato Doge Marin Grimani con grandissima allegrezza, e giubilo di tutta la Città, che fu dimostrata specialmente dal popolo, il quale non cessò per molti giorni di acclamare con incessanti voci il nome, e la famiglia del nuovo Doge, abbrucciando il legname, che era in Piazza preparato da fabricar le Botteghe per la Fiera dell'Ascensione, e con nuova maniera di applauso, portò fuori del Palazzo i Banchi de Magistrati, abbrucciandoli in Piazza.'

[3] ibid, p. 630: 'Li furono fatte regatte, e solennissime Feste, & una in particolare di cento Gentildonne, delle più belle, e più ricche della Città, vestite tutte di pretiosissimi, e ricchissimi vestimenti, ornate poi di tante gioie, in tanta copia, e di tanta bellezza, e valore, che stupirono i Prencipi, la Corte, e quanti si trovarono à questa festa.'

[4] G. Rota, *Lettera Nella Quale Descrive L'Ingresso Nel Palazzo Ducale Della Serenissima Morosina Morosini Grimani Principessa Di Venetia Co'la Ceremonia Della Rosa Benedetta, mandatale A Donare Della Santità Di Nostro Signore* (Venice, 1597).

[5] Biblioteca Marciana, MSS. Italiani, Classe VII, DLII (8812), *Compendio di me Francesco Da Molino de Missier Marco delle cose, che reputerò degne di venerne particolar memoria:*

before, given three times a year where one had previously sufficed. When Grimani died, and was buried to a Requiem Mass composed by Giovanni Croce,[6] Venice was a sad city.

It is not difficult to imagine the difference such a monarch must have made to the musicians of his chapel. It was not simply that the resources were larger than previously; the frequent opportunities to use them enabled the composer to gain experience in exploiting them. The results of this experience are to be found in the two volumes of Gabrieli's *Sacrae Symphoniae*, in those works which extend the double choir usage to compositions for three or even four groups of musicians. There may have been many more works which were never printed and thus perished with much of the other manuscript material of the time. Most of the surviving pieces are Mass movements, Magnificats, or settings of verses from some psalm of rejoicing which would do for any regal occasion. Any motets with texts relating specifically to the event would have been of little value to the publisher; in any case none have survived. What is left still can give us a good idea of how Venetian composers took their opportunities.

Cori spezzati on a larger scale than usual

The division into two choirs being normal at St. Mark's, was naturally the starting point for grander ventures. There was some tradition of adding a third choir by Giovanni Gabrieli's time. Willaert had included a 'Magnificat à tre cori' in his *Salmi spezzati* as long ago as 1550, and Merulo included a number of such pieces in his *Sacrorum Concentuum 8 10 12 et 16 vocibus* of 1594, settings of Mass movements and Magnificats rather than motets, which may well date from his Venetian years. But the primary model for all the younger generation must have been the pieces which form the last part of the religious music of Andrea's *Concerti*, the Mass, Magnificat, and two motets for twelve voices. Some of this may have been written as late as 1585,[7] but they were still epoch-making works, whose magnificence was unknown even in the most splendid music of Lasso or Palestrina.

The expansion of the medium of *cori spezzati*, however logical it might seem, presented new problems. The foremost practical problem must have been where to put the third choir. The gallery over the main West

'... alle 10 hore nella Chiesa di S. Marco per udir la messe santiss[a], che fu soleniss[a], piena di diversi concerti d'instrumenti et voci musicali nobiliss[i] ...'

[6] Caffi, I, p. 203.

[7] See Chapter Two above.

entrance to St. Mark's seems an obvious place. It is spacious enough to accommodate a large choir of singers and any number of instruments, including, if desired, an organ. It is on the same level as the other two organ lofts. But it is far enough away from them to make accurate ensemble difficult. Visibility between the galleries is not good, and pillars obscure the view of the organs from the West loft so that without at least one subconductor, coherence would be virtually impossible. The solution was to place the third force somewhere nearer, even at the expense of erecting a platform of some kind;[8] this is what they did, as the paybook for 1586 tells us. According to Sansovino it was not uncommon for musicians to perform from the pulpit. 'At the side of the balustrade are two pulpits, left and right after the Greek custom. One, the higher and made in two levels in the form of a pyramid, has a dome. The other is octagonal, but much lower. In this one they sing the Gospel and from time to time preach on the more solemn days of the year; in the other they present the newly created Doge to the people, and usually when the Signory come to church, the musicians are there to sing the divine offices'.[9] How often scaffolding was erected for the musicians is not clear, since payments to joiners and carpenters often leave vague the purposes for which they were engaged; but the *palco* for musicians is mentioned from time to time,[10] so that it was probably not very unusual. No doubt the platform was to minimize the lack of direct contact consequent upon having the musicians at different levels. An organ had to be brought into the basilica to support the third force, and at one time indeed a third organist was added to the other two on the payroll, though he was paid much less.[11] It was more usual to hire a player for individual occasions, as at Christmas 1602, when a payment of two scudi was made to Giovanni Priuli for playing the little organ on the *palco*[12] during two separate services (he did the same in 1604).[13]

[8] A.S.V. Proc. de Supra Registro 4, entry for 19 August 1586; see Chapter Six, fn 29 above.

[9] Sansovino, p. 101. 'Da i lati del parapetto sono due pulpiti alla usanza greca dalla destra, & dalla sinistra. L'uno altissimo, & fatto in due suoli in forma piramidale, finisce in cuba. L'altro è di forma ottangola, ma molto più basso. In quello si canta il Vangelo, & talhora si predica ne più solenni giorni dell'anno, in questo si appresenta al popolo il Doge creato di nuovo, & per l'ordinario, quando la Signoria va in Chiesa vi stanno i Musici à cantar gli offici divini.'

[10] A.S.V., Proc. de Supra, Registro 5, entry for 10 May 1595 and Registro 6, entry for 30 December 1604.

[11] Caffi, I, p. 33ff.

[12] A.S.V., Proc. de Supra, Registro 6, entry for 3 January 1604 (Venetian style 1603).

[13] ibid, 30 December 1604; the porter who carried the organ from the Seminary and back received 1 ducat 7 grossi.

Expansion of cori spezzati techniques

The main difference between writing for double choir and for further fragmented ensembles was simply one of size and colour. There is, after all, not much more that can be done in the way of dialogue than is possible with two choirs. Once the element of surprise has been lost with the entry of a third group the potentialities of variety of phrase lengths and of the cut and thrust of alternating forces are basically the same as in double-choir pieces. The gain comes in the sheer weight which the additional singers and players can bring, and the greater sophistication of contrasting timbres which they make possible. The differences between the two choirs had been gradually growing from the 1560s onwards, and the introduction of a third allowed a considerable expansion of such contrasts. The two choirs up above could be pitted against the one below, the tutti against any one of the three, or one high and one low against the third on the other side of the altar, or a single choir could emerge magically from the tutti.

Three choirs imply twelve distinct melodic strands, and given traditional modes of thinking, there were inevitably some adjustments to be made to the idiom. Doubling the bass lines of the various choirs was, of course, a great convenience to the composer, and while doubtless it was even more necessary if the harmony was to seem complete to listeners stationed at different angles and different distances from the divided musicians, it also made it less difficult to keep the counterpoint of the lines independent of one another. Nevertheless to write in at least ten 'real' parts was still a test of skill. One way of easing the problem a little further was to expand the tonal range. In the double-choir motets both Gabrielis could write bottom B flat for the lowest line, and top A for the highest; but these are recognized as extremes, used sparingly and for specially powerful moments. The added lines in three-choir works bring them into general usage, so that the composer has a greater number of notes available. The *tessiture* of individual parts is nonetheless limited. In Andrea Gabrieli's 'Kyrie a 12 voci' from the *Concerti*, the cantus has a range of a fourth—D to G; the bassus does not go below F, and remains around G for most of the piece. Such parts must be played on instruments to make their effect; and it is in the role of the instruments that composers sought to make the most of the new expansion of forces.

Meaning of the word 'cappella'

It is impossible in the double-choir motets to be sure that Giovanni Gabrieli envisaged specifically different roles for instruments and voices. In the three-choir pieces, however, we find the first actual markings in the partbooks which indicate a conscious effort at 'scoring'. In a sense these are negative, for they do not indicate the instruments to be used but the fact that voices *must* be employed. In Andrea Gabrieli's large Mass, the several lines of one choir are marked 'cappella'. It is a word with many meanings, ranging from simply a building to the whole musical establishment of a duke or a cathedral, and Michael Praetorius, writing his *Syntagma Musicum* some years after the younger Gabrieli had died, devoted several pages to its exact meaning.[14] He tried to define it under three headings. One defines it as what today would be called *ripieno* as opposed to *solo*. Another takes it to mean a complete assembly of musicians 'with all kinds of instruments and men's voices', and another shows how to divide such forces in various ways so as to make a full sound. He goes on '. . . and of such *Cappelle* I have seen many different excellent examples in Johann Gabrieli's Concertos'. But then he proceeds to more technical matters.

In the same [= Gabrieli's Concertos], however, as also in his *Cantiones Sacrae* [= the *Sacrae Symphoniae*] published first in the year 1597, one finds the word *Cappella*, which signifies to him the same as when I use the marking *Chorus Vocalis* or *Chorus Vocum*: that is the chorus which must be assigned to [boy] singers and men's voices. Thus when in a Concerto in which one choir has cornetts, the other violins, the third trombones, bassoons, flutes, and similar instruments, with, however, at least one concertato singer put with each choir, on most occasions there is one choir which has singers on all four lines [stimmen]. This [group] is called by Giovanni Gabrieli *Cappella*. And such a choir or *cappella*, because they belong essentially to the principal choir, must never be left out, can be recognized immediately by its use of the *Claves Signatae*; and from time to time can be performed with viols da gamba or violins.

From this it is clear that the way the clefs are distributed in the various choirs of a concerto is, for Praetorius, the key to its orchestration. So he proceeds to a thorough examination of the various possibilities, taking up twenty-six closely descriptive pages.

[14] op. cit., Vol. III, p. 133ff.

Instructions of Praetorius for orchestrating polychoral music

The fact that it was written for German musicians must be borne in mind when we apply Praetorius' explanation to the music of the Gabrielis. Conditions in Venice were not identical with those north of the Alps. Many of the instruments which Praetorius advocates do not appear in the records and descriptions of St. Mark's which we possess today; shawms, pommards, crumhorns only appear occasionally in the documents. But Praetorius also tells the reader how to dispose cornetts, trombones, flutes, bassoons, and strings among the choirs, and his information on these may well be applicable to the music of the Gabrielis and their Venetian contemporaries and it does help to explain certain features of their festival music.

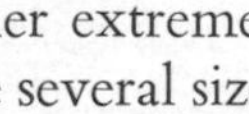

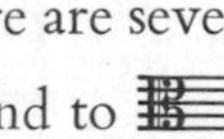

In general, Praetorius favours a homogeneous sound for each 'choir' in a polychoral work. Although mixtures of timbre are not ruled out, his discussion mainly centres around what he called *Flöten Chor*, *Violen Chor*, *Posaunen Chor*, or some such grouping of a single instrumental type. This in itself must have caused a composer to think in terms of distinct ranges, for although most instrumental families were more comprehensive than today, few of them could cover the complete range of notes from soprano to bass. Cornetts, to take the example with which Praetorius begins, were made in several sizes, covering loosely the notes of soprano and alto voices, but lacking anything which could truly be called a bass. Thus they were just the thing for a 'choir' in which the clefs were [music example] If an alto, tenor, or bass clef was added to these, a bassoon or trombone had to be used. This was not particularly unusual, but clearly the *coro acuto* with the 'cornett' clefs, which is not uncommon in polychoral music around the turn of the century, allowed for the monochrome effect which Praetorius liked. The cornetts were interchangeable with violins in such a grouping, though since a few cornetts could reach a low E or D, attention had to be paid, since the normal violin only went to G (though tenor violins were also known at this time). At the other extreme comes the trombone and bassoon 'choir'. Here again there are several sizes of instruments, the range being restricted at the upper end to [music example] ; though it could extend the available notes in the bass to [music example] (the descant and double-bass trombones which allow for extensions at both ends were not in general use). This fitted perfectly the *coro grave*, notated by such clef combinations as: [music example] Again, if there were upper parts, a cornett or a violin would be used, but the dark hues of trombones and bassoons must have inspired composers, so often did they write for such groupings. The widest-ranging instrumental family was that of the flutes and recorders, of which there existed eight distinct sizes, although in practice it was less useful because its lowest members were so quiet that it was better, according to Praetorius, to limit it to choirs in which the tenor clef was the deepest in use. Strings were more versatile. They could be employed for the complete range of the human voice, and either gambas or the modern *viole de braccio* (violin family) were recommended for the choir with the following clefs or Praetorius also remarks that gambas are useful in place of trombones or bassoons for lower groupings.

These last arrangements of clefs are precisely the *claves signatae* which indicate the Gabrielian *chorus vocalis*. It was necessary to mark such a clef combination as *cappella*, to show that all lines must be sung, because voices were used in other choirs in a comparatively free way. Praetorius encourages the mixing of voices among his instrumental groups. In a choir of upper range, a tenor might take the lowest line, or a boy, if available, an upper one. The *coro grave* of trombones or bassoons might well have the uppermost of the two upper parts sung. Whatever the arrangement, to have one voice in each choir is essential, even if all the lines are taken by instruments, to preserve the verbal text intact. It is not certain whether Praetorius's idea that single voices must be placed among the instrumental groups was also Venetian usage during Gabrieli's middle years (the situation had changed considerably by 1619 with the introduction of the solo motet), or whether a number of singers held a line to vie more equally with the instruments. It seems likely, however, that parts with awkward *tessiture* for the human voice were either doubled by instruments or simply played rather than sung. The fact that words are laid under each part of a grand motet does not mean that the Gabrielis did not want a mixture of timbres. It merely made possible a variety of performance as occasion arose. And as we look at the massive three- and four-choir pieces written in the last two or three decades of the sixteenth century with the information given us by Praetorius, there emerges a system which amounts to a method of orchestration no less real than later systems because its notation is somewhat sketchy, and which allows for considerable flexibility in its application.

Andrea Gabrieli's Grand Mass (1587)

What was to be the classic disposition of clefs is found in the elder Gabrieli's largest-scale Mass.[15] The most massive part of this is the Gloria, where the forces are divided into four choirs, to which the methods of Praetorius are so obviously applicable that we can imagine its sound from a score apparently unrevealing of timbres. The first choir is exactly as prescribed for a group of cornetts or violins on its three upper lines. The two higher parts are indeed almost tailor-made for cornetts, using their most forthright register, while the lowest of the three, with its range extended only to the A below middle C, would go well on the alto of the family. The *bassus* of this choir lies too low for a cornett, although if strings were used, an alto violin (i.e. viola) could complete the ensemble; but its range from d to D reminds us that Praetorius expected at least one line to be borne by a singer. For this range is that of the most effective part of the light tenor voice, not stretched to its upper reaches as it was to become in later secular music, but exactly as it is revealed by the solo motets of the early seventeenth century. The second and third choir are both notated in the *claves signatae* of the Praetorius *chorus vocalis*, though the second choir concentrates on ranges slightly higher than those of its fellow. They tend to interlock, often forming a solid phalanx against which the outer choirs are contrasted, and it could easily be that the ripieno singers of the basilica were deployed in both. If only one of these choirs was taken by the singers, the uppermost *coro secondo* is less in need of instrumental participation than the other, the *tessitura* of which suggests gambas or the violin family to help the low notes of bass and tenor. The fourth choir returns to a characteristic and distinctive Praetorian formula, its clef combination exactly fitting the *Posaunen Chor* with a high tenor or alto as its *cantus*. It is noticeable that the trombones are kept in their middle and low registers while the voice part is placed higher so that there can be no chance of its being overwhelmed by what were the loudest instruments then available.

The safe distance kept between the *cantus* and the other parts of this choir is typical of Andrea Gabrieli's skill in tackling a new problem. With such huge forces, any thematic development or a style of dialogue which involves extended phrases to contrast with short climaxes, is impossible, especially for a composition destined for an audience such as Doge and Senate. Nor is harmonic subtlety appropriate. This Gloria is astonishingly consonant—astonishingly dependent even on the major chord. Perfect cadence follows perfect cadence, the chord of A minor constantly turned

[15] See Chapter Two above.

into the major by the musica ficta *tierce de picardie*. There is some variety in the rapid movement from one tonal centre to another but the sophistication of the double-choir motet is much reduced in this grand manner, to which variety is not really appropriate. In the closing bars of the Gloria Gabrieli's flair for sonority is seen at its most characteristic. The total range from deepest bass to highest soprano is just a third short of four octaves, in itself impressive for music of this epoch; but it is to the details of the layout of the various strands that the music owes its grandeur. The way that the two top 'cornett' lines maintain a register in which the trumpet rather than *vox humana* quality of the instrument is prominent; the filling-in of the middle octaves with notes which, if sung, exploit the upper notes of tenors and altos; the wide spacing of the trombones to make full use of the low octave of the ensemble without overwhelming everything else with the indiscreet forte of the heavy brass at its upper extremity; these are features which show an awareness of problems of balance which go far beyond the conventions of the contrapuntist. It is, of course, skilful music, in that there are sixteen strands, all kept distinct from one another, with no doubling even of the bass lines. Yet it is obvious that this kind of score is the antithesis of true counterpoint. Even the occasional cross-reference between parts (as, for example, the working out of a scale in the *cantus* of Choir III and the *altus* of Choir IV) cannot disguise the fact that the parts have little separate identity. Limited ranges, and much repetition of single notes reveal that each has become, to a degree never before known in ensemble music, subordinate to the total effect. The general bass, with its harmonic idiom depending on the polarity of its extreme parts, is not far away.

Development of Andrea's techniques by his nephew

This work was clearly the model for his nephew's larger ventures in both the *Sacrae Symphoniae* of 1597 and later volumes. We have only to glance at the score of the 'Gloria à tre cori' of the 1597 Mass to see the points of resemblance. Admittedly the choral groupings are all equally disposed, being written in the *claves signatae* which would denote three choirs of voices without any instrumental participation; it could, indeed, be performed in this way. However, not only the marking 'cappella' for one group, but also the way that the other two have the lion's share of the argument indicates a fundamental inequality. Praetorius might have suggested strings or flutes as protagonists in these groups; but the lower three strands of each could be taken by trombones quite comfortably, and indeed one or two turns of phrase would be easier. In addition, there is a feeling that the uppermost parts of these choirs are slightly more melodious and thematically akin to one another than the rest, so that two of St. Mark's sopranos might have been given them.

There is a basic difference between the two works, and the use of the same dynamic triple-time sections to conclude these canticles, the similar attitudes towards the individuality of the melodic strands do not obscure the diverse cast of mind of uncle and nephew. For the first twenty bars of Giovanni's setting, neither harmony nor texture seems far from Andrea's style. There are major chords and perfect cadence progressions in plenty; the homophony and regularity of harmonic change equally belong to the manner of the elder. But from then onwards the harmonic range becomes wider. Although the basic material still consists largely of triads, more of them are minor or imply the minor key; the *tierce de picardie* is by no means invariable, the modulatory scheme allowing for more variety. Cadences also imply suspensions more often, and there is space within the phrase to produce such sophistication as this passage of genuine counterpoint:

The main divergence from Andrea's manner lies in Giovanni's gift of melody. We have already some evidence of this in the dialogue-madrigal 'O che felice giorno'.[16] In the Gloria much the same process is at work in the interplay between the two soprano parts of the non-cappella choirs. The way the two fit in with each other, at times repeating the motif or phrase,

[16] See Chapter Five above.

sometimes extending it, can be seen if the two choirs are arranged as a duet:

Whether this was a conscious effort to make the parts which would be most likely to be sung also most pleasing to the ear is impossible to say. Nonetheless, there is evidence of a similar approach to writing for what must probably be considered semi-accompanied voices elsewhere in this Mass, especially in the first Kyrie, in which the cantus parts of the two choirs, although of different *tessiture*, seem to have more thematic material in common with one another than with the remaining members of their respective groups. The Sanctus shares this trait, too, in spite of an opening in which the first choir seems to be used in an almost Palestrinian way, the extended, smooth, vocal thematic material being given some elaborate imitative counterpoint, which is then expanded by the other two choirs, whose more homophonic texture does not preclude flowing lower parts. But with the 'in nomine Domini' section of the Benedictus, the melodiousness returns, the uppermost voices of the non-cappella choirs showing and developing their material as in the Gloria. The overall effect of this trend is to make Giovanni's setting appear less forceful but more prayerful. A comparison with Andrea's Sanctus is in fact very revealing from this point of view. That Giovanni was copying the general idea from his uncle is evident from the similarity of the proportions in each setting. Both open with extended single choir music, both bring about a massive climax at the words 'Pleni sunt coeli', then engage in dialogue at the Benedictus, and have further massive part-writing at the final 'hosanna'. The differences are in emphasis. Giovanni's most impressive and characteristic music comes in the non-climactic passages, where the tunefulness and more sophisticated harmony give a depth of feeling quite lacking from Andrea's setting. Andrea's interest is in the grand moments of rejoicing, where all twelve melodic strands are set in motion. For though the harmony is simple and obvious, the rhythmic life is astonishing, contorted with dynamic syncopations in a way only a member (and associate) of the Lasso-Munich group could exploit at this time. Giovanni's rhythms compared with this seem staid, almost classically Palestrinian. Comparison with the grand Masses of his colleague Croce confirms this view of the younger Gabrieli. In such a work as his *Missa Percussit Saul*, published just a year before Giovanni's *Sacrae Symphoniae*, and almost certainly contemporary with Gabrieli's 'grand' Mass, Croce shows his interest in Gabrieli's bright sonorities, admittedly on the more restricted scale of the double choir, but enjoying the extended range allowed by the use of cornetts on the uppermost lines of each choir. But the feeling of splendour comes from the intensity of the rhythms which seldom have the repose of the younger Gabrieli's. The 'Christe' of this Mass, with its continual misplacing of the accent, encouraged by the shorter note values made possible by the use of the madrigalian *misura comune*, shows exactly how restrained is Gabrieli's manner, confirming once again that not he but Croce was his uncle's true successor (see Example 3).

Differences between the two Gabrielis

There are works where Gabrieli seems nearer to his uncle and colleague, though they are seldom quite as carefree. The Magnificat for 12 voices (1597) does indeed stem from Andrea's setting, published just ten years earlier. The disposition of the choirs is virtually identical in each: a *coro acuto*, probably for cornetts or violins, the *cappella*, and a *coro grave* probably for trombones and tenor voice. And these are used in much the same way in both works, the upper register of cornetts exploited to the full, as are the low C and D of the trombone. There are many other details connecting the two—the general proportions of the distribution of phrases between choirs in the opening section, the nervously close dialogue at the word 'dispersit', the repeat of various semi-paragraphs in the doxology,

numerous turns of the harmony. Even so, it is in the harmony that differences appear. Comparing Andrea's treatment of one of the few verbal phrases in the Magnificat which allows some break in the general rejoicing, 'Et misericordia eius', which relies solely on the darker hues on the low choir to express its meaning, with Giovanni's exploitation of the mood not merely with the same colour but by a chromatic chord progression, extended cadential suspensions, and the general change of tonal direction, shows a total difference of emphasis between the two. The quasi-military rhythms used by his uncle to convey the strength of the Almighty's arm are also softened by Giovanni, who manages to work in yet another emotional chromaticism at 'misericordiae suae'. There can be no doubt that Gabrieli the younger was much more aware of the truly religious needs of the text than his uncle had been; no doubt, as well, that this greater sensitivity to shades of mood makes the later setting the more interesting of the two.

Yet it would be wrong to over-emphasize this devotional attitude to the exclusion of the grandeur which Giovanni understood extremely well. The Mass and Magnificat are not typical Venetian texts, for they are the staples of religious observance. The Republic found its fullest musical expression in motets; and so did Gabrieli. In the *Sacrae Symphoniae* of 1597 about a dozen seem to go beyond the normal scale of sixteenth-century ceremonial music, either by using three or even four choirs, or simply by expanding the double choir by an increase in the number of 'real' parts. This latter expedient tends in itself to encourage the composer to use the extremes of instrumental ranges as he had done in Mass and Magnificat. 'Quis es iste', for example, uses contrasting choirs, in which the uppermost and lowest parts imply cornetts or violins, and trombones. Its ten-part climax when the Lord is declared 'mighty in battle' reaches from low C to the cornett's brilliant A above the stave; and indeed the 'scoring' is as brilliant as anyone could desire. But in motets where there is less of this expansion of choral tessitura, sonority is the chief interest. A church less devoted to St. Mark might perform the ten-part 'Deus qui beatum Marcum' with voices alone, though in the Doge's Chapel, its full realization surely demanded at least a quartet of trombones to give its *coro grave* the maximum effect. Even in this lack-lustre clothing, the listener could scarcely fail to be overwhelmed, if only because the full resources of the choir are employed nearly all the time. The movement of the dialogue is less in evidence than the magnificence of the tutti, which indeed is kept in use for about four-fifths of the whole motet.

Comparison between Gabrieli and Bassano

A comparison with Bassano's setting of the same text is revealing. Bassano, supreme player of the cornett, seeks his effect in the brightness of upper sonorities. Both his choirs suggest cornetts or violins as the instrumental support (though the title page of his book of motets[17] does not give the usual formula 'per voci e stromenti') and the result is a lightness surprising for double choir music. This effect is increased by the fact that, although there is no neglect of the total resources, the main burden of the argument

[17] *Motetti per Concerti Ecclesiastici A 5.6.7.8 & 12 voci, di Giovanni Bassano Musico della Serenissima Signoria di Venetia Et Maestro di Musica del Seminario di San Marco. Composti et dati in luce In Venetia Appresso Giacomo Vincenti 1598.*

is carried on in dialogue, developed between the choirs, or sometimes in genuine counterpoint. Compared with Gabrieli's piece, Bassano's seems lacking in weight, but neither is emotionally very sophisticated; it is just that Bassano prefers brightness, while Gabrieli chooses darker hues, constantly varied in combination.

In Gabrieli's celebration of Easter Day, 'Surrexit pastor bonus', the tutti is used even more; and although in the more sombre 'Judica me, Domine' the opening section seems to show that slow build-up to a climax, with the resources of a single choir, favoured by Giovanni's uncle, it is noticeable that where this climax does arise, it comes only a third of the way through the motet—and thereafter there is a continuous tutti. There are one or two exceptions, notably another motet for St. Mark's Day, 'Virtute Magna', which seems technically nearer to the eight-voiced motets. Its working out of some short thematic figures in the concluding section is very close to that in 'O Domine Jesu Christe' with its almost equal choirs, highly developed flowing phrases, and highly charged close alternations of choirs. There is nonetheless logic in its application of larger forces, for when certain parts become animated in the development of dynamic rhythms the depth of sound is created by other parts holding fast, which again creates a sense of splendour not obtainable within a lesser framework (see Example 4).

Gabrieli's grandest motets for great ceremonies

In these works, many of the trends seen in the smaller-scale pieces come to fruition. There, if it had been possible to depict some of the changes of mood inherent in a text, the tendency was still to concentrate firmly on the main issue. In the grander pieces, shades of meaning are of lesser importance. Texts used at Easter, Christmas, St. Mark's Day, and the festivals of the Blessed Virgin are treated in almost exactly the same way, now that the relative intimacy possible in, say, 'O magnum mysterium' or 'O Jesu mi dulcissime' has given way to a more political attitude. Indeed, these texts are virtually interchangeable; extended passages in most of these motets are devoted to setting a single word, applicable to any feast of rejoicing: 'alleluja'. In a most splendid motet in praise of the Virgin, 'Regina caeli', and in 'Hodie Christus natus est' more than half of the music is taken up with this; in the 'Plaudite' for three choirs it is scarcely less. There are musical reasons for such an expansion; the 'alleluja' has become a structural device. The repetition of the word during a motet comes from liturgical usage and throughout the sixteenth century composers took

Ex.4
CHOIR I
CHOIR II
al – le – lu – ja, al – le – – – – –
al – le – lu – ja, al – le – – lu – ja,
al – le – – lu – ja, al – le – lu – ja, al –
al – le – lu – ja, al – le – – – – –
al – le – lu – ja, al – – le –
al – le – lu – ja, al – le – – – – –
al – le – lu – ja, al – le – – – – – –
al – le – lu – ja, al – le – lu –
al – le – lu – ja, al – – le – lu – ja,
al – le – lu – ja, al – le – lu – ja, al –
al – le – – – – – – – –
al – le – lu – ja, al – le – – – – –

– – lu – ja, al – le – – – – – lu – ja,
al – – le – lu – ja, al – le – lu – – ja,
le – lu – ja, al – le – lu – ja,
– – – – lu – ja, al – le – lu – – – – – – ja,
lu – ja, al – le – lu – – – – ja,
– – – lu – ja, al – le – – – – – – lu – ja,
– – lu – ja, al – le – – – – – – lu – ja,
– ja, al – le – lu – ja, al – le – lu – – – ja,
al – le – lu – ja, al – le – lu – ja,
le – – lu – ja, al – le – – lu – ja,
lu – ja, al – le – – – – – lu – ja,
– – – lu – ja, al – le – – – – – lu – ja,

advantage of the fact.[18] Palestrina, whose work is closer to strict liturgical requirements than that of any Venetian, on several occasions binds the sections of a bipartite motet together with a repeated extended alleluja setting.[19] In his lesser works Gabrieli does not show marked interest in such a device. There are allelujas, in both 'Ego sum' and 'Jubilemus singuli' of the *Sacrae Symphoniae*, which could easily be made to yield unifying music; but, as in the early 'Angelus ad pastores' (1587), Gabrieli prefers to set 'alleluja' to fresh music each time it comes, not even keeping such sections equal in dimension or manner. In 'Jubilemus singuli' the first alleluja is scarcely more than an incident in proceeding to following words, while the final one is an extended and majestic setting. In 'Ego sum' there are no less than three allelujas, totally different in manner; the first short but rhythmically exciting, the second scarcely more than a prolonged cadential formula, the third a massive triple-time coda of the most pompous kind. Yet in the larger-scale pieces, Gabrieli nearly always repeats the music of his 'alleluja' at least once. The reason is not hard to find. In most sixteenth-century contrapuntal music unity is achieved by the repetition of thematic motifs by the several voices of the texture. In double-choir music it is brought about by the constant repetition of phrases during the dialogue. Where this feature is diminished, some other element must take its place, and so a refrain, without the necessity to set new words to old music, is a valuable aid to the composer. Thus 'Quis est iste' employs its alleluja no fewer than five times and 'Hodie Christus natus est' the same. Even though in 'Regina caeli' the alleluja only occurs four times, the motet is so short that the refrain still dominates the whole piece.

This rondo technique was obviously likely to attract an audience of the musically untutored nobility. The repetition of a complete and often fairly brief section is the easiest design for anyone to appreciate. All music of a harmonic (as opposed to a polyphonic) kind was to rely on some such expedient in the seventeenth century, before more sophisticated means involving key relationships became possible; and even then, the da capo aria, and the first movement of the Vivaldian concerto, are not very distant from this simple but radical reorganization of musical thinking. Nor is it surprising that Gabrieli exploited this formal pattern more than other composers at this time. An organist used to the *canzona francese*, a composer of instrumental music experimenting with concertante effects

[18] O. Strunk, 'Some motet-types of the sixteenth century', *Papers of the American Musicological Society*, 1939 (1944), p. 155.

[19] For example in 'Canite tuba' from *Il 2º Lib. de Motetti a 5, 6, & 8v* (1572) and 'Tempus est' from *Il 5º Lib. de Motetti a 5v* (1584).

where a *concertino* is offset against a recurring tutti, is just the man to see how similar patterns can be applied to vocal music. Perhaps it was not he who had the original idea, for his former colleague and another organist, Merulo, had published a similar motet—also a setting of 'Regina caeli'—some three years before Gabrieli's *Sacrae Symphoniae* appeared.[20] Nevertheless, his interest in the device is characteristic. Only a composer to some

[20] Modern edition, ed. D. Arnold, in 'Formal design in Monteverdi's Church Music', in *Monteverdi e il suo tempo* (Parma, 1968), p. 194.

extent away from the mainstream of musical trends, not affected by the current theories of a combined art-work, could show that the concept of a pattern in sound was not always to be set aside, even if the old contrapuntal methods of organization were dying.

'Alleluja' refrains

The setting of the word 'alleluja' essentially presupposes a mood of rejoicing, and is thus somewhat limiting. Even so, it is surprising what variety Gabrieli finds within the emotional limits; though perhaps it is not quite so astonishing if we take into account the way he could use the similarly stereotyped conception, the canzona rhythm, which infected so much of his instrumental music. Probably today Gabrieli's 'Regina caeli' is considered a typical Venetian alleluja. It is in triple time, which, with firm cadences, divides it off from the body of the motet. It is, even more than most, triumphant music wrought from perfect-cadence progressions, with scarcely a minor chord anywhere. It signals its conclusion by the use of the hemiola and a suspended dissonance (the only discord in the passage) (see Example 5).

This derives from Andrea's model, whose 'Deus qui beatum Marcum[21] has an almost identical pattern, and whose passages of praise are often in precisely this vein. Both Merulo and Croce also used such a pattern in their motets. But a closer examination of the younger Gabrieli's works reveals how rarely he adopts it, and when he does, it is not quite as simple as in 'Regina caeli'. In 'Plaudite', the alleluja seems of this kind, with the triumph emphasized by cross-rhythms; yet here a certain disturbance of the mood is caused by the fact that the one minor chord is placed more prominently on an accented part of the bar. It is, moreover, a tonic chord, after a prolonged emphasis throughout the motet on the major.

More common still is the alleluja type of 'Quis est iste' and 'Hodie Christus natus est'. These too are in triple time, segregated from the remainder of the motet; but here the rhythms are made to spring by the syncopation in the second bar. The minor chord is by no means shunned (see Example 6).

In fact, it is liveliness of rhythm which is the hallmark of Giovanni's alleluja sections, rather than his uncle's solidity. Comparison of the short alleluja which emerges from the first section of 'Surrexit pastor bonus' with a passage using an almost identical theme in Palestrina's motet 'Rorate caeli' shows that training in the more secular atmosphere of

[21] Modern edition, ed. D. Arnold, No. 96 of *Das Chorwerk* (Wolfenbüttel, 1965).

Munich could obviously result in music which was exalted rather than staid, whatever its ostensible political background might be (see Example 7).

Occasionally, as in 'Virtute magna' (Example 4 above), the rhythms become so animated that we may wonder how precise their original performance can have been.

Comparison between Gabrieli and Croce

Gabrieli's essays in this grand manner were not as simple as they appear at first sight—nor, perhaps, so simple as those of some other composers of the Venetian school. In the passage from 'Virtute magna' the technique is nearest to that of Monteverdi, in whose Vesper psalms of 1610 such rhythmic animation is common, and Monteverdi was certainly not just a composer of large-scale occasional music in this work or any other.

Another comparison helps to make Gabrieli's true attitude even clearer.

The final work in this first volume of *Sacrae Symphoniae* is a sixteen-voice setting of verses from Psalm 46, 'Omnes gentes', for use on Ascension Day: 'God is gone up with a merry noise and the Lord with the sound of the trumpet'. The musicians are divided into four groups, to deploy all possible sonority. There is the usual choir marked *cappella*; another with the 'cornett' clefs; a third a *coro grave* with its upper line for alto: and finally, another *coro grave* with its appropriate part for soprano. Both these latter suggest trombones and there are low Cs and Ds on the bass line. Since '*all* people' must clap their hands, the tutti arrives in the second bar, with a chord scored over the full range of three octaves and a fifth, and left to resound with the slowly moving harmony. Excited and nervous dialogue ensues, first in triple time, then more dignified in a duple-time passage, from which the various choirs emerge and develop material quite extensively. Indeed the *cappella* and one of the 'trombone' groups expand their material at some length before the Lord's ascension provokes triple measure, treated with almost Andrea-like majesty and regular changes of harmony and accent. 'Omnes gentes' thus seems a comparatively unsophisticated piece, from the emotional if not from the technical point of view. Yet a brief examination of Croce's setting of the same words in a motet published in his *Motetti à otto voci* puts a new perspective on Gabrieli's style. Both settings, allowing for the more restricted sonorities permitted by Croce's resources, begin similarly, the second choir in each reinforcing the statement of the first on a single chord; but Croce's is a major chord, Gabrieli's a minor. At 'subjecit populos nobis' Croce's plain statement of the phrase contrasts with Gabrieli's modulatory scheme which crams four tonal centres into a couple of bars. In the dialogue for 'et gentes' both composers make use of the same chordal progressions, but the succeeding phrase shows Gabrieli's more intense nature by another quick change of tonal centres involving a temporary ambiguity between major and minor, at a point where Croce brightens the mood by further major chords which establish a modulation to the dominant. It is, in fact, only when each sets the phrase 'with the sound of the trumpet' in the pictorial manner usual throughout the sixteenth century that the two really coincide; and here the very sophistication of what has gone before makes Gabrieli's triumphant statement of faith more emphatic. And his extended allelujas, not in the standard triple time but emerging from the trumpetings full of syncopations and vital counterpoint, outshine Croce's mass-like setting. This is not to depreciate Croce's piece as a whole; it merely underlines once more the fact that the extrovert manner of Andrea Gabrieli was handed down less through his nephew than through other Venetians.

Gabrieli's setting of 'Nunc Dimittis'

Such a view of the music composed in Giovanni Gabrieli's first dozen years at St. Mark's makes his later development less surprising. Nevertheless, it is undeniable that his grandest works of this epoch are very grand indeed. The canticle 'Nunc Dimittis' is one of the most splendid, if hardly the most profound of the *Sacrae Symphoniae*. For most English composers, for whom it became a traditional part of Compline, it was a prayer; for the Venetians it naturally became a thanksgiving (as it originally was). Gabrieli's setting may have been meant for the festival of the Purification of the Virgin, which the Doge celebrated at the church of S. Maria Formosa and incidentally simultaneously celebrated a victory of the citizens of the district of Castello (in which the church stands) over the Triestini in the tenth century.

If, as is possible, Gabrieli wrote the work for the festival in 1595, he had at his disposal the five players of the Basilica's ensemble, and Giuseppe Bonardi and his company, who from the payment of 2 ducats, 21 grossi, and 21 piccoli might also have been five in number,[22] which would explain the disposition of the choirs. For there is the customary *cappella* of four voices, written in the equally customary *claves signatae*, and two other groups, each of five parts, both obviously requiring instruments. The *coro*

[22] A.S.V., Proc. de Supra, Registro 5, entry for 14 February 1595 (Venetian style 1594).

acuto has the bright colours associated with cornetts, though its two lower strands might have had voices supported by the bassoons, whose players are named periodically in the St. Mark's paybooks. The *coro grave* seems appropriate for trombones, with its uppermost part sung perhaps by Croce himself, or by Ser. Battista of S. Pantalon, of whom Donato reported that he had 'a big voice and secure'.[23] The opening tutti makes clear the scale of the piece. As in most works of this size, interest is less in individual parts than in the overall effect, though the harmony gains vigour with some abrasive clashes in one of which a major and minor third of the chord are sounded in a way that would have delighted Tallis or Byrd. But there is some neat counterpoint in the episodes with which each of the three groups in turn displays itself, before the final splendour of the whole ensemble. The doxology comes, and the grand tutti is given triple time to express the glory of the Trinity. As it cadences with the customary hemiola, the effect is as mighty as Andrea could have imagined. Whereupon the music actually broadens out in a return to duple time, the bass taking its B flats below the stave. As Gabrieli prolongs the final chord with much contrapuntal elaboration in various voices, while their fellows hold their long notes apparently indefinitely, it is as though he was as confident of immortality as were his patrician masters that the Most Serene Republic would last for ever.

[23] See Chapter Two above.

CHAPTER EIGHT

The Scuola Grande di S. Rocco

ONE of the advantages to a musician of living in Venice lay in the fact that so much musical activity went on throughout the whole city. There were entertainments in private houses;[1] there were over a hundred churches, many of them with organs; and there were other official bodies, like the hospitals and confraternities, maintaining chapels at which music was to be heard quite regularly. The Doge's annual visits to some of these institutions were the occasions of elaborate music-making, and saints' days were always celebrated with figural music, as opposed to the usual plain chant. The musicians at St. Mark's were naturally in demand outside their own church, and we find their names turning up as the temporary, and even permanent, employees of other bodies. Not surprisingly, many of these engagements were on a freelance basis; Monteverdi reported in 1620 that he could add two hundred ducats to his current salary of four hundred by such means, so there must have been many opportunities. More surprising are those cases in which the employment was so regular that it apparently interfered with the musician's duties in the basilica. How, for example, did Giovanni Croce manage to combine being *vice-maestro* in the Doge's *cappella* with a post at S. Maria Formosa? Admittedly this was not a major church, but nonetheless it had its own music, sometimes quite prolonged: as a stern patriarchal letter indicates.

Lorenzo Priuli . . . to P. Giovanni Croce, Priest in the Church of S. Maria Formosa, salutations in the name of Our Lord.
Having information that when music is given at Vespers and Mass on solemn festivals, the majority of the singers who are engaged in this said music are without gowns [*cotta indossa*] and that the Vespers are not finished and completed by the hour laid down, which is contrary to the orders of Our Synod; for which reason We inform you, under pain of suspension, or other penalties under Our jurisdiction, that Our orders must be observed, and that your singers must wear

[1] See the regulations which allowed the girls of the Pietà to give concerts to raise funds for the orphanage in 1575 in Pullan, p. 415.

gowns during the said offices, as in the regulations published from time to time: otherwise We order that they must not come to sing any more on any solemn festival. We further admonish you and inform you that they must perform grave and devout music, and that everyone must serve with decorum and modesty, as is suitable for the [divine] office and holy place so that the faithful shall be brought to devotion and to the Spirit.[2]

It is hardly conceivable that Croce would have absented himself from his own church on those 'solemn festivals' to attend St. Mark's, especially as much of his religious music, for resources of the kind available in parish churches, was presumably composed for his own choir. Either he arranged that his engagements did not conflict, or, more likely, his presence in St. Mark's choir was not essential except on major state occasions. Many of the singers were in holy orders, and had some allegiance to monasteries in the city, so Croce was not untypical; perhaps the Procurators saw it as a way of keeping their salary roll reasonably low. It is more difficult to understand their leniency with the organists, who were paid quite well and whose attendance was absolutely necessary; but there is ample evidence that they did other jobs. Giovanni Gabrieli was one of the most fortunate holders of a plurality, since all the time he was organist in St. Mark's he was also organist to the Scuola Grande di S. Rocco.

Religious confraternities in Venice

The institution of the *scuola grande*, as developed by the sixteenth century, was unique to Venice. Thomas Coryat wrote in 1608:

The third feast was upon Saint *Roches* day being Saturday and the sixth day of August, where I heard the best musicke that ever I did in all my life both in the

[2] Museo Correr, Codex Cicogna 2583: . . . 'Lorenzo Priuli . . . P. Gio: Croce Tit^{o} nella Ch^{a} di S. Mª Form^{a}, salute nel Sig^{e} Habbiamo informazione che nelle musiche che si fanno alli Vesperi e Messe nelle solennità la maggior parte dei Cantori si trovano presenti ad esse musiche senza cotta indossa, et che li Vesperi non sono finiti, e terminati alle hore debite, ilche e contro li nr̄i ordini sinodali; Per tanto vo cōmettemo sotto pena di sospensione, et altre pene a nostri arbito, che dobiate osservare essi nr̄i ordini, e farli osservare alli vostri Cantori tanto nel portar le Cotte indosso mentre si celebrano essi officij, quanto nel terminarli ad hora e tempo che habbino ordinato, e facendosi in ciò alcuna trasgressione, vi com̄ettemo sotto le pene sop^{te}, che non debbiate trovarvi presente, ma partirsi, et venirsi, a dar aviso di quanto fosse seguito, altrimenti provederemo, che non andaranno più a cantare in alcuna solennità. Vi am̄onimo di più, et com̄ettemo, che si facciano Musiche gravi e divoti e che ognuno in simil ministero servi decoro e modestia a conforme all'officio, et luoco sacro p eccitare li fedeli alla devotione, et spirito

Dati die 14 Xbris 1595

morning and the afternoone, so good that I would willingly goe an hundred miles a foote at any time to hear the like. The place where it was, is neare to Saint *Roches* Church, a very sumptuous and magnificent building that belongeth to one of the sixe Companies of the Citie. For there are in Venice sixe Fraternities or Companies that have their severall halles (as we call them in London) belonging to them, a great maintenance for the performing of those shewes that each company dothe make . . . In this [the lowest] roome are two or three faire Altars. For this roome is not appointed for merriments and banquetings as the halles belonging to the Companies of London, but altogether for devotion and religion, therein to laud and prayse God and his Saints with Psalmes, Hymnes, spirituall song and melodious musicke upon certaine daies dedicated unto Saintes.[3]

The *scuole* had begun as confraternities dedicated to flagellating themselves in procession, to atone for the sins of mankind and to prepare themselves for death. They originated in the thirteenth century, and the element of flagellation persisted throughout the following three hundred years. But the members of the Venetian confraternities favoured less primitive ways of reminding themselves of redemption and of seeking grace. Substitutes could be hired for the flagellant processions; priests could be employed to say Masses which would speed the souls of their members through Purgatory. Moreover they could alleviate poverty, help the sick, see that orphans were provided for (a very cogent consideration in an era when the marriage age was high and the average expectation of life low). Lastly, one could glorify God and His Saints, which in Venice, with its taste for public pomp, hardly required justification.

Their charitable works seem to us to lack the altruism which the word charity nowadays implies. The benefits derived from the activities of the *scuole grandi* were largely directed to their members. Thus the numerous almshouses, the payments to the sick, the masses for the dead, the provision of dowries for the daughters of the less affluent were all for the most part provisions for a membership who had joined the club specifically to achieve greater security. But it would be unsympathetic to be cynical over this. The musicians who appear in the *mariegola*, or list of members, of the Scuola di S. Rocco in the first half of the sixteenth century are poor and otherwise unknown singers and players.

Andrea [son] of Zuane, singer at S. Geremia
Alvixe [son] of Thomaxo, trombonist
Alessandro relative of Zuan, singer
Andrea [son] of Pietro from Barena, singer

[3] T. Coryat, *Coryats Crudities* (London, 1611).

Andrea [son] of our Pietro, singer
Batista from Lagano, singer
Domenego from Stai, singer at S. Sofia
Geronimo [son] of Antonio, player
Jacomo [son] of Matio, player.[4]

Significantly, none of the singers mentioned is a priest, as they would have been in the *cappelle* of most churches, and they came from the ranks of the lower, or at most middle, classes. When musicians were hired, one of their perquisites was to be 'made brothers of the fraternity without fee'; which in turn may explain why their salaries were rather low.

Ceremonial life of the confraternities

As the confraternities ceased to have the character of flagellant communities, there was some division of thought among the state authorities about the essential nature of the *scuola grande*. In times of hardship they stressed their charitable functions; orders went out to reduce expenditure on anything except the giving of alms.[5] Singers or players would be laid off, either the whole company being dismissed[6] or their numbers being reduced.[7] Sometimes, new taxes forced the governing body of the confraternity to take such steps. This happened at the end of March 1588 to the Scuola della Carità:

As it has seemed prudent to Their Excellencies of the Most Excellent Senate that the *scuole grandi* should be obliged to contribute to the exchequer galley tax, in the execution of which order Their Excellencies the Board of Admiralty, on 4 August last, have imposed on our *scuola* the obligation to pay fifty ducats to the Exchequer each month, and it being beyond our power to make this payment and to continue with the holy work which we do; thus considering that the expenditure that our *scuola* makes on players of the *lironi* and on singers is very considerable, since to the players are given eighty ducats per annum and to the singers fifty ducats, in total being one hundred and thirty, to which must also be taken in consideration the fact that these have many times been absent from their duties, as we know from the testimony of the Magnificent Warden [of the *scuola*], it being claimed [by the musicians] that they have no necessity to serve the *scuola* on the day of its patron saint if they are not paid extra, which is insupportable and must not be tolerated, thus

It is decided by the Magnificent Messer Zuan Balbi, Grand Warden, that the said players of *lironi* and singers be dismissed, and that *de cetero* no salary be paid,

[4] Archivio di S. Rocco, Mariegola, f. 55v. [5] Pullan, p. 126.

[6] Scuola della Carità, Notatorio (1607–23), f. 170v–171.

[7] A.S.V., S. Rocco, Rubbrica Generale Sonadori, 30 October 1543.

liberty being granted to the Warden to make arrangements, as appears necessary for the festivals and solemn days, with someone to be paid for each separate occasion, it not being allowed to give any kind of salary without the authority of Our Grand Council.[8]

But at other times, as different people were in office, the reverse happened. Pomp and splendour would be desired by everyone from the members to the officers of state, and the lack of music would seem a disgrace. The following report of the English Ambassador, Sir Henry Wotton, indicates why the Scuola di S. Rocco had none of its customary superb music on 16 August 1622:

Among other notes of this week, let me tell your Lordship that we have seen one great solecism, a St. Rocco's Day uncelebrated with music, even their peculiar Saint; which in common discourse is attributed either to the avarice or the spite of an apothecary, on whom that confraternity did lay the charge of those rites this year against his will. This omission to many ears may perchance sound like a trifle; but the Pope's instruments work upon it, and say it is no marvel if his authority be decayed here (as hath been lately seen in violating the Court of Inquisition, and in a round proceeding against the Bishop of Padova) when their own saints (for Rocco is not yet in the Roman Canon) are so slighted.[9]

In 1585, the Council of Ten ordered the *scuole* to increase their expenditure for a special St. Mark's Day procession, which the Scuola di S. Rocco calculated would cost them some three hundred ducats.[10] The magnificent turn-out of the *scuole* to celebrate the peace treaty between France and Spain in 1598 must have cost even more;[11] and no doubt during the interdict of 1606–7 the state encouraged them to show how well these

[8] A.S.V., Scuola della Carità, Notatorio (1581–1607), f. 92: 'Così come prudentissim^{te} sua Ser^{ta} ha deliberato per parte dell'Ecc^{mo} Senato che tutte le scole grande siano obligate a far deposito de galiotti in Cecca, in essecution della qual li Ecc^{mi} SS^{ri} Presidenti della Militia maritima, sotto 4 Agosto prossimo passato e stato tansato la Scola nostra a dover portar ogni mese ducati 50 in cecca per conto di detto deposito, ne dovendo ancor noi mancar con quel che può le forze nrē di farsi che questa buona, et santa opera sia essequita con quel manco interesse sia possibile; impero conoscendo che la spesa che fà la scuola nrā in sonadori de Lironi, et cantori e molto importante, perche a sonadori se li da d. 80 all'anno, et à cantori d. 50, che in tutto sono d. 130 li quali anco il più delle volte mancano del loro debito, so come di ciò ne può render testimonianza li mg^{ci} Guardiani; che sono stati asserendo anco non esser obbligati servir la scola il giorno dlla nostra festa, se non vengono, pagati, cosa certo insopportabile da non esser tolerata, però
L'anderà parte che mette il mag^{co} M. Zuan Balbi, Guardian grande che li ditti sonadori de lironi, et cantadori siano licentiati; et che de cetero non li debba correr salario alcuno, essendo in libertà delli mag^{i} Guardiani servirsi de chi, et quando li parerà per le feste, et giorni solenni da esser pagati de volta in volta, non possendoli assegnar salario di sorte alcuna se non con l'autorita del Cap^{lto} nō General.'

[9] L. Pearsall Smith, *Life and Letters of Sir Henry Wotton*, I, p. 245.

[10] Pullan, p. 127. [11] See Chapter Seven above.

Plate 4 The procession at the coronation of the Dogaressa in 1597, one of the many elaborate ceremonies which Doge Marino Grimani devised during his reign (1595–1605). (*Devonshire Collection, Chatsworth: Reproduced by Permission of the Trustees of the Chatsworth Settlement*)

Plate 5 One of the six wind players of the Doge, for whom Gabrieli wrote his canzonas and sonatas. (*Museo Correr, Venice*)

Plate 6 One of the singers in the choir of St. Mark's. (*Museo Correr, Venice*)

Venetian institutions could do without Papal support. At this time 'the *Scuole Grandi* in particular made many fine floats, with scenes which alluded to the rightful claims of the Republic against the Pope, because on one float appeared a Christ and two Pharisees with a motto which said "Reddite quae sunt Cesaris Cesari et quae sunt Dei Deo".'[12]

Clearly charity and ceremonial were of roughly equal importance, and if we compare the sums spent on alms and on processional pomp during Gabrieli's lifetime of service at S. Rocco we can see how important the *scuole* must have been for such people as musicians, not to mention the carpenters and joiners who made the floats. In the latter 1590s the amounts were more or less equal, and in Marin Grimani's reign more was spent on the processions than on almsgiving, a state of affairs which only began to be reversed in the last years of Gabrieli's life.

It is interesting that the players most commonly mentioned as employees of the confraternities are called *sonadori di lironi*, though harpists and lutenists are also mentioned.[13] All these instruments, significantly, are portable, for although the term *lirone* was probably a vague term used by un-musical secretaries of the governing body, it could most easily refer to the 'lira da braccio', an instrument especially suitable for *al fresco* processions, since they could play chords as well as single melodic lines.[14] But it remains a little puzzling that the cornetts and trombones in common use in St. Mark's were not also employed. In any case, the S. Rocco players had plenty to do.

Summary of the supplication and letter given by the aforementioned players of violins

Most Magnificent Signory, your players, much aggrieved by the most arduous duties which we have in this confraternity of S. Rocco: on which we have all agreed to serve Your Excellencies for the whole of the present month, and having thus deliberated well, [declaring] that we wish to have twenty ducats per annum for each man, and if we do not merit this do not let it be given us, in the light of the duties that we have, and in the light of what the other confraternities pay their players; that is they have as salary fourteen ducats per annum each man, and they do not have half the processions that we do, since we have double the processions they have, which are forty-one in number, as Your Excellencies will see written hereunder, so that if Your Excellencies do not give us the said salary, we shall take our leave at the end of the month . . .

12 Pullan, p. 60: 'Render unto Caesar the things which are Caesar's; and unto God the things which are God's'.

13 A.S.V., S. Rocco, Index 6 entry under *Sonadori*.

14 Howard Brown: *Sixteenth-Century Instrumentation: The Music for the Florentine Intermedii* (American Institute of Musicology, 1973).

[List of Processions]

First Sundays as usual	12
Processions to the *scuole grandi*	6
To St. Mark's 7 times	7
thus	
St. Mark's Day	1
St. Mark of the Rose Water	1
S. Isidore	1
St. Mark's and Sta Justina	1
St. Mark and S. Vio	1
St. Mark's on the day of Corpus Domini	1
St. Mark's and Sta Marina	1
To S. Zaccaria and S. Stefano	1
To S. Giovanni and to the Cross and to S. Andrea	1
On [the day of] Corpus Domini to S. Andrea	1
To Castello	1
To S. Andrea	1
To Sta Maria Maggiore in August	1
To the Angel Raphael and S. Maria Maggiore	1
To S. Bastian	1
To the Madonna of the Mercadente all'horto	1
All Saints	1
On [the day of] the Trinity	1
On [the day of] the Holy Spirit	1
To the Maddalena	1
To the Apostles	1
To S. Pantalon	1
To S. Stin	1

And several times to S. Iseppo, and also several times to S. Niccolò of the sailors, as on [the feast of] S. Antonio, without taking into account several others.[15]

Two facts become clear from this document. Firstly there was a tremendous amount of music-making in the confraternity; secondly, as far as the

[15] Archivio di S. Rocco, Registro delle Terminazioni, No. 3, f. 7: 'Tenor della supplicatione, et scritt^{ra} posta per gl'oltrascritti Sonadori di violini

Sig^{ri} mag^{ci} li vostri sonadori molto aggravati di grandiss^{a} fatica qual noi femo in questa scola de ms. S̄. Rocho, onde tutti noi siemo deliberati di servirle S.V. p̱ tutto il mese presente, et in questo mezo fatte bona deliberatione, se quelle vora che servirmo noi volemo ducati 20 all'anno per homo, et se non li meritemo non li datti. Vardati le fadighe che noi femo et vardati come le altre schole pagha li suoi sonadori, et gue ne, che hanno de salario ducati 14 p̱ homo all' anno, et nō dan̄o la mittà delle processiō, che femo noi, p̱ c̄h noi femo il dop̄io precessiō di quello, che fan̄o loro, le qual sono n° 41, como le S.V̄. vederà qua di sotto, si che le S.V. nō farā la provvision ditta, finido che sarà il mese sopra ditto piliaremo licentia . . .' [a list of processions as in the English].

players were concerned it was mainly done in processions. It seems unlikely that they played during the Mass when they arrived at the churches. When they went to St. Mark's on grand festivals, they would scarcely have taken their place alongside the musicians in the basilica. There is no evidence that the *sonadori di lironi* were highly skilled. Their names rarely appear in any other context than that of the *scuole*, and mention of one of the men employed at St. Mark's is rare. One wonders what they can have played in these processions. There is some guide in a resolution of the governors dated 14 April 1550.[16]

To be rid of certain undesirable things that are seen to happen on the days of processions and on ordinary masses, done by our players of the *lironi*, who have on their own responsibility, when accompanying our confraternity, played many songs [*canzon*] and other things more lascivious than devout which are certainly not pleasing to Our Lord, nor are these honest things for our masses and processions, these kinds of pieces and songs as aforesaid. [So] for the reverence of Our Lord and the honour of our confraternity, The Most Magnificent M. Jacomo di Olizzi, our honourable Grand Warden, now orders that to be rid of the above mentioned errors, and so that the confraternity's actions should be to the honour of Our Lord, and our Protector S. Rocco, by the authority of the Banca and Zonta, fully assembled, our players of *lironi* be given one ducat per man as a special gift, the players being obliged to play motets, and *laudi* to the honour of Our Lord and our Protector S. Rocco and other Saints, and nothing else; and if at any time the aforesaid players are found to be playing *canzoni* and love songs [*cose amorose*] as said above, they shall be dismissed and sent away by

16 Archivio di S. Rocco, Registro delle Parti, II, f. 103v. 'Per oviar alli inconventi che si vede per zornata occorra nelle procession, e messe nostre ordinarie delli sonadori nostri de liron, li quali fine della creation sua fin'ora nell'andar della Scola nostra fora de casa [?] vanno sonando molte canzon, et altri soni più presto lassivi che devoti cosa qual certo al nostro Signor Dio non è da piacer ne honesta cosa e nelle nostra messe e Procession Se soni d. [?] sorti de soni et canzoni come de sop^{a}. Per el che per reverentia del nostro Sig^{r} Dio et honor della Scola nostra el mag^{co} ms. Jacomo di Olizzi nostro honor, ando Vardian Grando al pn̄te

Mette parte per obviar alli errori sopraditti, et che le cose della scola passano ad honor del nostro Signor Dio, et Protettor nr̄o ms San Rocco che per autorità della pnte Banca et Zonta redotta al N^{o} perfetto sia dado a ditti nostri sonadori de Lironi per una volta tanto D^{to} uno per homo essendo obligati ditti Sonadori sonar motteti, et laude ad honor dal nostro Signor Dio, et Prottetor nr̄o ms San Roccho, et altri Santi, e non altrimenti. Et se per tempo alcun di d^{ti} sonadori se troverà sonar canzon aut'cose amorose come di sop^{a} è ditto detti Sonadori se intendino privi, et casi della Scola Nostra, e de Sonadori della detta essendo obbligati sonar tutto l'anno iusto li ordini nostri some appar nelle Creation sua fu mandà le Parte attorno

Della Parte B.19 } presa.'
De non B.3 }

The banca and zonta (or giunta) were the two major committees of the confraternity.

Our Scuola; and the players of the same shall be obliged to play all the year after our orders, as appeared in the statute hiring them.

Votes in favour	19	
against	3	agreed

Motets of the contrapuntal style customary around 1550 are not, however, easy to play in processions. There was no repertoire of sophisticated music suitable for these occasions, and these players were probably more used to performing dances and songs. Gabrieli can have found little musical stimulus among them.

Singers employed by the confraternities

The singers may have been more accomplished; for though they were seldom great Venetian virtuosi, the Scuola Grande di S. Rocco did from time to time employ some exceptional performers. The tradition of having a group of professional singers for the processions dated back to the last years of the fifteenth century. In 1493, the four paid singers, like the instrumentalists, were expected to attend on the festivals, and Sundays and for all the processions. An agreement was probably made with a leader who arranged their attendance. Their salary was gradually raised, and other perquisites, such as candles for the processions and the palms for Palm Sunday, were added. By mid-century they were full members of the *scuola*, being excused the entrance fee, and still allowed their candles at its expense. With such munificence the Scuola Grande di S. Rocco was able to attract some quite distinguished men, and on 4 March 1577 they elected a quartet led by Baldissare Donato (tenor), D. Galleazo of Pesaro (bass), Fra. Angioletto of the Minorite order (perhaps an alto), and Father Nicoleto of Castello (soprano),[17] the first three at least being in the service of St. Mark's. But by the following January, this obviously superior company had departed.[18] The men who replaced them included two Spaniards (Spain and the Spanish-dominated Papal States were the home of the virtuoso castrati of the time). Again there were difficulties. Antonio Spagnolo, the soprano of the new quartet who was almost certainly a member of the St. Mark's *cappella* was dismissed in 1578. Although we do not know the names of all the singers who served the Scuola of S. Rocco in the succeeding years, the links with St. Mark's were

[17] Archivio di S. Rocco, Registro delle Terminazioni, II, f. 379.
[18] ibid, Vol. III, f. 6v.

apparently maintained. In 1607, for example, a resolution of the governors tells us

> that since our bass the Rev. Father Agostin of the Frari Church has left the city and it being necessary to elect another in his place at the same salary and emoluments,
>
> It is decreed by the Most Magnificent Messer Andrea Stagiera, our honoured Grand Warden, that the Rev. Father Homobon of the *cappella* of St. Mark's be elected as said above.[19]

Father Agostin had been a very experienced singer,[20] and his living literally next door to the Scuola di S. Rocco in the Frari monastery must have been extremely convenient for all.

Duties of the organist at the Scuola Grande di S. Rocco

With four singers and six string players, circumstances were obviously very different from those in St. Mark's, and it might seem strange for the younger Gabrieli to come into the employ of the confraternity. But the *scuola grande* needed someone to take charge of its music, and this lot gradually fell to the organist. This post was founded later than those of singers and players, for processions and public display did not require someone who could only perform in church. The first indication of such an appointment comes in February 1539 [Venetian style 1538] when they proceeded

> to elect an organist, who shall serve throughout the year
> as follows
>
> All Fridays at Compline
> Every first Sunday of the month at Mass
> The Days of the Nativity, Resurrection, and Ascension
> The Day of Pentecost at Mass and Vespers
> The Day of the Most Holy Cross and the Days of Saints Appolonia, Giacomo, Bastiano at Mass and Vespers
> All the Votive Masses—the Vigil and Feast of S. Rocco at Mass and Vespers
> All the other Masses and Vespers taking place in church

19 Archivio di S. Rocco, Registro 4, f. 131; entry for 4 March 1607: 'Essendo Partito da questa Citta il Rdo P. fra Agostin di frari Bassa della scola nra et dovendo in loco suo farsi elecione de altro sogietto con il medesimo salario et Regalie che egli havea
l'Andera Parte che mette il Magco ms. Andrea Stagiera nro Hono do Gn Gde che si eletto per Cantor del Basso il Rdo Pre Homobon de Capella de S. Marco in tutto come di sopra'.

20 See Chapter Two above.

With a salary of six ducats per annum
and was elected
Father Domenico Tenestrer.[21]

Tenestrer's duties (like his meagre salary) were less than those of their other musicians, since he did not need to attend the processions. There was one exception: whereas the singers and players were apparently not expected to appear at votive masses, the organist was. And although it is impossible to say exactly how many times a year these memorial masses were celebrated, the requirements of those who left money to the confraternity clearly grew as the years passed. So did the post of organist assume importance.

The next organist, Mario Serafin, elected in 1541,[22] received ten ducats a year, and his equally unknown successor in 1549 was Angelo Lupini. A new organ was installed in 1558 'over the door of the church'. A new organist was immediately elected with increased status. From an entry in the resolutions of the governors we see that 'this player of the organ shall be (*illegible*) and efficient to play the said [new] organ . . . and the organist elected must come personally to play the organ as obliged nor must he ever send others to play the said organ except in the case of a just impediment, and the salary he shall have from our scuola for his service is twenty-four ducats per annum.'[23] This salary indicates that the confraternity were at last taking the office seriously; and the list of required attendances is now formidable.

Each first Sunday of the month except during Lent and Advent
Then
Item The Day of Epiphany to play at Mass and Vespers
Item The Day of S. Sebastiano to play at Mass and Vespers
Item The Day of the Purification of the Madonna to play at Mass and Vespers
Item The Day of S. Poloneo to play at Mass and Vespers
Item The Day of S. Matteo to play at Vespers
Item The Day of the Annunciation of the Madonna to play at Mass and Vespers
Item Easter Day to play at Mass and Vespers

[21] Archivio di S. Rocco, Rubrica Generale Organisti. [22] ibid, 10 July 1541.
[23] Archivio di S. Rocco, Registro delle Terminazioni, II, f. 294v: '. . . uno sonador che sia [illegible] ꝑ sonar ditto organo p̲ onor di ditta nostra giexia . . . la persona di uno sonador de organo che sia perito et sufiziente p̲ sonar ditto organo con tutte le obligazione che apartiene a dita giexia et qual sonador eletto chel sara debi personalmente sonare sempre l'organo juste le sue obligazione nō podendo maj mādar altrij ꝑ luj a sonar ditto organo salvo justo in pedimento et abj dj salario dj benj de la ascuola nostra ꝑ suo servitio di d̲ⁱ vinti quattro al ano.'

Item The Day of S. Filippo to play at Vespers
Item The Day of the Invention of the Cross to play at Mass and Vespers
Item The Easter [Festival] of March to play at Mass and Vespers
Item The two festivals at Easter to play at Vespers
Item The Birth Day of St. John the Baptist to play at Vespers
Item The Day of S. Pietro to play at Vespers
Item The Day of the Visitation of the Madonna to play at Mass and Vespers
Item The Day of S. Rocco to play at Mass and Vespers
Item The Day of S. Bartolomeo to play at Vespers
Item The Birth Day of Our Lady to play at Mass and Vespers
Item The Day of S. Matteo to play at Vespers
Item The Day of S. Simeone to play at Vespers
Item All Saints Day to play at Vespers
Item The Day of Our Lady's Assumption to play at Mass
Item The Day of S. Tommaso to play at Vespers
Item All Sundays to play at Vespers except in Advent, and Lent and all Fridays to play at Compline.
Item The Day of S. Andrea to play at Mass and Vespers.[24]

This shows that the organist was in the church of the confraternity about twice a week; he was hardly less important than some of the chaplains. So it is not surprising that at last a man who made some mark in Venetian musical life appeared on the scene. He was Vincenzo Bellavere, a colleague of Giovanni Gabrieli at St. Mark's, and he remained in the service of the *scuola grande* until 1585 when a minute of the governors for 1 February records that

M. Vincenzo Bellavere having left us and vacated the post of organist on his removal to Padua, as he told us, and not being able to do without [an organist], to proceed to elect a new man in his place,

It is agreed . . . that an organist be elected in place of the said M. Vincenzo Bellavere, to have the salary of twenty-four ducats per annum, with the same obligations and conditions of service as had the said Bellavere, the person elected not being allowed to send others to play, but attending in person, at the will of the Banca and Giunta.[25]

[24] ibid.

[25] ibid, II, f. 91v: 'Essendo partito ms. vic^zo Bellaver et lass^o il carico d'organista per esser stato conduto à Padova, com'egli disse, et non potendosi far di manco di far nova ellettione nel loco suo.

L'Anderà parte, cħ mette il m^co Guardian Grande oltras^to che sij elletto un'organista in loco del detto ms vic^o Bellaver che habbi il carico di organista con il salario de duc^i 24 all'anno, et con gl'oblighi, et conditioni, cħ haveva il detto Bel'haver, nō posendo l'elletto far sonar altri, ma essercitarsi lui in persona, et sij à beneplacito di m^ca Banca, et Gionta.'

An account book tells us the name of Bellavere's successor: '4 August 1585, Received by me. Jovanni Gabriello [*sic*], organist, from the Most Magnificent Grand Warden, twenty-four ducats as the salary for the year beginning 13 February.'[26]

Gabrieli as organist of the confraternity

Gabrieli was the first organist of St. Mark's to have such a post, though the Scuola di S. Rocco may have had some dealings with his predecessor, Merulo, who had been the tenant of one of the confraternity's houses for a short time.[27] Looking at the formidable list of festivals at which he needed to be present we may well wonder how he managed to fulfil his duties: or indeed why he took the job in the first place. He may have been short of money, for it is unusual to find payments at the Scuola di S. Rocco made in mid-year; and certainly later he sometimes received his stipend in advance at St. Mark's, which suggests temporary financial difficulty. He remained in the Scuola's service for the rest of his life, and there is no record of discontent on either side. His salary was never raised, nor does any petition asking for more survive: singers and players retired and were appointed as need arose, so that all appears to have run smoothly.

Annual festival of St. Roche

The music of the confraternity became more impressive, and on at least one day each year, the feast of its patron saint, it was quite magnificent. It is difficult to discover what had happened on this day, 16 August, in the earlier part of the sixteenth century, since the relevant documents have not been discovered. But clearly when a musician from St. Mark's was brought into the *scuola grande*, it was possible to arrange sumptuous music there. The Venetians had their own reasons for beatifying S. Rocco (not a saint in the Roman calendar), since he was a protector from the plague, from which, as a seaport receiving ships from all the Mediterranean, Venice suffered more than most. Although his miracles had largely been wrought in France, there were important relics in Venice and the Veneto.[28] So, in spite of the fact that 16 August was also the festival of the Assump-

[26] A.S.V., S. Rocco, Busta 423; entry for 4 August 1585: 'Riceve io Jovanni Gabriello organista dal Mag$^{\underline{ci}}$ Guardiā grāde ducati vinti quatro p̲ il salari de ano uno precipiado a 13 febraro 1584 [Venetian style 1585].'

[27] A.S.V., S. Rocco, 2ª Consegna, Vol. 121, f. 26v and 31v.

[28] K. Jeppeson, 'A forgotten master of the early sixteenth century: Gaspar de Albertis', *Musical Quarterly* (1958), p. 311.

tion, the Doge and Signory went in solemn procession across the Grand Canal by boat to the confraternity's church and hall. The musicians of St. Mark's went with them; and some stayed for the remainder of the day.

The receipts for musicians' payment are on flimsy pieces of paper, now devastated by damp and old age. Luckily they contain a wealth of detail:

Account of the money spent for the Solemn Ceremony and Feast of San Rocco this present year of 1595 as below, and first . . . [payments for hire of carpets, etc.]

Item to the Singers, both companies of the same		lire 372
Item to the 4 singers of the *Scuola* as usual		14
Item to the Chiozotto [Giovanni Croce] as *maestro di cappella*		14
Item to M. Giuseppe Bonardo on behalf of the Bassani players		124
Item to M. Francesco Laudi on behalf of Fauretti's company of players		124
Item to M. Giovanni Gabrieli, organist, with his company		112
Item to the same for the hire of Organs	21	
and to those who assembled the bellows	6	27
Item to the players of the violins	20	
and to that of the violone	10	
with the pourboire	7	53[29]

This indicates a magnificent assembly. The two companies of singers mentioned must surely have included the choir of St. Mark's, if the *vice-maestro* of the basilica was in charge. Bassano's company were probably the six salaried instrumentalists, while Fauretti may have assembled the part-timers who adorned the Doge's music so frequently. Gabrieli's own 'company' is more of a mystery, but might easily be a group of organists, for it was clearly the custom to hire several organs (this entry is a constant factor thereafter). There are a number of other puzzles, especially the rather low payment to Croce. As this is only his payment 'as *maestro di cappella*',[30] it may well be that he was paid something on commission for making arrangements in connection with the choir (the *vice-maestro* at St. Mark's often acted as a go-between, since he was essentially one of the singers, rather than a state official). Certainly, the assembled company was virtually the most distinguished which could be drawn from native Venetian resources.

The receipts for the next few years are missing, but when the series resumes in 1602, the situation is much the same. There are payments to Croce and Gabrieli of sixty-two lire each, a large bill for a choir, with six

29 A.S.V., S. Rocco, Filza 26, 'Polizze di Spese da 1500 a 1600', Busta 418.

30 A.S.V., S. Rocco, Busta 156, Cauzioni 1602.

organists now mentioned, two companies of players with some extras not apparently belonging to the established groups, two violinists and a violone.[30] Moreover, it looks as though the music was being taken more seriously since there are separate entries for additional rehearsal fees, most unusual at this time, from which it seems as though rehearsal rates were about a quarter of the usual fees. In 1603 Croce, having become *maestro di cappella* at St. Mark's, has been replaced by the new *vice-maestro*, Bortolo Morosini. The usual choir and companies of players are back, and Gabrieli has hired six organs in addition to one called the *organo grande*. There are again the string players; but there is now a separate entry for 'two priests who sang'; this might at first sight seem to be just a payment to two men who could not be hired through the usual intermediaries, but the accounts for the following year suggest that they are soloists. The list of payments shows how Gabrieli had been developing the music for this grand feast day.

This day 16 August 1604 in Venice
Money spent for the Feast of St Roche

Paid to S. Giovanni Bassano for the players of the company	ducats	40
Paid to the usual 2 violinists	lire	248
Paid to the 4 exceptional [*straordinarii*] violinists	lire	307
Paid to the said Bassano for 4 additional players for attending the rehearsals	lire	36
Paid to the same as his fee	lire	18
Paid to Sig^r Giovanni Gabrielli for 7 organs at lire 21 each	lire	147
Paid to the same for 4 lutenists	lire	48
Paid to the *violone*	lire	20
Paid to the said Gabrielli as his fee of 10 ducats	lire	62
Paid to Father Bortolo [Morosini] for his company and the money for the singers who came from Padua and their rehearsals	lire	360
Paid to the Rev. Father Don Vido, to Father Reventio, to Father Benedict, singers from Padua, for coming to the rehearsal and singing on the day of the Festival	lire	180
Paid to the Rev. Father Giacomo and Father Giovanni Battista, Father Ottavio and Bortolomeo, singers from Padua	lire	96
Paid to the Polish bass, singer at St Mark's	lire	18
Paid to the other special singers	lire	28
Paid to the 4 singers of the scuola	lire	14
Paid to the Rev. Father Bortolo [Morosini] for the rehearsal fee	lire	60[31]

[31] A.S.V., Scuola di S. Rocco, Busta 157, Cauzioni 1604–5.

This shows a very different attitude from the earlier years. Whereas in 1595 the ensemble could be like that at St. Mark's, with trombones and cornetts to support and contrast with the full choir, nearly ten years later these are only a small part of the *cappella*; the string players are more prominent, and there are also such quiet instruments as lutes. As for the singers from Padua, it is clear that they are virtuosi, since three of them seem worth a fee just half that of the whole choir directed by Morosini. In the next years the tendency towards the virtuoso singer continues. Some Paduans appear in 1605 (probably the same, though the names are unfortunately obliterated by damp on the receipt). They do not appear in 1606, but there is an entry for two *cantori falsetti*, while in this same year the music for Holy Week included something sung by a castrato 'who sang soprano . . . to the pleasure of the Most Magnificent Grand Warden'. The file for 1607 is missing. But that for 1608 is unusually forthcoming, and to it can be added a description by a visiting Englishman, Thomas Coryat, so vivid that it brings to life in a quite extraordinary way what had by now become one of the greatest events of Venice's musical year.[32]

This feast consisted principally of Musicke, which was both vocall and instrumentall, so good, so delectable, so rare, so admirable, so super excellent, that it did even ravish and stupifie all those strangers that never heard the like. But how others were affected with it I know not; for mine owne part I can say this, that I was for the time even rapt up with Saint Paul into the third heaven. Sometimes there sung sixteene or twenty men together, having their master or moderator to keepe them in order; and when they sung, the instrumentall musitians played also. Sometimes sixteene played together upon their instruments, ten Sagbuts, foure Cornets, and two Violdegambaes of an extraordinary greatnesse; sometimes tenne, six Sagbuts and foure Cornets; sometimes two, a Cornet and a treble violl. Of those treble viols I heard three severall there, whereof each was so good, especially one that I observed above the rest, that I never heard the like before. Those that played upon the treble viols, sung and played together, and sometimes two singular fellowes played together upon Theorboes, to which they sung also, who yeelded admirable sweet musicke, but so still that they could scarce be heard but by those that were very neare them. These two Theorbists concluded that nights musicke, which continued three whole howers at the least. For they beganne about five of the clocke, and ended not before eight. Also it continued as long in the morning: at every time that every severall musicke played, the Organs, whereof there are seven faire paire in that room, standing al in a rowe together, plaied with them. Of the singers

[32] See also *Les remarques triennales di Jean-Baptiste du Val, advocat en Parlement de Paris et secrétaire de la royne, pendant l'ambassade de Messire Jean Bochard, s^r de Champigny . . . ambassadeur à Venise*, Bibliothèque nationale, ms. fr. 13977.

there were three or foure so excellent that I thinke few or none in Christendome do excell them, especially one, who had such a peerelesse and (as I may in a manner say) such a supernaturall voice for the sweetnesse that I thinke there was never a better singer in all the world, insomuch that he did not onely give the most pleasant contentment that could be imagined, to all the hearers, but also did as it were astonish and amaze them. I alwaies thought that he was a Eunuch, which if he had beene, it had taken away some part of my admiration, because they do most commonly sing passing wel; but he was not, therefore it was much the more admirable. Againe it was the more worthy of admiration, because he was a middle-aged man, as about forty yeares old. For nature doth more commonly bestowe such a singularitie of voice upon boyes and striplings, than upon men of such yeares. Besides it was farre the more excellent, because it was nothing forced, strained or affected, but came from him with the greatest facilitie that ever I heard. Truely, I thinke that had a Nightingale beene in the same roome, and contended with him for the superioritie, something perhaps he might excell him, because God hath granted that little birde such a priviledge for the sweetnesse of his voice, as to none other: but I thinke he could not much. To conclude, I attribute so much to this rare fellow for his singing, that I thinke the country where he was borne, may be as proude for breeding so singular a person as Smyrna was of her Homer, Verona of her Catullus, or Mantua of Virgil: But exceeding happy may that Citie, or towne, or person bee that possesseth this miracle of nature.[33]

Virtuosity of the performers

Clearly S. Rocco employed some very fine musicians at this time, and the accounts of the treasurer[34] tell us who they were. The Director of Music was, as in 1604, Bortolo Morosini, *Vice-maestro di Cappella* at St. Mark's, and he was paid for bringing along 'two companies of singers', of whom the majority must have been from the basilica. Bassano had also brought along two companies of players, in addition to which there were the players led by Nicolò Dalla Casa not to mention the special violinists who were given separate fees. There were seven organists, of whom we only know the names of one Gianbattista (probably Grillo, eventually to succeed Gabrieli as organist for the confraternity), and Gabrieli himself, though the organist at SS. Giovanni e Paolo might have joined them—he was certainly a pupil of Giovanni, and may have been a certain Giacomo Barbarini, whom we know to have been in this post a few years later.

But it was undoubtedly the virtuoso singers who were the greatest attraction; and in this year they were evidently very good indeed, for we can identify some of them with certainty and even find some of their

[33] op. cit. [34] A.S.V., Scuola di S. Rocco, Busta 158, Cauzioni 1606–8.

music. There was the Spanish castrato from St. Mark's, Mattia Fernando, and, as in 1604, a group of singers from Padua. Though one of these, Gratiora, has left no trace of his activities, the two counter-tenors were quite famous. A gentleman called Da Piove was Father Vido Rovetta (not to be confused with Giovanni Battista Rovetta, later *maestro* of St. Mark's), known to be a falsettist of some distinction. A demanding solo motet by him is in Simonetti's *Ghirlanda Sacra* (1625). The other counter-tenor was Bartolomeo Barbarino, who published a book of solo motets in which the dedication to a former patron, Giuliano della Rovere, refers to performing them 'to the chitarrone with my raucous and bad voice' (the mock modesty is obviously to be taken with more than a pinch of salt); this explains why Coryat heard them singing to the lute. His two volumes of motets, though not of any great merit, show how a virtuoso singer of the Venetian school around 1600 displayed his art. Barbarino, who had come from Pesaro in the central part of the Italian Adriatic coast, seems to have been little affected by the novelties of the Florentine singer-composers; he uses decorative figures more in the manner of Bassano, or indeed Gabrieli himself, working out a rhythmic or melodic pattern in a quite orderly way:

There is real music in his display pieces, triple-time sections which flow along in pleasant sequential phrases, obviously derived from the familiar 'alleluja' refrains of Venetian motets (see Example 2) and perhaps a hint of passion at times, when a chromatic turn of phrase suggests itself (see Example 3).

This was something from which Gabrieli could learn; no one else was writing this kind of music in Venice at the time, though when Giulio

Cesare Martinengo arrived in 1609, he may have taken up the genre, as Simonetti's anthology contains his 'Regnum mundi' in a non-virtuoso but pleasant style.[35] Gabrieli seems to have enjoyed such music, for the virtuosi were back in 1609:[36] Rovetta, Barbarino, the three violinists, the singers from St. Mark's, and Bassano's players augmented by 'six extras' [*sei agionti*]. And although there were only six organs, one was an *organo grande* and one of the players was Giovanni Priuli who was much used as a

[35] Printed in H. J. Moser, *Heinrich Schütz: Sein Leben und Werk* (Kassel, 1936; English translation by C. F. Pfatteicher, St. Louis, Missouri, 1959).

[36] A.S.V., Scuola di S. Rocco, Busta 159, Cauzioni 1609–10.

deputy at St. Mark's. The cost of the festival in 1610 was down from the 2,650 lire of the previous year to only 2,075 lire, but the castrati and falsettists are still in the lists—it was the instrumentalists whose services were more expendable. Similarly in 1611, the last St. Roche's Day of Gabrieli's life, it is the singers who continue to appear in the somewhat reduced accounts:

Paid to the Singers	lire	310
Paid to the Players	lire	186
Paid to the Violone	lire	18 g 12
Paid to Sr Gabrielli to give to the priest Da Piove (10 ducats) and to the Pesarino [Barbarino] (10 ducats) and for the two priests who sang (5 ducats) and for 4 organs (84 lire) and for the hire of same (22 lire) and to give to Rev. Father Bartolo [Morosini] (40 lire) and to the said Gabrielli (10 ducats) in all	lire	363
Paid to the Vicar of St. Stin as a present for having sung	lire	18
Paid to the 4 singers of the Scuola	lire	14[37]

Possible works by Gabrieli for the confraternity

Little is known about the music which Gabrieli himself wrote for these grand occasions. There is no extant motet specifically dedicated to St. Roche, nor even one with words which could obliquely be thus construed. There may be one or two clues, nevertheless, in the musical style and resources needed for the music in the posthumous volumes of 1615. Firstly, it is noticeable that there are some pieces which rely little if at all on the general concept of *cori spezzati*. These would certainly be appropriate for performance in the hall of the Scuola di S. Rocco, which has no galleries or other architectural adornment. Such pieces are not necessarily just those written for single choir, although such a canzona as no. 15 of the *Canzone e Sonate* certainly seems the kind of music to go well in the circumstances. The *Sonata à 14* from the same collection, with its use of isolated instruments taken from the various 'choirs', could fit such surroundings just as satisfactorily as St. Mark's. Motets using soloists are even more appropriate, of course. It is significant, too, that much of the late instrumental music has stringed instruments among the named parts. No. 10 of the *Canzone e Sonate* requires two violins whose music is suitably *passeggiata*—as indeed is the bass line of the first choir, which might provide a test of skill for the player of the violone, or 'violdagamba of an

37 A.S.V., Scuola di S. Rocco, Busta 160, Cauzioni 1611–12.

extraordinary greatnesse'. No. 17 fits the information given by receipts for the 1608 festival and its successors even better, for each of its three 'choirs' has a violin on its uppermost line, while the other instruments designated are cornetts, and the unspecified parts look as though they are destined for trombones.

Gabrieli's sonata for 3 violins

This is all speculation: but one work fits our knowledge of the 16 August festival so exactly that there can be little doubt that it was composed for the confraternity. This is the 'Sonata à tre violini', the final work in the 1615 volume of instrumental music, and unique in Gabrieli's *oeuvre* in belonging purely to the new musical style of the early seventeenth century. The organ bass or continuo part though labelled *Basso se piace* in the partbook, is in fact vital to the piece, which makes it unique. It is an essay in the small *concertato*, little investigated by composers of instrumental music in Gabrieli's lifetime, though quickly to become popular thereafter. Comparing his work with the occasional pieces in this vein by his contemporaries, such as the canzona included by Viadana in his *Cento Concerti* of 1602, or those of Giovanni Cima published in Venice in 1610, it is evident that Gabrieli's sonata has the characteristic technical assurance and emotional content that only a great composer can give to a new genre. Viadana's piece looks like a double-choir *canzona* cut down for use by a four-instrument ensemble, and Cima attempts a kind of instrumental *motetto passaggiato*; Gabrieli takes the model from the sixteenth century which can be most readily adapted to the new circumstances. His three violinists are capable of decorating what is in effect the madrigalian style of melody. The following shows the working out of a contrapuntal motif, which recalls the madrigalists of Venice, and indeed England:

Yet the whole work is instrumentally conceived. The traditional canzona rhythm begins and pervades it; the up-beat patterns of some of the motifs remind one of the 'Sonata pian e forte'; there are places where one violin echoes another, to be in turn echoed by the third; and the climaxes come with a resurgence of the favourite *battaglia* repeated notes. As always Gabrieli shows his skill in using the sequences derived from the ornaments of Bassano and Girolamo Dalla Casa, while the juxtaposition of major and minor at cadences adds that bitter-sweetness which we have seen elsewhere in Gabrieli's music:

Above all, there is a sense of intimacy. The texture and the motifs are reminiscent of such a madrigal as 'Deh di me non ti caglia' with its interweaving sopranos, but the whole conception seems to belong to chamber music. Coryat had to stand near the singers to hear them at all, which he could in the hall of S. Rocco, but not in St. Mark's. The violins were no doubt more forceful than the singers, but nonetheless, there was no need to play loudly when the audience was so close to the performers.

The fate of the music of the confraternity after Gabrieli's death

After Gabrieli's death Priuli seems to have taken charge, and the music for S. Rocco's Day was maintained in 1612 on the usual scale, with Barbarino and another falsettist in attendance, and one of the choir of St. Mark's, Gasparo Locatello, who taught singing at the Seminary, directing the assembled company. The following year there seems to have been no music of any distinction. The situation is rather obscure in the documents during the next few years, but by the end of the decade, it was in good shape again. Giovanni's successor as organist, Gianbattista Grillo, obviously re-established the necessary relationships, especially after his appointment in St. Mark's in 1619. Vido Rovetta and Barbarino continued to be engaged up to 1624. But the composers who now provided the music for 16 August were no less than Claudio Monteverdi and his disciples Alessandro Grandi and Francesco Cavalli, all of whom were fully acquainted with the art of the solo motet, and its ability to display the dexterity of singers. These were still sought from far afield; Alvise Grani, collector and editor of Gabrieli's music, was sent to Modena to find suitable performers. Not until the glory of the Most Serene Republic was seriously diminished by the plague of 1630 was the tradition eroded. Yet, as so often in Venice, habits are hard to break: today the singers of St. Mark's still cross the Grand Canal on 16 August to celebrate the festival of St. Roche, and visitors are invited to join in the thanksgiving in the heart of the district of Santa Croce.

CHAPTER NINE

The Pupils

GIOVANNI Gabrieli was one of the most famous music teachers of his time. The names of a number of his pupils are known: they came from all over Europe. Some of them were distinguished men in their own right. All of those known to us by their compositions are interesting in some way. This is surprising. Teaching has never been one of the favourite occupations of practising musicians. Monteverdi made no bones about the fact that it was not a requirement of the post of *maestro di cappella* which contributed to his happiness in Venice.[1] A man in a similar post at Padua Cathedral in 1565 was dismissed for his negligence in teaching the choirboys. Why then did Gabrieli occupy himself with it? The fact that the *maestro di cappella* did not teach may have diverted such activity to the organist: we have already seen that Giovanni's uncle was a good tutor. It may thus have been an inheritance from Andrea.

We have no written record of Giovanni Gabrieli's teaching methods, but we know of a very large number of pupils. The minute book of SS. Giovanni e Paolo records on 26 July 1602 'a pupil of Sig. Gio: Gabrieli was appointed as organist with a salary of 30 ducats per annum, on the condition that he also teaches Father Pietro Martire of Venice, *Profetto* in the Noviciate'.[2] Francesco Stivori in 1599 dedicated a book of instrumental music to 'The Most Magnificent, my dear master, Signor Giovanni Gabrieli'.[3] There was no material gain for Stivori in dedicating it to a musician, whereas a nobleman, or even the rector of the order to whom he was organist might have been more forthcoming. Clearly Gabrieli inspired uncommon devotion.

Whether Gabrieli received much money for such teaching is doubtful.

[1] Letter of 10 September 1627. Translation in *The Monteverdi Companion*, ed. D. Arnold and N. Fortune (London, 1968).

[2] A.S.V., SS. Giovanni e Paolo, Registro 12, f. 82v: '. . . fu eletto in organista un scolaro del Sr Gio: Gabrieli cō di 30 ducati all'anno cō patto ch̄ anco insegna a fra Pietro Martire da V^a^ Profetto in Noviciato.'

[3] Printed in C. Sartori, op. cit., p. 102.

When the pupils came from farther afield, it was sometimes a different matter. Alessandro Tadei[4] came from Graz to Venice in March 1604, and remained there for two and a half years. The documents show that Gabrieli taught him the organ, but instruction may also have included composition, since on his return Tadei showed his mastery of the Gabrielian style of polychoral church music. He must have studied well, for he became court organist to Archduke Ferdinand on his return to Graz while he was probably still in his early twenties. The bills presented by Gabrieli to the Graz authorities are revealing. Gabrieli paid the doctor's and apothecary's fees and saw to it that Tadei had a confessor and a barber and was provided with clothes, he even reimbursed him for the expenditure of the journey to Venice. Gabrieli's fee was twelve silver crowns per month, about one hundred and fifty ducats a year. Since his total pay from St. Mark's at this time was two hundred ducats per annum, this was good recompense, even allowing for the expenditure of board and lodging which were presumably included. He may have had additional payment for music bought on Tadei's behalf, and the *objets d'art* for which he appears to have negotiated when the Archduke Maximilian was visiting Venice in 1604. Finally on his departure Tadei was reminded by the Venetian Signory that 'a pupil [sent] by a prince or other gentleman had never gone away without giving a present from their master'. So in 1609 a handsome gift of a hundred florins, or about eighty ducats, was sent from Graz.

Gabrieli had many other foreign pupils sent by princes anxious to *fare bella figura* after the Venetian manner (and apparently willing to pay for it). The first to arrive were a group from Denmark, an organist, Melchior Borchgrevinck, two choir-boys, Mogens Pedersøn and Hans Nielsen, and two other singers. They arrived in 1599 and remained in Venice at their royal master's expense for a year. They were succeeded by another group including Hans Brachrogge, and Nielsen who stayed two more years; finally Pedersøn came back in December 1605, to remain until 1609. By this time, two German musicians had arrived, Johannes Grabbe from Westphalia and Heinrich Schütz from the Saxon court. The former came in 1607 and stayed until 1610, the latter from 1609 until shortly after Gabrieli's death in 1612. Another German, Christoph Clemsee, was probably in Venice in the last years of Gabrieli's life. These were all composers (though Clemsee is known only by a single madrigal book). There were

[4] H. Federhofer, 'Alessandro Tadei, a pupil of Giovanni Gabrieli', *Musica Disciplina*, VI, p. 115, from which article the rest of the information concerning Tadei is taken.

certainly a number of other musicians who studied the organ with Gabrieli and subsequently became instrumentalists.

Music by Gabrieli's pupils

Though the instrumentalists left no record of their teaching or repertoire, the composers left a small but extremely interesting collection of their music, the more valuable since it was published in the years during which we have little other evidence of Gabrieli's stylistic development. Most of them published a collection of Italian madrigals, perhaps as a sort of graduation exercise. Madrigals by Borchgrevinck and Nielsen were published in 1606–8, and pieces appeared in most of the intermediate years until Schütz's famous madrigals of 1611 (Clemsee's were issued in 1613, but since the only surviving copy is incomplete, it is difficult to consider them in this context). Moreover, with the exception of Borchgrevinck, whose early biography remains obscure but who was clearly a man of some experience when he arrived in Venice, these musicians were all young men on whom Gabrieli must have had considerable influence; they all acknowledge their debt to him in their prefaces. One may therefore assume that their madrigals reflect the sort of music to which he directed their attention; and this in turn may tell us something about his own development.

Models for the pupils' madrigals c. 1605

Borchgrevinck's contribution is especially significant because not only did he compose, he compiled a couple of anthologies of Italian works for his royal patron. These anthologies, both called *Giardino novo bellissimo di varii fiori musicali sceltissimi*, are not at all old-fashioned for 1605 and 1606, when they were published. Monteverdi is included, as are de Wert and Salomone Rossi; and indeed most of the compositions come from madrigal books published within the previous few years. The five madrigals by Leone Leoni and Simone Molinaro (famous as the editor of Gesualdo's madrigals) come from the last five years of the sixteenth century; those by Santini and Fattorini were even newer. But the music in the first book is on the whole no more advanced than Gabrieli's own at the turn of the century. There is little of the fashionable *fin-de-siècle* gloom; of the five settings of Guarini, only one, Monteverdi's 'Ah dolente partita', really reflects the avant-garde. The other two madrigals from Monteverdi's epoch-making *Quarto libro* are lighter pieces. 'Non più guerra' is for the most part cheerful and at its most serious scarcely more advanced than some of the madrigals he had published as early as 1592; while 'Quel augellin che canta' is a virtuoso piece in the Ferrara style, with the usual prominent parts for the ladies' voices. And this clearly is the aspect of Italian music which affected Borchgrevinck most strongly, for his own contribution to the volume, 'Amatemi ben mio'. similarly stresses the trio of upper voices and delights in the new sonorities. Yet when Tasso's verse does suggest a 'modern' idiom, the composer refuses the hint:

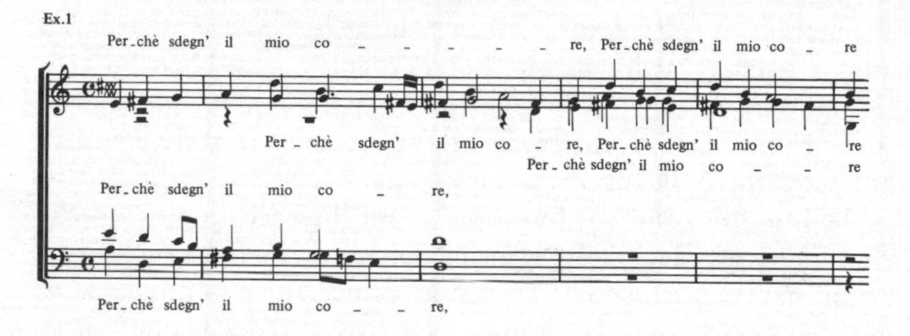

This is just what we would expect from a pupil of Giovanni Gabrieli—the same bright musical colours, the same refusal to take poetic imagery too seriously. Borchgrevinck's style is essentially an offshoot of that of 'Queste felice herbette' or 'Se cantano gli augelli', those madrigals in which Gabrieli has mastered the manner of the 1580s.

Borchgrevinck's second anthology came out during 1606, and significantly it was probably during the intervening months that Monteverdi's celebrated *Quinto libro*, with its promise of a reply to the attacks of Artusi, appeared. Borchgrevinck included the most famous of these madrigals in his volume, 'Cruda Amarilli', which had not only achieved notoriety in the pamphlets but also comes first in Monteverdi's book, almost as a challenge by the avant-garde to traditional ways. It appears, however, as the eighth number in Borchgrevinck's anthology, and on the whole the contents do not seem very different from those of the previous year. Nicolò Gistou apparently provides a parody of Monteverdi's older style in his setting of 'Quel augellin che canta' (see Example 2).

Borchgrevinck's own contribution shows a greater concern for the 'modern' ways, with a passage full of sustained dissonances for the words 'O dolcezza d'amor rara e infinita', but in fact for the most part he still writes in the Gabrielian idiom, and cannot by any stretch of imagination be said to be revolutionary. Even so, there is a change in emphasis in the choice of Italian music. There are a couple of composers from Northern

Italy who must have known the work of Gesualdo; Pietro Maria Marsolo actually followed him to Ferrara. Monteverdi's Mantuan colleague Benedetto Pallavicino, is represented by some mature madrigals, including two from his *Sesto libro* in which the new style is explored. Again the lesser men show the tone of the volume. The Venetian, Francesco Sponga, is perhaps the most conservative, and his 'O se torni il mio sole' is not very different from Gabrieli's settings of similarly light verse. Nevertheless, his opening phrase, given to a single voice and not developed very much contrapuntally thereafter, reminds us of the recitative melody of the newcomers:

Another contributor, Giovanni Paolo Nodari, belonged to the Mantuan circle, working for Andrea Gonzaga at Sabbionetta, and publishing some of the earliest, if rather simple, imitations of the Viadana *Concerti* in 1605. Borchgrevinck includes his setting of Guarini's 'Parlo misero taccio', the opening of which shows a distinct awareness of the new means of expression. The chromaticism, the homophony, and the sense of colour-change evinced by the octave leaps in the upper part are the work of the younger generation (see Example 4).

Still more striking is one of the madrigals by Leoni, who also apparently had Mantuan connections. The opening of 'Dolci baci e soavi' is conventional enough, and the use of triple time for 'baci, segni d'Amor' might be

Ex.4

the work of Marenzio. The passage which follows is very different, for although it is not at all dissonant, the written out ornament is very much of the kind used by Monteverdi in 'Cruda Amarilli':

Ex.5

Another Monteverdian trademark is the descent of the sixth in the melody of the closing section, one of those extravagances affected by the expressive school brought up in the knowledge of the skill of contemporary singers.

Both of Borchgrevinck's collections were published in Denmark; but it is interesting that almost all the music taken from printed sources came from Venetian printing houses. The omissions are significant: there was no music by Gesualdo, first printed by Baldini in Ferrara. Nor is there any truly revolutionary music: Caccini's *Nuove Musiche* had been printed by Marascotti in Florence (it was eventually reprinted in Venice, but only in 1607), as was *L'Euridice*. Thus we may assume that it was only after the years around 1605 that the Serenissima really had much opportunity to discover the effects of the musical revolution.

Later models for the pupils' madrigals

Pedersøn's anthologies show a gradual approach to the new style, and this impression is confirmed by Nielsen's madrigals, published by Gardano in 1606. It was in all probability the composer's first publication[5] and in the

[5] See *Dania Sonans*, II (Copenhagen, 1966). This volume and the succeeding one in the series (Copenhagen, 1967) contain virtually the complete corpus of madrigals by Danish composers.

dedication to his patron, King Christian IV, he proudly mentions '. . . that time, when by your command I was in Venice under the discipline of the most excellent Signor Giovanni Gabrielli, organist to the Most Serene Republic, a man of such worth that everyone knows it, [a time] which was not spent in vain'. In 1606 Nielsen was in fact in Wolfenbüttel, although this dedication is dated from Venice. The contents may be the work of a number of years, for Nielsen had been in Venice since 1599, when he was still a choirboy. Nevertheless they do show an awareness of the novelties of the first years of the century and in any case they are of extreme interest, as work done under the immediate influence of Gabrieli.

Nielsen chooses some verses by Guarini, but even the unidentified majority have traits to which the up-to-date madrigal composer attached great emphasis—a high level of intensity, 'affective' words, and that use of oxymoron which Gesualdo much favoured. 'T'amo mia vita' had already been set by Monteverdi, 'Ch'io non t'ami' by Benedetto Pallavicino; several others are, in effect, paraphrases of verses set by the avant-garde, notably 'Ite, amari sospiri' and 'Corre al suo fin', while Guarini's 'Fuggi, fuggi, O mio core' not only received later a fine setting by Schütz, but was put to music by so advanced a composer as Domenico Mazzocchi as late as the 1630s.[6]

There is some sense of modernity in Nielsen's music also. The tricks of style are largely those of the Italians of Borchgrevinck's second anthology, such as the descending sixth in the final section of 'Fuggi, fuggi, O mio core', which is very reminiscent of the madrigal by Leoni mentioned above:

In the same way the use of written-out decoration in 'Quasi nobil pitrice' is provoked by the words 'd'ogn'ornamento hor scosso'. Above all there is that compression of melodic material which is so characteristic of the avant-garde, who were less interested in contrapuntal development than in conveying the smallest detail of meaning. From this point of view, 'Ite, amari sospiri' might have been written by Gesualdo. Its spare, lean phrases

[6] Included in D. Mazzocchi, *Sechs Madrigale zu 5 Stimmen, Das Chorwerk* 95 (Wolfenbüttel, 1965).

set the words in a minimum of time, rarely repeating them in any single voice, and for the most part allowing no expansion by the ordinary procedures of counterpoint. But only from this point of view does the work seem 'modern'; and Gesualdo's settings of similar texts use an entirely different musical language. The materials of Nielsen's madrigals are conventional enough. There is no chromaticism, and the setting of its climax, 'A la durezza vostra, al suo languire', has none of the harmonic asperity Monteverdi would have given it:

Such purity is more old-fashioned than Gabrieli's in even his earliest madrigals, and certainly seems curious in the year 1606. In general, though, it is clear that much of Gabrieli's own madrigalian style had influenced Nielsen. The most obvious common feature is the relatively square rhythmic structure. The increasing concern for natural Italian declamation from the 1580s onwards never affected Gabrieli very much, and many of his secular works appear almost like French chansons in the regularity of their rhythms ('Chiara angioletta' is fairly typical in this respect). This is exactly what we find in Nielsen's work. 'T'amo mia vita' not only begins with the famous canzona motif, but is written throughout in the stilted, measured rhythms of the genre, and ends with a refrain, like Gabrieli's 'Lieto godea'. The love of false relationships in Gabrieli's music, too, is found in Nielsen:

A comparison of Nielsen's setting of 'Ch'io non t'ami' with that of the up-to-date but (in this work at least) by no means revolutionary Pallavicino reveals his backward-looking attitude. The Italian's madrigal is very much in the Ferrara style, with prominent parts for the three upper voices, and Nielsen may perhaps have known it, since there are similarities of phrase, and one or two moments of the same kind of trio texture. Neither setting is particularly dissonant, although Pallavicino contrives by sustained passing notes to produce a more intense, sophisticated atmosphere than does Nielsen. But the essential difference between them lies in the fact that Pallavicino gains his effects within the modern homophonic, declamatory style while Nielsen is full of suggestions of polyphony. The way they put to music the line 'Fonte d'ogni mio ben' shows the wide gap between a Mantuan writing for the court virtuosi with an audience which needs to hear the words distinctly, and a pupil of a Venetian, more interested in musical device:

There is thus little sign in Nielsen's music that Gabrieli had taught him much about the new idiom.

The increasing modernity of the pupils' music c. 1608

It is another story with the next book of madrigals by a Gabrielian pupil to be issued. Mogens Pedersøn's first published volume of his own music, which came out in 1608, reminds us that while Nielsen had remained largely North of the Alps since his return home, his colleague had returned to his teacher. Admittedly the verse chosen by Pedersøn is very little different from that set by Nielsen; some of it goes back rather more to the pastoral idiom of the 1580s. 'Ecco la primavera', 'Tra queste verdi fronde', and 'Dimmi caro ben mio' are indeed very like the poems in Wert's later and Monteverdi's early madrigal books. But there is enough fashionable sophistication to show the composer's awareness of the latest trends. The popular 'T'amo mia vita' is here once more and a version of 'Donna, mentre i'vi miro', by Guarini which Monteverdi had already set in his fourth book in the altered form 'Cor mio mentre vi miro'. The favoured oxymoron is the whole basis of 'Morirò, cor mio' and 'Care lagrime mie'.

At first sight the musical style also shows conservative features. 'Se nel partir' is a Venetian piece which, with its interplay between pairs of voices, and its short, singable, diatonic motifs could have been written by any pupil of Andrea Gabrieli. 'Non voglio più servire' has a less clear stylistic basis but is certainly a polyphonic piece mostly in the conventional manner of the late sixteenth century. 'Tra queste verdi fronde' not only sets the Tasso-like verse favoured by Wert; it also adopts his musical style, and the whole madrigal is most reminiscent of 'Vezzosi augelli' from his *Ottavo Libro de Madrigali à cinque voci*, originally published in 1586, or 'Ecco mormorar l'onde' from Monteverdi's second book. Even madrigals which, as we shall see, contain novel ideas, or a new way of working out the clichés of the time, have extended passages which could well come from an early madrigal by Gabrieli or some madrigalist of the 1580s. 'S'io rido e scherzo' is built up from contrapuntal motifs, and 'Se del mio lagrimare', in spite of a diminished fourth in the melody of its opening phrase, in fact has little that could have shocked even Zarlino.

Nevertheless, the volume belongs to the new century, and the analogies with Wert and Monteverdi suggest what music Pedersøn may have studied with Gabrieli. Admittedly there is none of the real harmonic violence for which Artusi had criticized Monteverdi, though there are one or two aggressive clashes, mainly towards cadences, and some unorthodox resolutions of dissonances:

When, in 'Non voglio puì servire' (bar 44) one voice sings a C natural while another holds a D which is about to come to rest on C sharp, this reminds us that Pedersøn may have known the English composers such as Gibbons and Byrd for whom this was a normal usage. In 'O che soave baccio', the phrase 'Fatti pur ladro' is expressed by a shift from F to F sharp and C to C sharp, culminating in some unusual melodic turns at the end of the phrase. There are similarly mild harmonic changes in 'T'amo mia vita'; yet if we think of what some of the composers of the 1570s had done, not to speak of the works in Gesualdo's third and fourth books which had been reprinted in Venice in 1603 and 1604, it is obvious that Gabrieli, while looking forward, had still not directed his pupils to real extremists.

Surprisingly, Monteverdi seems to have been considered a safe model. There are many signs that Pedersøn had looked at a number of works from the now well-known fourth and fifth books. 'Son vivo e non son vivo', for example, is a study in trio textures such as we find in Monteverdi's 'Cor mio mentre vi miro' and 'Era l'anima mia'. 'Morirò, cor mio' opens with Monteverdi's motif for 'Non più guerra'; 'S'io rido et scherzo' takes up an idea similar to one used for the 'smile' in 'A un giro sol' and, more particularly, 'Io mi son giovinetta'. 'Cor mio mentre vi miro' is never far from mind in Pedersøn's setting of the same words; 'sospir' is set almost identically. Pedersøn does not achieve the superb climax at the words 'O bellezza vitale' which crowns Monteverdi's madrigal, but his own work is fine enough to show that he has understood fully the principles of the style. One particular device is apparent in his own music. In 'Cruda Amarilli' Monteverdi used, not only harsh dissonance, but also written-out ornamentation to make the words more expressive. Artusi had indeed attacked these 'irregularities'; Monteverdi's defence was that these had long been in oral, if not printed, use. In Venice such ornamentation had become a traditional usage, and Pedersøn had discovered its value for his madrigals. There is a simple *gruppo* on the word 'guai' in 'Morirò cor mio', and a more ambitious *passaggio* in the closing bars of 'Nell'apparir dell'amorosa Aurora'. The dotted rhythms in 'Come esser può' are more adventurous, and the application of a simple figure makes one bar of 'Dimmi caro ben mio' in total opposition to Artusi's ideas:

Ex.11

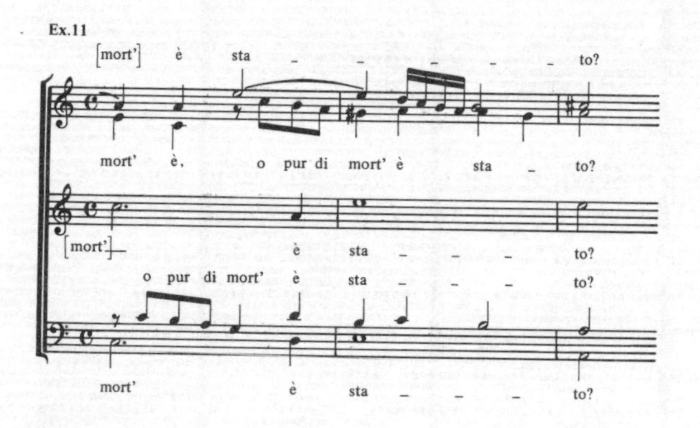

'Madonn', Amor ed io' one of the final linked pair of madrigals, is practically a textbook in itself of the modern techniques. Almost every line has a word in it which had some distinct musical association: Love and the Lover sing together (cantiam' insieme); an attempt at flight provokes a sigh (sospiro); Venus, after a pause, makes a counterpoint over the canto fermo of the tenor: and so it goes on. And inevitably almost every up-to-date musical device is used. The Monteverdian downward leap of a sixth expresses the 'dolce cantar'; 'giro' obtains a decorative turn in the *quinto*; 'sospiro' is preceded by the inevitable rest, and 'pausa' is followed by one; 'fugghette' suggests a short imitative section. More interesting still is the passage where four voices hold the long notes of the canto fermo, while the tenor 'extemporizes' using a *gruppo* often used by Gabrieli:

Ex.12

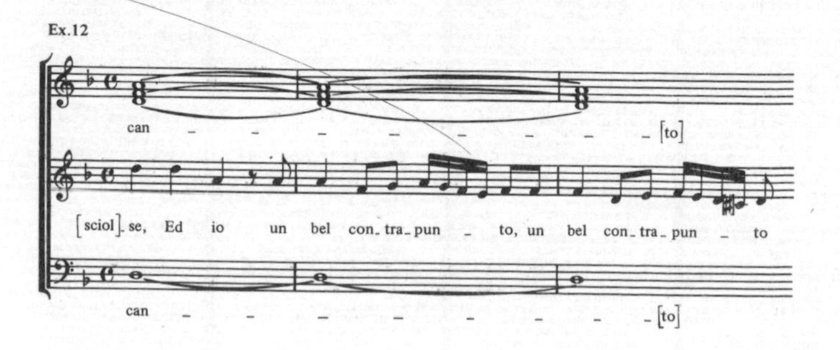

The word 'passaggi' is naturally set by a flurry of ornamental figures and 'legature' by some unusual suspended dissonance. There are chromatic changes for the 'dolce l'armonia' and a broken line for 'Ma stanca fermò il canto' (But wearily she ceased to sing). Though it exemplifies all the latest musical resources its emotional attitude makes it obvious that this is music by a pupil of Gabrieli. It has that detached, witty quality which is typically Venetian, and the whole layout of the madrigal never departs from the contrapuntal style as the Venetians interpreted it. The *gorgie*, for example, are not those delicate and irregular ornaments which make Caccini's madrigals and arias for solo voice so expressive, but those which Bassano and the other sixteenth-century theorists applied to ensemble music, requiring a more precise rhythm and clear-cut harmony. Such chromaticisms as are used are temporary, and do not destroy the overall tonal scheme. The new style is throughout the volume only superficially observed: some minor notational novelties, of which the use of the tie, to provide some rhythms otherwise impossible, is the most common; a feeling of more rapid mood change which comes from the close following of the verbal image; a cautious use of some harsher dissonance—that is virtually all.

The German pupils and the trend towards the avant-garde style

The revolution really reaches Venice in the madrigals of the two Germans who came to study with Gabrieli around 1608. Johann Grabbe was the first to publish the result of his studies in a madrigal book published by Gardano in 1609[7] and he seems to begin at the point where Pedersøn had stopped. The advanced poets are his commonplace, though his 'Lasso perchè mi fuggi' uses the same verse by Guarini which Monteverdi and Pallavicino had set as 'Crudel, perchè mi fuggi' twenty years earlier. But it is the musical treatment the verse receives which shows the next stage of development. Grabbe obviously knew Monteverdi's setting; his concluding phrase uses the same contrapuntal motif as in Monteverdi's. But the latest declamatory madrigals interest him more. His rhythms spring from the natural pronunciation of Italian, and he knows how to stress important words with a homophonic coming together at the cadence. This, as well as such vivid musical symbolism as the cries of 'ohimè' in 'Cor mio deh mio languire' show an intimate knowledge of Monteverdi's

[7] See *Nordische Schüler Giovanni Gabrielis: Neun Madrigale zu 5 Stimmen, Das Chorwerk* 35 (Wolfenbüttel, 1935), and *Denkmäler Norddeutscher Musik II,* ed. H. W. Schwab (Kassel, 1971).

fourth and fifth books. So does the opening of 'Alma afflitta', a single voice declaiming the words to the downward sixth leaps, in the manner of 'O Mirtillo' (and indeed the 'Lamento d'Arianna').[8] Ornaments are now used with complete freedom, dominating whole phrases as they come several times on a vital word. There are more dissonances, often the result of pedal notes in the manner of Monteverdi's 'Era l'anima mia'. Above all, the short phrases allow the music to follow the words in exact detail, producing the nervous, discontinuous atmosphere typical of the modern madrigal.

But the revolution is not yet complete; Gabrieli's style is simply taken to its farthest limits. The ornaments, for example, are still closely akin to Bassano's. They are often applied contrapuntally, as at the opening of 'Lasso perchè mi fuggi', to produce a phrase which the real moderns would have found much too regular in development, too 'musical' and lacking in the immediacy at which they were aiming:

The harmony, despite its dissonance, is still tonally organized, built from motifs which imply the dominant-tonic relationships which give Venetian music its characteristic clarity. This mixture of close attention to the expression of the individual word and the desire to develop these purely

[8] The 'Lamento d'Arianna' was not yet in print, but may well have been known by this time.

musical elements gives a curious mingling of old and new, which infects the harmonic rhythm itself. The *misura comune* means that the basic unit of movement should be, as in virtually all madrigals around 1600, the crotchet; in the melody it usually is, with the expressive ornaments and declamatory motifs creating the impression of a fast tempo. But the fact that these motifs are developed contrapuntally in the older manner suggests that, on the contrary, Grabbe is thinking essentially in the *misura di breve*, with a rate of harmonic change measured in minims and even semibreves.

The pupils of Gabrieli's final years

This metrical ambiguity comes to its height in the two books of madrigals by Gabrieli's pupils published in 1611. The pieces in Pedersøn's second volume, only recently discovered in a British Library manuscript,[9] indeed use the *misura di breve* for their time signatures, as do certain madrigals by Schütz. But in the works of both we can see that the conventional madrigal *senza basso continuo* is very nearly at an end of its useful life. Much of the quasi-polyphony inherited from the last years of the sixteenth century has now become no more than a set of clichés, while the actual novelties in the idiom fit much better into music with keyboard accompaniment. Perhaps the best integrated pieces in style (though not necessarily the most interesting) are indeed those that frankly look backwards; and, as might be expected, there are several such numbers in Pedersøn's volume, such as 'Non garir Augellino', a light-hearted piece in Wert's tradition, and its *seconda parte* 'Importun Augellino', which ends with the chanson-like rhythms of 'Lieto godea'. 'Tu fuggi' and 'Lasso io prima morire', for all that they set highly emotional, modern verse, do not go beyond the style of Monteverdi's middle-period madrigals, with occasional asperities in harmony and an even more occasional use of *gorgia*.

Elsewhere there are signs that the genre is now borrowing material from the *concertante* madrigal. 'Udite, amanti' has a cantus which often seems quite independent of the lower voices, these passages being extremely effective, with chromatic progressions, dissonance, and an expressive vocal line. The only difficulty is to reconcile such vivid, terse music with the working out of contrapuntal figures which require extended development and thus tend to distract the listener from the essential emotionalism of the verse. 'Son morta' suffers from the same contradictions. The opening section is

[9] Mss. Egerton 3665. This manuscript is fully described in B. Schofield and T. Dart, 'Tregian's Anthology', *Music and Letters* (1951), p. 205.

a slow-moving passage developed at length in a thoroughly competent old-fashioned way. The difficulties arise with the next phrase, 'con un sospir' d'Amore', which uses not only a rest for the 'sigh' but an ornamental figure for the word 'Amore'. Again this is highly expressive, but Pedersøn can hardly reconcile its power with the necessity to provide extensive music for the succeeding phrase. In spite of some chromaticism and some well written counterpoint, there is too great a disparity between the two manners for the madrigal to be unified.

The most successful madrigals in Pedersøn's volume are those where he constantly uses material which can be developed at length, such as his setting of 'Lasso perchè mi fuggi', which is less extreme than Grabbe's madrigal on the same verse and better balanced. Dissonance and chromaticism are used extensively, and there are unconventional melodic turns of phrase. Nevertheless, there is ample room for the development of all this material and the sudden juxtaposition of opposing moods and ideas seems quite natural. If, for example, the first phrase, the slow-moving setting of the single word 'lasso', had been left to contrast with the closely imitative counterpoint for the words, 'perchè mi fuggi', without any repetition of the idea, the whole would merely appear bizarre; by repeating 'lasso' as part of an extended section, and amplifying the counterpoint of 'perchè mi fuggi' by using five voices instead of three, he knits together the opening section as tightly as any conventional polyphonic madrigal of the sixteenth century. The chromatic alteration for 'senza dolore' occurs first in a short, terse version, which is then expanded into a larger paragraph:

There are no ornaments in this piece, and the basic metre is clear throughout. Perhaps Pedersøn founded his style on his first visit to Venice, before

Gabrieli was fully aware of the revolution, and found it difficult to adapt to the newer tastes—indeed if he had been inclined to the up-to-date idiom, he would surely have turned to music with *basso continuo* as had the Italians of his generation.

Schütz as a Gabrieli pupil

Much more surprising is young Schütz's composition in the dying genre. He was in his early twenties when he arrived in Venice and it is some measure of the powerful influence of 'il famosissimo Gabrieli',[10] that he followed his master's other pupils in practising the style. Throughout his life he quickly absorbed new ideas, and on his second visit to Venice he proved very receptive for a man in his forties. But these madrigals are far from conventional for the period around 1610, and certainly not in the older style of Gabrieli. It is difficult to deduce exactly what models Gabrieli gave to Schütz. Monteverdi may have been one, for the setting of 'Ride la primavera' is reminiscent of some of his lighter madrigals. Some of the ornamentation in 'O primavera' recalls that in the madrigals of Marco da Gagliano's fifth book, and there are points of similarity between the two men's settings of 'Di marmo siete voi'. The Venetian influence may be detected in 'Vasto mar', which is a homage madrigal for double choir, thus continuing the polychoral tradition so often found in the madrigal books of the state composers of the Serenissima. Beyond this, Schütz's music seems highly original in its general effect. Looked at closely, however, the music is full of clichés. Schütz had learned the language of madrigalian symbols very thoroughly, and there is little that is actually new in the detail of his music. The word 'sospiro' will produce rests; 'ridendo', melisma; 'duro', dissonance; 'fuggi', closely woven imitative counterpoint; 'giro', a motif which revolves around a single note. Dissonance is not much more intense than in the works of Pedersøn, even in such a passage as the following from 'Quella damma son io', where the most violent discords are short in duration (see Example 15).

Sevenths are now not in the least unusual, and the diminished fifth is taken without preparation; but again these involve not so much new chords as a new method of applying dissonant intervals. Any dissonance which was previously only allowed if it was treated as a suspension or a passing note, can apparently now be used at any time. It need not resolve conventionally and it may be as long or short as the composer wishes. But

10 As Schütz called him in the dedication of his book of madrigals to his patron the Landgrave of Hesse.

Ex.15

this is not very different from the methods of Monteverdi and goes little further than the suggestion of Galilei in his 1589 treatise.[11] Schütz's use of ornaments is also, in itself, not particularly advanced. Following the practice of the older madrigalists he confines himself to *gorgia* which will not disrupt the metric structure of the work, and usually repeats a rhythmic pattern several times, as in the following examples from 'O primavera' and 'Vasto mar':

Ex.16

[11] See C. Palisca, 'V. Galilei's Counterpoint Treatise: a Code for the Seconda Prattica', *Journal of the American Musicological Society*, *lx* (1956), p. 81.

Again these ornaments are so short that they are hardly noticeable in performance; and that Schütz did not mean them to seem dissonant is clear from the words to which he puts the ornaments: 'venti' and 'canto' in 'Vasto mar', 'il cor' in 'Ride la primavera', 'divino' in 'Mi saluta costei'. These are words which need emphasis but are not in themselves highly emotional.

Thus the individual traits of Schütz's madrigals are not particularly original, but nevertheless the whole is so unexpected as to seem revolutionary. In part, this is because of the scale on which the composer works. Using the same sort of material as Gesualdo and Monteverdi, Schütz often expands it to twice their usual length. Thus an idiom developed for the purposes of a compact, intense form is now used for one in which shape and long-range emotional planning are necessary. The results are naturally not always satisfactory and there are longueurs in Schütz's madrigals simply because a *coup de theâtre* loses its point on repetition. But in the best of them, the very prolongation of the intensity produces a music with a neurotic atmosphere of its own, of great power and expressiveness. The other characteristic of Schütz's madrigals lies in the consistency of the thematic working out in a contrapuntal texture, in the refusal to depart from the older traditions of the sixteenth century. It is rare for a theme not to be fully developed throughout the complete five-part texture, something which the Italian avant-garde rarely did. There is learned use of contrapuntal motifs in inverted or invertible counterpoint, ingenious combinations of two themes simultaneously, and so on. This may be predictable for the young composer, desirous of displaying his skill; and it is certainly not unexpected from the pupil of the old organist, brought up on Andrea's solid polyphonic teaching.

The pupils' music as evidence of Gabrieli's own changes of style

Schütz's madrigals have a flavour which is quite different from the music of any Italian composer. The one exception is Giovanni Gabrieli himself. Since he had long given up writing secular music, we have to look in his motets, which is why the relationship between his pupils' works and his own late music has been overlooked by the historians. Nevertheless a man who can show his pupils a way to a style more advanced than his own (and this is the sign of a good teacher) is unlikely to have closed his mind when he comes to write his own music, and an awareness of his links with the younger generation helps to explain a number of his late works which otherwise seem to be completely outside his natural development. The evidence that his pupils' music provides shows that he was not a revolutionary. Indeed, the future of German music might have been very different if Schütz had studied with a true modern such as Caccini or Monteverdi. But it does show that Gabrieli was a progressive who knew much of the music being issued by the Venetian publishers in the vital first decade of the seventeenth century. This is part of the explanation of the great works of his final years. It would have been easy for him to have repeated himself in that highly satisfactory idiom developed in the years before his fortieth birthday. Because he was receptive, his style was enriched and his last music is his greatest.

CHAPTER TEN

The Later Instrumental Music

THE great retrospective collections (the *Musica Nova* of Willaert, the *Concerti* of Andrea Gabrieli, the *Sacrae Symphoniae* of Giovanni, and later, Monteverdi's *Selva Morale*) so favoured by Venetian composers and publishers might appear to have had little general musical influence. They were rarely reprinted, while a favourite book of madrigals or motets would often appear in a new edition almost annually. But in fact much pirating went on. The Antwerp publisher Phalèse included many of Willaert's motets in his own collection a couple of years later. Friedrich Lindner and his publisher Catherine Gerlach in Nuremberg published some of Andrea's *Concerti* of 1587 in the following year. Kauffmann borrowed some motets and canzonas from the 1597 *Sacrae Symphoniae* within a matter of months. These pieces thus achieved wider diffusion in the more practicable form of anthologies.

These volumes also gave an impetus to other composers. As we have seen,[1] the *Concerti* sparked off the vogue for double-choir music which arrived in the 1590s; and the *Sacrae Symphoniae* led to the popularity of large-scale instrumental music in the early part of the seventeenth century. The *Concerti* perhaps changed the face of church music; its publication led to the development of the Mass and motet written for instruments and voices, and the concertante motet with general bass. The church music in the *Sacrae Symphoniae* had less effect. The emotional richness which is Giovanni's real contribution to festal music was less easily imitated than Andrea's brilliance. The instrumental music was similarly difficult to follow, being written with a special ensemble in mind when comparatively few similar ensembles were in existence. Even so significantly more instrumental canzonas and sonatas were composed in the *spezzato* manner in the decade following 1597, and many of these show Gabrieli's influence.

1 See Chapter Three above.

Raverii's anthology (1608)

These works first appeared appended to collections of music for smaller groups. Of the *Canzoni da Suonare* (1600) of Francesco Rovigo and Ruggier Trofeo, all but two pieces are for four instruments, each composer contributing one for eight. Similarly, the Brescian Don Floriano Canale's *Canzoni da Sonare a Quattro*, published in the same year, contains, as well as seventeen four-part pieces, two on a larger scale, one of them 'La Bevilacqua' in honour of its dedicatee, a famous Veronese patron of music. In 1607 Giulio Radino, son of the organist of a church in Padua, included four canzonas 'a otto' in a collection called *Concerti per Sonare e Cantare* (the volume includes a Mass on Andrea's pattern, though like Giovanni's collection, most of the contents are motets). In the following year a recently established but prolific Venetian publisher, Alessandro Raverii, assembled a vast anthology called *Canzoni Per Sonare Con Ogni Sorte Di Stromenti, A Quattro, Cinque & Otto, Con il suo Basso generale per l'Organo, Novamente raccolte da diversi Eccellentissimi Musici & dato in luce, Libro Primo.*[2] There was in fact no second volume, and Raverii disappears from the publishing scene in the following year, so perhaps his project was unsuccessful. The volume contains thirty-six canzonas, twelve for large forces, including one piece *à 16 voci*. It was the most ambitious publication of instrumental works until Gabrieli's posthumous *Canzoni e Sonate* seven years later. But also in 1608 a Milanese, Agostino Soderino, included some similar instrumental music in his Opus 2, and the organist of S. Maria delle Gratie in Brescia, Cesare Gussago, made up almost half a substantial volume with 'Concerti a Otto', six of which are canzonas after the Gabrielian models. A couple of years after this Viadana dedicated to Archduke Ferdinand of Austria a book of *Sinfonie Musicali A Otto Voci commode per concertare con ogni sorte di stromenti* and Monteverdi's massive 'Sonata sopra Sancta Maria' (on, unusually, a plainsong tune) appeared in his Marian Vespers in the same year. Though minor compared with other forms such as motets and songbooks, this steady trickle of instrumental music was significant. Gussago dedicated his book of sonatas to two 'most excellent virtuosi', one a cornett player, the other a very distinguished violinist, confident that his works would, as he declared, have 'the strongest of champions'. This indicates the availability of musicians competent to play this kind of music. The Venetian ensemble was increasingly imitated elsewhere as was its music. Indeed, practically all the composers

[2] For a full discussion of this collection see L. E. Bartholomew, *Alessandro Raverij's Collection of Canzoni per sonare* (Michigan, 1963).

involved in the new movement were connected in some way with the Venetian organists. Several contributors to Raverii's anthology had been pupils or associates of Merulo: Frescobaldi, Luzzaschi, Giuseppe Guami. Another, Giambattista Grillo, later became organist at St. Mark's. The Milanese composers seem to have no such connection, but among several Bolognesi Banchieri had written a Magnificat on 'Lieto godea' in 1596 and continued using Venetian techniques all his life.

All these composers came from northern Italy, where the grand manner in instrumental music flourished, and the source of their inspiration is clear in their music. The two canzonas of Canale, for example, show unmistakable Venetian characteristics. 'La Bevilacqua'[3] has the same bright sonorities for its two choirs that Gabrieli had used in 'Chiar'Angioletta', the same cheerful melodiousness which had given that piece its sub-title 'aria da sonar'. Harmonic details confirm Gabrieli's influence, although the dialogue is less imaginative. 'La Canobbia'[4] from the same collection is more interesting. Its rondo technique, using a triple-time alleluja-type section as its refrain, is reminiscent of 'Regina caeli' or the ten-part 'Hodie Christus natus est' of the *Sacrae Symphoniae*. Similarly Bonelli's 'Toccata La Cleopatra'[5] is another canzona after the 'Lieto godea' pattern, with a prolonged triple-time middle section with sequences making for attractive melody, and a short recapitulation with the 'choirs' reversed. Gussago[6] is more accomplished, and seizes on more interesting features, such as the rich counterpoint in the sonatas of the *Sacrae Symphoniae*, which he imitates in the 'Sonata 17' of his collection, even using repeatedly the cadential cliché in which a suspended dissonance has a scale figure passing through it:

[3] S. Kunze, *Die Instrumentalmusik Giovanni Gabrielis*, II (Tutzing, 1963), p. 75.
[4] ibid, p. 80.
[5] ibid, p. 84.
[6] ibid, p. 96.

Gabrieli's contributions to Raverii's anthology

The six works of Gabrieli included in Raverii's anthology show the same mixture of conservatism and progress. The four 'canzone à quattro' were not new; 'La Spiritata' had appeared in an organ version in 1593,[7] and the others are in a similar style. The two larger pieces for eight voices are no more revolutionary, but it is clear that they are later, maturer works. In Raverii's volume, they both significantly have titles which spell their principal themes in solmization syllables. The double-choir 'Canzon sol sol la sol fa mi' is the simpler of the two, short and apparently without contrapuntal learnedness. Two cornetts (probably) play a cheerful tune in canon, without accompaniment of any kind. The full ensemble now joins in with gay rhythms and major harmonies, and the triple-measured instrumental 'alleluja' maintains this mood, though there is the occasional minor chord to enhance the return to the duple metre which arrives with a string of tierces de picardie. Here the original tune returns, its canon this time in four parts, the two cantus lines and two basses of the 'choirs', while the altus and tenor parts play an inversion of the theme and the quaver figure of the theme provides a bass to the descending motif of its first bar. The triple-time alleluja is now repeated, and again the main theme arrives to clinch the major. More canonic writing leads to a straightforward harmonization of the theme and the coda broadens out the music, though its rhythms are still derived from those of the first tutti. It is as taut a work as Gabrieli ever wrote—and yet it is one of the most approachable, not grand but gay, not stately but happy.

The other canzona 'a otto' is more sophisticated, with a less memorable theme and a less readily perceptible structure. Its title, 'Fa sol la re', refers not to the opening notes of the cantus, but to a bass figure which arrives in the third bar. This is a sign of the times; the repeated bass had become fashionable with the invention of the figured keyboard part. By the year when Raverii's anthology was published, strophic variations were in common use; Monteverdi had used this extensively in *L'Orfeo*.

Ex. 2

[7] See Chapter Six above.

The way Gabrieli uses it here, however, is ahead of the fashion, for the idea of a short ostinato-like figure only became popular in the following decade (the earlier composers tended to think in larger patterns).

Monteverdi used an almost identical figure in 'Chiome d'oro: (Ex. 2), but Gabrieli's organization is less predictable than Monteverdi's and this adds to the interest of the piece. Surprisingly the canzona motif, always found in duple time in the sixteenth century, here appears as triples until the final section, when the inclusion of some bars of common time act as a kind of written-out ritardando. The work uses the 'fa sol la re' theme as a point of punctuation, above which Gabrieli modulates from tonality to tonality with startling subtlety and originality. The change of time at the coda also has a powerful effect. It first occurs about 20 bars before the end, where fa sol la re appears in an augmented form in the bass. Triple measure is then resumed, coming again to the same 'improvised' broadening out—but this time, at the end of the fa sol la re bass, the improvisation continues, transposing the motif again and adding a dignified and final plagal cadence. The piece is notable for its mastery of form, its tunefulness, the regularity of its rhythms, and the variations of texture. The motifs are conceived in duet form, often in thirds, occasionally with a hint of cross-rhythm or hemiola so that one acts with a gentle abrasion against the other. The result is that for the clarity which distinguishes the texture of Gabrieli's earlier instrumental music we have substituted a kaleidoscope, the segments coming together in a host of different ways. It is on too large a scale to be called intimate, but the post-Lepanto splendour has substantially diminished, and a new style has emerged. This canzona is characteristic of Gabrieli in its mixture of gaiety and wistfulness, and it is not hard to understand why his pupil Father Thaddeo reprinted it in the 1615 collection of *Canzoni e Sonate*.

The influence of the basso continuo on instrumental music

In the absence of evidence for a more personal explanation we may ascribe the new manner of this final corpus of his ensemble music to his discovery of novel technical devices which encouraged a new mode of thinking. In the canzona on 'Fa sol la re' there is nothing that a sixteenth-century composer could not, technically, have written; but he would never have thought in these terms. The manipulation of texture in particular is new. This canzona does not rely exclusively on counterpoint (as the big motets of the Lasso school had done) nor on the dialogue of *cori spezzati*. Its texture is much freer than in any of his earlier works. This is even more true in the *Canzoni e Sonate*, where the sound is surprisingly sparse and unvoluptuous. The fact of the matter is that after 1602, the basso continuo had arrived, and Gabrieli was aware that it had altered everything.

Gabrieli's colleagues Croce and Bassano were among the first to supply a printed *basso seguente* to their motets; his follower Banchieri was equally quick off the mark. It is surprising that Gabrieli had not insisted on Gardano printing one for his first book of *Sacrae Symphoniae*, since the virtuoso 'Canzon in Echo con l'organo' obviously requires one. Viadana published his *Cento Concerti Ecclesiastici* in 1602, the first printed musical book to explain thoroughly the purpose and method of the organ bass, and by the time Gabrieli died, Vincenti had issued eight impressions, in addition to which there was the usual pirating in Germany, not to mention a host of imitators.

The composers of instrumental music did not immediately take up the fashion. Only one or two volumes which showed an understanding of the basso continuo were published in Gabrieli's lifetime. The whole concept is based on accompanied melody; it has left counterpoint behind. This is a position to which Gabrieli had been aspiring in his church music for some time. There is no longer any compulsion to write for double choir in terms of chordal blocks. All parts in the ensemble no longer have to be (or appear) equal. The status of 'melodic' parts—which is to say the upper instruments of the various groups—is not disguised. They bear the *passaggi*, while the lower voices are unornamented. There is a new sense of freedom, a move away from the monumental into an idiom which gives more scope for variety. To a composer like Gabrieli, becoming less interested in the statuesque and more in the expression of subtle shades of mood, the new manner had obvious attractions.

Gabrieli's use of the basso continuo

The concertante style quickly acquired its own clichés and imposed its own limitations. The Viadana basso continuo was easy to compose, and dilettanti could, and did, turn their hands to it. But Gabrieli's method was to graft the new discoveries onto established techniques. So the volume of *Canzoni e Sonate* is a virtual compendium of the devices of instrumental music of Gabrieli's lifetime. One or two works are almost old-fashioned. The 'Canzon Prima' for five instruments could belong to his very earliest music, in its determined counterpoint, and the strong chanson element with its da capo shaping. Even the harmonic adventurousness which leads to chromatic sequences is of the same kind that can be found in such motets as 'Miserere mei' in the first book of *Sacrae Symphoniae*, and some of the sequential writing, prominent after the opening section has completed its contrapuntal course, is no stranger to the instrumental music of that collection. The sense of its belonging to Gabrieli's maturity comes from the free use of diminished intervals in its melodic strands, the interest in grouping the instruments to gain colour contrasts, and the crispness of some of the motifs, especially a skipping cross-rhythm pattern which has the effect of compression:

This device is used quite frequently throughout the *Canzoni e Sonate*, and it adds a touch of gaiety to pieces otherwise slightly pompous. 'Canzon 5' uses cross-rhythms in precisely this way. It is a work reminiscent of the 'Canzon Noni Toni' (1597) in the opening bars, though less preoccupied with the minor, especially when the bass instruments enter with bell-like major scale passages. Any shadows in the clarity of the pompous C major, in a series of confrontations between high and low groups, are soon dispelled by *passaggi* of the older virtuosic kind, which not only are given to cornetts or violins, but also to the lower instruments, perhaps to give Ser. Nicolò Mosto a chance to display his dexterity on the bassoon. There is a *battaglia* climax when all the seven instruments come together in Andrea Gabrieli's manner; but then the dancing rhythms come in, and even a rather squarely phrased alleluja in triple time cannot dispel the joyous feeling (see Example 4).

The whole work is an excellent example of Gabrieli's emotional variety at this stage of his career. There is no tight formal pattern, no rigid groupings in the way of *cori spezzati*, but an infinitely malleable shape, coloured in kaleidoscopic textural patterns. The material may be highly developed or merely repeated once or twice with differing sonorities. The basis of the sound is a series of duet groups, not just in the upper voices as in many madrigals, but also between the lowest parts; and the fact that with seven strands to manipulate there must always be some imbalance, makes it the more intriguing. The extra voice joins the various groups, acting as treble to the lower instruments, bass to upper ones, or as part of a filling-in block while the outer duets continue.

Formal design in Gabrieli's canzonas

Describing this work as lacking a tight formal pattern does not imply that it also lacks form, for this term need not signify sectional repetition of the sort which flourished in Gabrieli's earlier music. In the 'Canzon Quinta', the shaping of its variety is unified by the nature of the material, which is always related to the basic opening canzona motif. Either the rhythm is preserved or the scale passage which acts as the continuation of the motif is suggested in some way. Even the passages for the virtuoso players, which at first sight seem pure Bassano-like finger work, are introduced by a single crotchet most probably derived from that opening material:

Ex.5

while a repeated note in a motif apparently little related to the initial theme recalls the canzona motto:

Ex.6

This shows, as does the 'fa sol la re' canzona, a genuine understanding of principles of development. There are many other canzonas in this collection which demonstrate it equally well. Of the single choir pieces, perhaps it is the Canzon 6 which shows it at its most subtle. Here it is not even the usual rhythmic motif which dominates the work, for the opening short duet for the uppermost instruments is not referred to again. It is the second phrase which assumes predominance, and it is material common to all instrumental music rather than a deliberate derivative of the canzona rhythm. Indeed it is its military quality which makes it memorable:

Ex.7

Its anacrusis gives rise to the next phrase, and it is this which in fact gives birth in turn to a whole host of motifs. It must be quoted as a harmonic entity since it is not merely its cantus which will be used throughout the work (see Example 8).

Ex.8

This is immediately stated in half note-values; later in a contrapuntal inversion, with the alto elevated above the cantus to give rise to a further imitative section; later still in an inversion of another kind, the motif rising instead of falling, which leads to its own crop of diminished and rhythmically altered versions. The original phrase, or its inversion, with different harmonizations, punctuates the work to make it fall into distinct paragraphs. A quarter of the way through, the statement pulls the tonal centre from the submediant back to the tonic; the versions around the halfway mark help to throw doubt on the main tonality; the last statement, some dozen bars from the end, marks the return to the tonic, which, after a lull of a couple of bars of duet which balance the very opening of the whole canzona, is flanked by two massive statements of the 'military' theme. This is in itself a highly sophisticated approach to shaping a canzona; but it is by no means all, for what is even more remarkable is the way subsidiary melodic fragments grow from one another. The continuation of the first restatement of a 'refrain' motif, for example, includes a turn (a) which might well have come from the treatises on divisions. Before the end of the section, its first two notes (b) have been isolated from the remainder of the turn, and assumed their own importance; in the next section the turn has been slightly straightened out (c); a slight alteration with one foreign note (d) proves convenient in a cadential figuration; and this in turn is deprived of its initial note (e) in a figure which pervades the canzona's second half (see Example 9).

Such close working out of themes is not the conscious academicism of the writer of ricercars, but the approach of a composer whose complete immersion in musical material results in one idea suggesting another, and yet another. It is essentially the method of the abstract thinker in music rather than one who finds inspiration in extra-musical considerations such as the grand festivals, religious texts, or even spectacular spatial effects. This canzona is doubtless 'effective' as occasional music; it is full of bright sonorities, and although no melodic strand exceeds vocal range, the continuous use of the upper registers of the parts written in treble clefs, and the rapidity of certain scale passages, shows the experience of the composer for state occasions. Displaying a theme in different contexts,

Ex.9

as in this piece, inevitably means a heightened sensitivity to shades of meaning.

There are only six double-choir pieces out of a total of twenty-two in the complete volume (those for three or more choirs must be granted a separate category for reasons which will emerge later), which may indicate some disenchantment with the medium of *cori spezzati*; or it may be that the larger works in the collection were meant for the Scuola grande di S. Rocco rather than St. Mark's. Whether or not this is so, it is certainly true that in place of the rich sound used so often at the beginning of the canzonas of the 1597 collection, they all start with a single instrument which states a contrapuntal motif. The counterpoint rarely lasts for long, but enough to show that these are not canzonas with which to *fare bella figura*. Indeed we may even wonder if the use of separated choirs was not simply due to the strict adherence to convention in the Doge's Chapel. Gabrieli seems little interested in those contrasts of colour which he had done as much as anyone to establish in Venetian music. In most of these works, the 'choirs' are identical; even where there are no indications of the actual forces to be deployed, the clefs are usually the same. Admittedly, Canzonas 10 and 11 require two cornetts for the first choir, two violins for the second choir. But in Canzon 14 the upper parts of both groups are allotted to violin (uppermost lines) and cornett (the second strand), as though homogeneity between the choirs was the aim. This represents a change of direction in accordance with general trends in the seventeenth century, during which the bright contrasts of colour of the late renaissance orchestra are gradually replaced by a monochrome, the final product being the string orchestra of Corelli.

The new methods of ornamentation

The nature of ornamentation is so important to Gabrieli's later music that it must now be discussed in some detail. The art of embellishment was showing signs of rapid development in Florence, Mantua, and Ferrara. Caccini, following the ideas of his more intellectual acquaintances in his book *Le Nuove Musiche* was concerned to reduce the amount of elaboration, to bring some order into the chaos of indiscriminate divisions. As a singer, his criterion for the addition of any ornament to the melodic line was whether it would enhance the word. Only significantly emotional words, such as *cor* or *languire* or *moro*, merited a display of skill. This meant that Bassano's continuous application of divisions was inevitably ruled out. The ornaments became less regular, more spasmodic. They occur, not to provide a natural musical balance or climax in the phrase, but simply because they are needed for extra-musical reasons. It is not difficult to find precedents for certain of Caccini's embellishments; the most startling difference between Caccini and his predecessors lies in their diverse concepts of rhythm. Caccini aims for a natural speech rhythm as the basis of his recitative, free from the tyranny of a notation built up specifically to make ensemble music possible. The irregularity of his ornaments reflects this desire. In place of the Bassano-esque:

we have:

A simple scale wise *passaggio*:

is not altered in notes; the note values are what must be changed to give a new crispness:

Ex.13

Even the only really original ornament in Caccini's preface, the *trillo* or rapid repetition of a single note, requires this sense of freedom, for this repetition must be carried out at a gradually increasing speed, not strictly measured but with a spontaneous sense of acceleration.[8] Only the *gruppo*, or trill in our sense of the word, is totally metrical, after its sixteenth-century usage. The basic difference is that, whereas previously the performer was allowed a vast choice, the number of ornaments is now restricted.

Modifications of the new vocal embellishments in instrumental music

Caccini's ornaments and methods clearly had logic in monodic song. In instrumental music, however, composers such as Salomone Rossi[9] and Biagio Marini[10] who tried to apply the new style in continuo-accompanied music for solo violin or cornett, were forced to compromise with more traditional ways. There were even more problems in vocal ensemble music, where too free an attitude to tempo rubato must inevitably cause chaos, and in the madrigals of such progressives as Monteverdi and Marco da Gagliano a similar compromise was arrived at, allowing some expression of the words, some use of the new 'irregular' embellishments—and some extended *passaggi* in the sixteenth-century manner. Instrumental ensemble music was least of all adapted to the new methods, and the new manner of ornamentation is scarcely apparent in Raverii's anthology or in Gussago's *Sonate a quattro, sei, et otto* (1608). There is a reliance on the older tradition even in the instrumental works of Giovanni Battista Grillo, who published a 'canzon pian e forte' and a 'canzon in ecco' in his *Sacri Concentus ac Symphoniae* in 1618.

[8] See H. W. Hitchcock, 'Vocal ornamentation in the Preface to Caccini's Le Nuove Musiche', *Musical Quarterly*, VI (1970), and R. Donington's article on ornamentation in *Grove's Dictionary of Music and Musicians*, V. This waywardness clearly only applies to cadential application of the *trillo*. In other places and in ensemble it is measured according to the composer's notation, as can be seen in Monteverdi's 'Duo Seraphim' from the Vespers music of 1610.

[9] See Riemann, *Handbuch der Musikgeschichte*, II (2) (Leipzig, 1912), p. 87.

[10] A. Schering, *Geschichte der Musik in Beispielen* (Leipzig, 1931), nos. 182–3.

Giovanni Gabrieli's use of the new style embellishments

There are works in Gabrieli's *Canzoni e Sonate* which in this respect go little beyond common sixteenth-century practice. Canzon 6 for seven instruments, the much larger scale Canzon 17, for twelve, contain nothing in the way of ornaments which cannot be found in the works published in 1597; Canzon 16 for three choirs constructs its motifs out of sequential repetitions of Bassano-esque figures in much the same way. But taking the 1615 collections as a whole, these are unusual. More typical is Canzon 10 for eight instruments divided into two groups. It begins conventionally enough with a long section for the first choir, the thematic motif worked out more contrapuntally than is usual in Gabrieli's *spezzata* music, and reaches its climax with decorated scale passages in duet for the violins:

Such figuration permeates the whole work, with extensive use of quavers, often in imitative pattern, giving the impetus and excitement of dynamic rhythms. This is not unknown in the earlier canzonas; but there is a new tautness derived from the sudden application of even faster moving embellishments. Most of these stem from the New Music. There is a kind of double mordent; a double fall, which is sometimes preceded by a tied note, to give a further irregularity[11]; a turn-like figure; and dotted rhythms, highly reminiscent of those used in the most 'modern' music such as Monteverdi's 'Sonata sopra Sancta Maria' (see Example 15).

To derive such embellishments from the music of the monodists, to compare the melody they create with that of such a modernist as Monteverdi is inevitable. Yet the total effect of the canzona is totally unlike anything

[11] These are the names given by Playford in his translation of Caccini's Preface. See O. Strunk, *Source Readings in Music History* (London, 1952), p. 377.

Ex.15

in the new style. The 'Sonata sopra Sancta Maria', for example, has an almost bizarre atmosphere which stems from the conflict between its organization around a plainsong cantus firmus and its virtuoso writing for cornetts, strings, and trombones. Gabrieli's music is, on the contrary, surprisingly well integrated. If it begins as a normal sixteenth century canzona and ends with a flourish of ornamental melody, the process seems utterly natural. The 'divisions', as we have seen, first arrive at the cadence of the opening section; they appear next when the first choir cuts short its opposing group, and it is while their implications are being worked out that the 'mordent' figure is introduced by the upper instruments of the second choir (interestingly, this figure is played only by cornetts, not by the violins). The cadence arrives, the rhythm returns in a derivative of the canzona motto on which the next new-style embellishment is superimposed, although it is an older type of figure, involving a cambiata-like tag, that leads the music forward to yet more virtuoso paths. The music again comes to a cadence and a moment of silence, following which the 'motto' rhythm reappears made more memorable by a D major–B major progression. The succeeding section reverts to 'old' ornaments—divisions punctuated once more by the motto, which in turn heralds a rhythmic alleluja. The 'turn' dominates the melody of all the parts, sometimes in inversion, sometimes the right way up, sometimes used in sequence, and sometimes simultaneously upright and inverted. Finally come the dotted-note embellishments, firmly applied to scale-wise melody, and played at the very top of the then range of cornetts and violins. The brilliance is kept up by giving all the instruments in each choir the fast movement, instead of allowing some to hold harmony notes. By introducing ornaments gradually, by reserving the real virtuosity to the end, Gabrieli follows a principle that has been known to all composers of variations. But since he is not writing a tightly organized pattern, he can overlap ideas, introduce faster note values, then revert to more stately movement. Unity comes from the exploitation of the canzona 'motto', which is given different harmonizations on each occasion it is used, carrying the music into unexpected tonalities, or acting as a mark of punctuation to conclude a section. Canzon 10 is an extravagant but not an eccentric work. To show the cleverness of the instrumentalists is not its primary aim, but their skill is an essential ingredient in making the music's growth possible.

The new rhythmic melody in Gabrieli's canzonas

New textures, new ways of unifying, new ornaments: the canzona has indeed been transformed. But perhaps the most obvious change to the casual listener in St. Mark's must have been the new rhythms that several of them use. The hallmark of the older canzona had been its 'motto', which was inevitably in duple time. The canzona 'Fa sol la re', on the contrary, was in triple time, with duple only acting as a ritardando in the final stages of the piece. Numerous pieces take up the suggestion. There had always been dances in triple time; vocal music, however, was almost invariably written in duples. There is only one piece by Gabrieli which goes against this pattern, the Magnificat for twelve voices, included in both the *Sacrae Symphoniae* and *Reliquae Sacrorum* of 1615, which, after a harmonized setting of the opening intonation, dances along in triple measure until the doxology forces it into a weightier metre. The four canzonas (including the 'Fa sol la re') which follow its lead are all remarkable. Most fascinating from the purely rhythmic point of view is Canzon 8 in which the triple time approaches the gaiety of a galliard, occasionally interposing a hemiolia cross-rhythm, though for the most part relying on different groupings of instruments for variety. Its main section is almost completely sunny in mood, its strong rhythms rarely frustrated, its consonant harmony only occasionally made a little more intense by a lightly touched suspension or seventh. Then, with duple time, the players seem to take to *contrapunto a mente*, the bass stating the cantus in long notes, while everyone else decorates above it. They start with the main theme of the canzona, but immediately launch out into all kinds of ornaments such as scales and dotted rhythms. Harmonic clashes, especially on the shorter note values, do not disrupt the texture. As ornament is encrusted on an already elaborate surface the excitement mounts until, in the final

bar, it is no longer enough to have, as formerly, a single note extending the last chord by arriving later and allowing the sound to be eased gently into the echo of the church. After this final chord arrives, all five upper instruments continue their florid ways.

The other canzonas in triple time are not so straightforwardly dance-like. Canzon 11 has equally gay rhythms, but the contrapuntal opening (very like that of the Magnificat for twelve voices) is one sign of greater seriousness; another is the layout for double choir, cornetts on the upper parts in one group, violins in the other. The dialogue begins after a dozen bars, but turns out to be strangely brief, and as the work goes on, it becomes clear that the places where both choirs are involved have only the structural function of a rondo refrain. The main burden of the work is carried on by the single choirs working in long sections, developing a sweet melody in which sequences play an important part, with mellifluous thirds in cornetts and violins, while the bass instruments hold fast to pedal notes (see Example 16).

Dialogue is largely carried on within each choir, cornett answering cornett, violin answering violin, sometimes with echo effects, achieved not by spatial separation but by 'forte' and 'piano' markings. There is a certain bleakness, an unexpected emptiness. The most remarkable expression of it comes in an echo passage for the 'violin' choir. 'Non sonate', Gabrieli tells his organist, and with no filling in of chords, there remain an uncomfortable number of bare fifths, and some distinctly chill minor thirds:

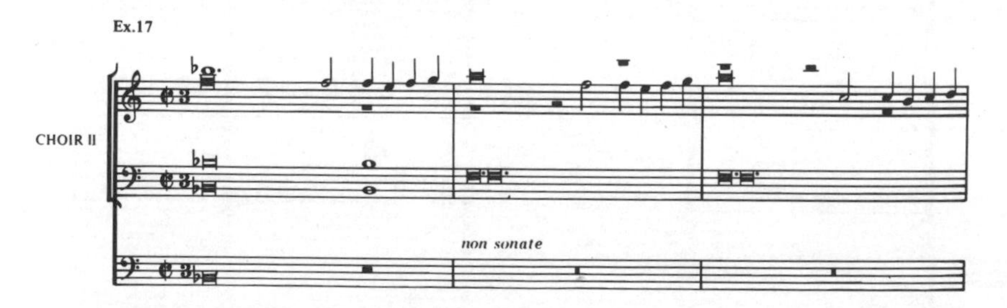

Canzon 17 is a big piece, scored for three choirs, each having a cornett and violin, plus two unspecified bass instruments (probably trombones or bassoons). Clearly each choir needs an organ to fill the gap between bass and melodic instruments, just as had Viadana's echo canzona. This massive piece of Venetian splendour starts with a brilliant fanfare, as confident as any of Andrea Gabrieli's post-Lepanto music, strong in its concentration on the notes of the major triad, and in its clean, forthright rhythms:

Ex.18

Gabrieli bases the whole canzona on this material. In some eighty bars it occurs over fifty times. Sometimes the derivation is obvious, for both the rhythms and the triad are kept the same. Elsewhere, it appears in inversion, diminution, in a syncopated version, slightly altered so that the triad appears in a different order, or changed from triple to common time. Yet its essence is always preserved. It remains strong, with firm accents; and the one version which suggests the minor is quickly banished in favour of its original:

Ex.19

There are subsidiary developments. The rounding off of the fanfare in its initial version gives rise to several variants, and there are other thematic links between material used as the argument proceeds; even so, the fanfare dominates throughout with a brilliance which indicates Gabrieli's full maturity.

Analysis of Gabrieli's finest canzonas

There is no set pattern in the volume of *Canzoni e Sonate*, for each canzona goes its own way, and yet there is not a single piece which does not bear the marks of being fashioned by a master of thematic integration. The most apparently unpromising works are sometimes the most subtle. Canzon 8, for example, looks ordinary enough, old-fashioned even in its division into *coro acuto* and *coro grave*. The opening admittedly has some cunning counterpoint, but the dialogue technique is not new, and there are the familiar 'battle' rhythms. But nearly half-way through, it departs from such well trodden paths to indulge in a measured cadenza, the two upper instruments of its 'high' choir displaying their prowess by scales, turns, and 'falls' of various kinds, accompanied by the basso continuo. Their duet owes a great deal to the echo music of the later sixteenth century, though to separate them spatially is out of the question since this effect is foreign to the remainder of the work. The passage shows how the predominance of upper voices was now made possible by the frank admittance of the organ bass (as opposed to its hidden presence as a *basso seguente*); it also shows the need for a greater variety of material than had been hitherto available in canzonas dominated by the 'motto'. The shape of the piece is also important; to call it a rondo would be misleading (although doubtless it was suggested by the rondo motets of the first book of the *Sacrae Symphoniae*) for the recurring motif in this case is not at the head of the whole piece. It is slipped in at the end of the initial phrase:

The leap of a diminished fourth in the cantus, the harmonization of the C sharp with an augmented triad, though not revolutionary, are uncommon enough at this time for the fragment to establish itself firmly in the memory. We hear it again, re-orchestrated for the lower choir, and with the parts re-arranged so that the diminished fourth is in an inner part, at the end of the second phrase. It recurs a dozen bars later at the end of that section. Syncopated rhythms and military repeated notes extend the next section even more, and the fragment appears again, reinforcing its impression by immediate repetition re-arranged for the tutti. The 'cadenza' gives way to dialogue between the choirs; but again the binding theme comes back, first in the lower choir, then the upper one, then tutti. The climax is full of fanfares on a perfect fourth: but the original pattern re-asserts itself with a couple of magnificent statements by the whole en-semble. The effect depends on the invention of new ways to lead from the recurring motif, and on the irregularities of phrase and section between these repetitions. Since there are eleven separate occurrences of the motif, the intervening material requires an uncommon creativity—and probably the new kind of ornament was a help in providing a stimulus to the com-poser. Without doubt, Gabrieli's flair for showing different shades of mean-ing by putting a theme in contrasting contexts is at its height. Though the piece is not as tuneful as the early canzonas, the ambivalence of the memorable motif, with its cadential functions and nature enriched by dissonance and angularity of melody, so that it is at once forthright and yet tinged with doubt, is ample compensation.

Canzon 8 is just over a hundred bars long, and lasts about five minutes in performance—rather longer than most of the canzonas of the 1597 volume. But its overwhelming feeling of space and grandeur depends neither on its length nor on the actual resources employed, but on Gabrieli's absorption in his material. This is equally apparent in Canzon 4, the best known of all the canzonas in the collection. At first sight, it seems to be an uncomplicated motet-rondo piece, a triple time 'alleluja' separat-ing five sections of the 'prayer', as it were. But it does not take long to realize that the real matter of importance is the manipulation of the opening phrase before the arrival of the 'alleluja'. In itself, this is no more than the working out of a fairly conventional motif on the canzona motto:

After the statement of the triple time there comes a link passage which leads to an apparently identical repeat of the opening. But an extension by means of further imitative entries casts a completely new light on the theme, giving it the darker hue of the minor, as well as changing the tonal centre (see Example 22).

The linking material to the next episode itself modulates so that the motif arrives on A and takes twice as long to return, by a series of perfect cadence progressions, to C major. The next episode suddenly modulates to D, and has to return via A, with a delicious progression from a C major to an E major chord. After this, Gabrieli displays his alleluja section twice, re-establishing the tonal status quo. The final section is announced with some of the new ornamental flourishes on the upper instruments. In two bars, a chromatic sequence stated twice opens up a glorious new vision from which the motif emerges in the greatest splendour, requiring six chords arranged in the circle of fifths to arrive at a satisfying conclusion with the usual plagal cadence (see Example 23).

Yet the resources for which it was written are not large: two violins, two cornetts (one line is unmarked but the duet textures make this inevitable), and two trombones which double up in the triple time tuttis. And although Gabrieli turns the use of the brilliant registers of the instruments to good advantage, it is clear that the feeling of breadth comes from the thematic argument, the tensions of opposed and related tonalities.

The sonatas

The sonatas, it is true, are less full of close thematic development, but they have their own virtues. The terminology of Gabrieli (or his editor) is not exact. The Sonata for three violins, as we have seen,[12] is closely related to the canzona, although the desire for a new name for so unusual a work is

[12] See Chapter Eight above.

easily understood. But Sonata 13, which begins with the canzona motto before dancing along in a joyous triple measure reminiscent of the 'Fa sol la re' canzona or Canzon 11, is little more dignified than Canzon 7. There are, it is true, markings of 'pian' and 'forte', but Canzon 11 has these too. The sudden turn to virtuoso *passaggi* in the stately coda is not unknown in other canzonas, nor are its echo effects. The other sonatas are another matter. All are massive, both in resources and scale, darker in sonority, and intensely serious in mood. Even Sonata 20, among its twenty-two separate parts, has none with a treble clef. The single part marked 'cornetto' takes that instrument only to F, thus neglecting those brilliant top notes of which Gabrieli made such play in other pieces. Sonata 19 is not so austere, but twelve of its fifteen parts are written in the alto clef or below, making it suitable for trombones. Sonata 18 is fully marked with the names of the instruments, revealing two choirs each consisting of two cornetts and three trombones, and as the third, a *coro grave* for trombones.

This Sonata is a brilliant display of virtuoso skill, while there can be no denying its serious intent. It has a sober rhythmic tread, with excitement brought about by sudden bursts of ornamental melody. The sonata opens with a variant of the old 'motto' theme, in longer notes than it normally has, and as it progresses the subsidiary material which emerges is often of the lighter kind found in the canzonas. But from the start, the counterpoint is denser, and soon, on the entry of the second choir, another type of formal pattern reveals itself. The initial duet in closely woven counterpoint is here repeated by the two lowest parts of the choir, while the other three weave their ornamental lines above them:

Then the third 'choir' adds its own development of the theme. This group of trombones can hardly compete with the cornetts, and works out the material in serious polyphony, dissonances and minor tonalities predominating. The cornetts add a coda to this section with a brilliant flourish reminiscent of the echo scenes in early opera:

There follows a full display of the tutti more typical of a sonata, the basses of each choir playing the theme while all the other parts weave an elaborate web around it. The idea continues to be worked out, free, almost cadenza-like passages for the cornetts alternating with counterpoint of the greatest skill. The decorative lines are sometimes as virtuosic as any in the Venetian repertoire, often lively in rhythm, always with the individual ornaments repeated several times, either in sequences within the phrase, or by echo effects, or by passing them from choir to choir, so that they never appear wayward or merely improvisatory. The rather slow movement of the main theme, especially as it often comes in the bass, ensures a steady movement of the harmony, and when, in the coda, the held chords are spread over three and a half octaves while the upper instruments vie with each other in displaying their dexterity, the sonorousness is splendid indeed. At the end, however, the final chord of C major dies away, for Gabrieli writes rests in all the parts but one. That one, the first cornett of the first choir, continues with an echo of the decorative figure just played by his colleague in the second choir.

A similar gesture is made in Sonata 20, physically the most massive of all Gabrieli's printed music. The final chord is decorated with various ornamental flourishes most of which are conventional enough; but one, in the cantus of the fourth choir, intrudes a flattened leading note as the highest point of the phrase. It is not unique in Venetian music; an almost identical progression can be found in Croce's *Missa Percussit Saul*, and the complex cadences of polychoral music encourage such confusions of tonality. But in this context, at the end of a long and massive piece, the lack of firm confirmation of the tonic seems of stronger emotional import and is curiously indecisive.

The tutti in fact comes together for only about a sixth of the whole; and when it does there is nearly always a hint of the minor, in spite of the strength of the major which pervades the rest of the work. It is in plan more conventional than Sonata 18, relying more on *spezzato* devices than do most of the canzonas in the volume, and there is both close dialogue and a monolithic alleluja after the manner of the grand motets. However, a dotted rhythm heard in the opening bars recurs from time to time, and the contrapuntal skill in manipulating twenty-two strands of melody is beyond praise. There is a certain amount of doubling, especially of bass lines, and some held notes made to appear more interesting by some fake cross-rhythms. It still remains astonishing how beautiful Gabrieli makes the complex dovetailing of passing notes, and how alive most of the melodic writing is. Detail is important. An ornament in one part is passed to another, one small figure suggests another; and yet all fits together in a simple but effective harmonic scheme, allowing for sonority of noble dimensions.

Yet it is Gabrieli's emotional power, even more than his skill, which distinguishes him from his contemporaries and imitators. Sonata 14 is the work nearest to the sonatas of the 1597 volume, reminiscent in both sonority and technique of the 'Canzon Quarti toni', one of the greatest pieces in that collection. There are things in it that the sixteenth-century composer could not do. The new century has made ornamentation a *sine qua non* of even the stateliest music, and the cantus parts of each of the three choirs give the cornetts (almost certainly) opportunity for virtuoso display. Thus the sonata seems to be orientated towards melody rather than counterpoint; though so, indeed, is the earlier 'Sonata pian e forte'. But in the main this solemn sonata is an offshoot of the old skill and mood. The sombre polyphony of the opening; the concentration on minor chords; the interruption of the steady progress by those biting ♩♩.♪♩|𝅗𝅥 rhythms; the way a harmonic formula is repeated with a new harmonic direction; the unequal phrases caused by intense dialogue; the stretching of the penultimate chord of the plagal cadence at the very end to give little brilliance in the ultimate major chord; all these are the characteristics of the Gabrieli whose fiery music had dominated Venetian artistic life for a quarter of a century.

Summing up of Gabrieli's achievement in instrumental music

In some ways, Gabrieli's instrumental works are a beginning from which a new idiom emerged. This is almost the first published music to 'put in the expression marks' and, more important, to use these means to some purpose (the manner in which a sudden change of dynamics can alter the whole mood can be seen at its best in Sonata 13). Specific instruments are indicated for specific parts; the writing shows that this arises from an act of creative imagination. For us, it is commonplace to think in these terms: in Gabrieli's lifetime it was not. That is one measure of his achievement. He is the first to use the word 'sonata', though, as we have seen, this was a fairly flexible term. Such things, however, are peripheral. More important is the fact that Gabrieli is the first composer for instrumental ensemble to see plainly how to write for his medium. In these later works, there is indeed little left of the canzona's vocal origins, still very evident in most such music of the time. Without words, old forms will not suffice; new patterns must be invented which will make instrumental music self-explanatory.

This had been done for the organ and for the lute by its virtuosi. Gabrieli did the same for the ensemble. He did it precisely because he was interested in pure music, and the invention of patterns in sound. In this respect he far outshines his highly professional uncle.

This in turn points towards Giovanni Gabrieli's real place in the history of instrumental music. He is not a beginning but an end. The Germans who were ostensibly his followers did not do much to extend this genre; they certainly wrote nothing so sophisticated. The Italians were quickly seduced by the delights of virtuoso fiddling, and although the Sonata for three violins has its successor in the trio sonata, Gabrieli's greatest achievements in the great canzonas and sonatas were soon forgotten even in Venice. Yet the very sophistication of these confirms that Gabrieli was the end of a road which had traversed some important ground. He is not so much the originator of the sonata as the climactic figure in the story of the canzona. The genre, itself a remnant of the *formes fixes* of the fifteenth century, and by now an anachronism in a world where the madrigal had superseded the chanson, justifies itself in the sophisticated clothing given it by Gabrieli. The simple repetitions, which were all the sixteenth century would allow it, led the canzona to a complexity hardly dreamed of even in the heyday of the chanson, and more important, into a world of the most subtle emotional expressiveness which goes beyond words. His works convey the finest shades of mood and thought. The fashions of the early seventeenth century decreed that absolute music was not allowed to possess such powers: hence Gabrieli's work led to no further development. But his achievement in instrumental music may in the long run be more to the taste of the twentieth century than the music which gave him his historical role as the symbol of a Most Serene Republic.

CHAPTER ELEVEN

The Later Church Music

BY Giovanni's later years, the mood of Venice had changed radically. When Doge Grimani died at Christmas 1605,[1] the Republic was in a state of political uncertainty. There had been a new Pope for more than half a year; Paul V was elected on the decease of Leo XI, who had himself occupied the throne of St. Peter for less than a month. Paul, a native Roman, considered his elevation a miracle from heaven, and felt that the world could scarcely be sufficiently respectful to one thus chosen by God. In particular, Venice was careless in showing its obedience when, a short time before Grimani passed away, the Republic arrested two priests charged with crimes under the civil law. The Pope declared the act illegal: *his* servants must be tried and punished by the Church, and Venice must hand over the two clerics to its jurisdiction. Venice refused and the Pope threatened excommunication of the entire population. Before the discussions could proceed much further, Grimani died. The Papal Nuncio to the Republic announced that any election of the new Doge would be invalid, until Venice had complied and been released from its threatened excommunication. Venice ignored this and proceeded to elect Leonardo Donato as its lawful Prince, providing him with a new Bucintoro to wed the sea on Ascension Day. Donato was in many ways a fortunate choice being, in Wotton's words 'a wise and beaten man in the world, eloquent, resolute, provident'.[2] And in this affair he had the advice of his friend Paolo Sarpi, a master of canon law, whose intellectual powers and wide knowledge made him a formidable adversary. He declared that the state had 'authority to legislate on matters temporal within its own jurisdiction. There was no occasion for the admonitions administered by His Holiness, for the matters in dispute were not spiritual but temporal.'[3] The Pope delivered a final ultimatum: either obey or be excommunicated. In May

[1] The exact date of Grimani's death has been the subject of some dispute since it was apparently kept secret for a short time. See *The Life and Letters of Sir Henry Wotton*, I, ed. L. Pearsall Smith (London, 1907), p. 339.

[2] ibid, p. 340. [3] Horatio Brown, *Studies in Venetian History*, II (London, 1907), p. 237.

the Republic was placed under an interdict. But nothing happened. Priests should, in theory, have refused to say Mass or administer the sacraments to heretics, for such the Venetians now could be considered. In practice, church ceremonial went on as before. Rome, after failing to gain support from its powerful allies for more militant action, was eventually forced to a compromise. The priests whose arrest was the original point of contention were surrendered to the French ambassador representing 'His Most Christian Majesty, King Henri IV' who turned them over to the Papal authorities. The interdict was then lifted, with moral victory to the Venetians.

Normally such political action would hardly be worth recounting in the life of a musician. There is no sign that the ceremonial at St. Mark's was lessened, and as we have seen, the *scuole grandi* turned out with even more splendour than usual on Corpus Domini.[4] Yet the ordinary citizen must have felt the dispute keenly, for Church and State both had claims on his allegiance, and in fact he was probably more deeply aware of his parish priest than any officer of state. The chroniclers[5] who recorded the reign of Grimani with joy have little good to say of the years which were to see the end of Gabrieli's life. Even Sarpi, who, after helping to bolster Venice's independence and surviving an assassination attempt in 1607, lived to be one of its heroes, towards the end of his days noted a distinct lessening of Venetian initiative and power.

The cappella at St. Mark's in decline

There are signs that this atmosphere affected the *cappella* of St. Mark's. In 1607 the Mantuan ambassador in Venice, seeking some singers with which to enhance his master's court, was told by both Croce and Gabrieli that there was not a single really good contralto in Venice, and that the choir of the basilica was in a parlous condition.[6] The registers of the Procurators seem to confirm that all was not well. In 1606, no singer or player was elected to the salary roll, although in the following years there were a number of new appointments; the next few months saw two singers departing for other regions,[7] something which had not happened on any scale since before Grimani's election as Doge. The increasing age of the men in charge of the musical establishment may have something to do

4 See Chapter Eight above.
5 For example, the writer of Biblioteca Ambrosiana Mss. H·5. Suss.
6 A Bertolotti, *Musici alla Corte dei Gonzaga in Mantova*, p. 87.
7 A.S.V., Proc. de Supra, Registro 140, entries for 14 September 1608 and 1 April 1609.

with this. Croce and Gabrieli were about fifty, and the latter was suffering from his kidney stone[8], as a number of absences from the basilica on festival days makes clear. Giovanni Bassano was perhaps five years their junior, and had apparently given up composition, for no grand motets by him were published in the new century. Not one of the lesser men—deputy organist, singers, or instrumentalists—was to make a real mark even locally in Venice in the next twenty or thirty years.

On Croce's death in 1609 the Procurators delayed the appointment of a successor, relying on the *vice-maestro* to act in the interim.

That since P. Fra Agostin Fasuol has acted as *vice-maestro di cappella* for seven months from the death of the quondam Giovanni †[=Croce] who was *maestro*, until the arrival of the new *maestro*, having put aside everything else to attend to this duty. Therefore we have decreed after a ballot, that P. Fasuol be given 25 ducats for the said service.[9]

The 'new maestro' was Giulio Cesare Martinengo, the son of a well-known musician who had been in the service of the Accademia Filarmonica of Verona in the 1560s and 70s. Gabriele, his father, as befitted his employment at the most colourful of musical clubs, was something of a madrigalist; he does not appear to have passed on his gifts as a composer to his son, who produced little music, none of it of any distinction. Still, Giulio Cesare was in 1609 the *maestro di cappella* at Udine Cathedral where they were evidently well satisfied with him.[10] Presumably he was an efficient choirmaster, which was perhaps what the Procurators wanted. But Martinengo was not a good manager of his own finances; he frequently asked for advances of pay and eventually took in a choir boy as a lodger (his apartment in the *canonica* being rent-free, he made a complete profit by this device).[11] Admittedly he was instrumental in finding a quartet of singers to whom he also gave lodgings.[12] Thereafter, nothing very much happened. When he died, in the year after Gabrieli's death, the Procurators looked further afield. The confines of the *terra ferma* of the Republic were clearly not wide enough.

[8] Caffi I, p. 178.

[9] ibid, entry for 31 January 1610 (Venetian style 1609). *Vice-maestro* in this context means literally 'in place of the *maestro*'. 'Che havendo il P. Fra Agostin Fasuol servito p Vice-maestro di Capella per mesi sette continui dopo la morte d^{l} G. Zuane †[= Croce] che era Maestro et fin all'entro d^{l} nuovo Maestro, Havendo tralassato ogni altra cosa p attender al d^{o} servitio. Però haño à. boss. et batty. terminato, che siano datti d^{t} vinticinq. al sop^{ra} padre Fasuol pla sevitu sopra . . .

[10] G. Vale, op. cit., p. 133.

[11] D. Arnold, 'The Monteverdian Succession at St. Mark's', *Music and Letters*, XLII (1961).

[12] A.S.V., Proc. de Supra, Registro 140, entry for 13 July 1610.

All these factors must incline us to the belief that St. Mark's was not, in Gabrieli's declining years, the musical force it had been at the height of his strength. This is confirmed by examination of the music by the Venetians which was published during this time. Bassano had retired from the field and Gabrieli was reluctant as ever to give the fruits of his labour to Gardano or Vincenti; so almost all the works to be considered are by Giovanni Croce. His madrigals continued to be published, and certainly his earlier music remained as popular as ever, as reprint after reprint (not to mention the usual pirating in Germany) showed. The line of the grand motets and masses, however, was substantially diminished; and in fact, Venetian music for *cori spezzati* is now less common altogether. We find some large-scale works of Croce, as of Gabrieli, in the massive choir books of the court of Graz,[13] and even from their fragmentary state we can see that he has not lost the art. In composing for Venice, he restricts himself to modest forces, and a modest manner. In place of the vigorous music of his earlier years, he tends to introversion and gentle melancholy. The dynamic rhythms of the works of the 1590s disappear; there is sometimes a beauty of melody, but no splendour of the old kind.

The basso continuo in church music

Similar changes will be found in some of Gabrieli's music, though the comparison is instructive mainly because it shows differences of character and approach, as do their differing attitudes towards the great innovations of the new century. Gabrieli's use of the basso continuo in his instrumental music seems a trifle uncertain; it is a liberating force from the older polyphony, and yet a source of confusion, for he produces virtually no music in which continuo instruments are consistently applied (the exception being the 'Sonata per tre violini'). Croce's major essay in concertante music was to appear as a book of motets which in its very title makes a point of the novelty: *Sacrae Cantilene concertate a tre, a cinque et sei voci, con i suoi ripieni a Quattro voci, et il Basso per l'Organo.*[14] These pieces are very different from anything in the Venetian tradition. Without doubt, they belong to the genre made universal by Viadana. They are for a small number of voices accompanied by organ, on which they rely for harmonic filling-in; and their simplicity must have been invaluable in St. Mark's in Croce's later years. Yet the *ripieni* which the title page mentions

[13] Now in the Vienna Staatsbibliothek, as Mss. 16703–8.

[14] For a full description of these works see D. Arnold, 'Croce and the concertato style', *Musical Quarterly*, XXXIX (1953).

are no less than the full choir of St. Mark's on a good day, singing what they have sung on many past occasions—rondo motets, full of alleluja refrains, or repeated triple-time sections to a more extended verbal phrase. The texture is simpler, but there is no mistaking the origins of this kind of passage.

Thus Croce has arrived at a compromise. One can even make these works into *musica spezzata* by placing the ripieni in different galleries and bringing them together in a splendid tutti at the end. Yet the pieces do just as well for the most modest occasion. They are not great music, not adventurous in idiom or resource. They are well composed, in a manner which Gabrieli had not as yet understood nearly so well—and he must have learnt much from them. It is indeed only against the background of such modest pieces that we can savour the grandeur that his colleague was to wrest out of means very little different.

Gabrieli's later church music for single choir

Looking at the three dozen or so works included in the two posthumous collections of 1615 which give us most of our knowledge of Gabrieli's late church music, it is not difficult to see the similarities of resources used. There are the motets for single choir in which the singers of St. Mark's must not be extended too much; the concertante pieces which exploit the skill of the few virtuosi while reducing the role of the ripieni to something well within their reach; and the polychoral pieces, somewhat less ambitious than those in the collections of the sixteenth century. Several of the finest pieces likely to belong to this later period are for single choir, and even when eight voices are used, Gabrieli prefers this simple format rather than the division of forces. Some of these works are in such a new manner as to require a separate discussion; but even those which do not materially depart from traditional ways show that Gabrieli, like Croce, was not deterred by limitations. 'O Jesu Christe', in the *Reliquiae Sacrorum Concentuum*, for example, is written for a choir without any real soprano tone, and does not require instrumental participation, although the text is suitable for brighter sonorities. Nonetheless, its allelujas, flourishing their dominant sevenths freely, are very spirited, and the darker hues of the choir are put to good use at the words 'defendat nos ab hostium insidiis'. The false relations and irregular resolutions of passing notes are very expressive.

The eight-part setting of 'Jubilate Deo' from the same collection[15] is more obviously a development of an older style, though here too, there are signs that the full resources of St. Mark's are restricted. There are sopranos, it is true, and cornetts would make their lines brighter, but they are not kept extended on their upper notes, as they are so often in the music

[15] Winterfeld, III, p. 32.

for double choir. The actual melodic style is also simpler, a cross between madrigal and chanson in the short phrases and incisive rhythms (the canzona is also suggested in a brief reprise before the final triple time). The opposition of contrasted groups of voices results in some closely woven dialogue. The same kind of opposition between changing, non-constant groups is to be found in the motet 'Alleluja' of the *Reliquiae,* which we know to be a contrafactum of the epithalamium 'Scherza Amarilli', published first in 1600, and this 'Jubilate Deo' evokes a similar atmosphere.

Works using cori spezzati

There are works which revert to the old, glorious manner, and seem to belong to a former world. The matter of chronology is complicated because the second volume of *Sacrae Symphoniae* and the *Reliquiae Sacrorum Concentuum* are posthumous collections. It is not possible to date the contents of either with any certainty, except those pieces which, like the setting of 'Deus, Deus meus' included among Andrea's *Concerti,* had been published in earlier collections. Some other works must also belong to Gabrieli's early years. 'Sancta et Immaculata Virginis', for example, is richly scored in the way of several Marian motets published in 1597, has the same kind of cross-rhythms, a similar repeated final section, and Gabrieli's favourite concluding drawn-out plagal cadence. The layout of the 'Magnificat' for fourteen voices of *coro acuto, coro grave* and *cappella,* is very familiar to us from earlier pieces, and the complex texture is the way of the younger man whose uncle has insisted on dozens of different solutions to the decoration of a *cantus firmus.* Other works, however, reveal details not within the scope of the earlier music. The eight-voiced 'O quam suavis' is another rich, harmonic, double-choir motet, developing its patterns in a way not unlike those in 'O Domine Jesu Christe' or some such highly emotional work. The chromatic changes which help to give its intense flavour could have belonged to a setting in a similar mood written in the 1580s. It is only in the later stages that a regularly applied ornament in the cantus parts of each choir, and some diminished and augmented intervals used both harmonically and melodically, exceed the limits of Gabrieli's normal sixteenth-century usage and begin to suggest that 'O quam suavis' is contemporary with other 'mannerist' pieces.

Occasional music

All this suggests that Gabrieli's style developed steadily throughout his life; and this must have been helped by the fact that his duties in St. Mark's do not seem to have changed very much over the years. Like the music published in 1587 and 1597, the church music of 1615 is still very much occasional music. Magnificats, a huge Mass, motets for Easter and Christmas or the festivals of the Blessed Virgin are the staples. Though the means had changed, the needs of the state church were essentially the same. And although the innovations of Viadana had substantially eased the problems of the musician in the smaller church, or even St. Mark's in its temporary decline, they did little more than add a new colour to Gabrieli's palette.

The grandest of his late published music is in fact nearest to his earlier work in spirit and means. The motet which comes at the end of the second book of *Sacrae Symphoniae* is not in essence different from that which had concluded the first. Like 'Omnes gentes', 'Buccinate in neomenia' sets part of a particularly splendid psalm, suitable for any civic occasion of joy or triumph. There are four choirs, one the customary *cappella*, the others five-voiced groups, one part of each carefully marked *voce*, so that the soprano, tenor, and bass soloists of the basilica (noticeably the contralto is lacking) shall be supported by instruments. One choir is a *coro acuto* and very suitable for strings or cornetts. The other two are both *cori gravi*, for trombones or bassoons or both, with an instrument capable of continuous low Cs; and the tutti makes a fine sound. The climax sees a chord of C major spread over three octaves and a fifth, made brilliant by a wide gap between the lowest parts and close spacing in its upper reaches so as to gain the maximum sonority. Doubling of the bass line is now a commonplace, but there is remarkably little doubling elsewhere, the variety of intricate rhythms and even an occasional melodic awkwardness, such as a clumsy leap of a sixth, being preferred. The rhythms are strong, almost military, as the word 'solemnitatem' is repeated over and over again, and there are fanfares for the phrase 'in voce tubae'.[16] Major chords abound, there is an alleluja refrain, though not in triple time and integrated more than usual with the body of the motet, and triple time for the words 'cantate et exultate'. It might be a work of the Grimani period,

[16] Compare the similar setting of the same words by Croce, reprinted in *L'Arte Musicale in Italia*, ed. L. Torchi, Vol. II (Milan, 1897; reprinted 1968), p. 323; and the passage in Palestrina's motet 'Exsultate Deo', from *Motettorum Quinque Vocibus, Liber Quintus* (Rome, 1584), reprinted in *Opere Complete*, XII (Rome, 1941), p. 88; the actual section is on pp. 90–91.

except that there are one or two features not to be found in 'Omnes gentes' and similar pieces. In spite of the usual triple time tonic-dominant reiteration, there is in general a somewhat greater subtlety of harmonic progression, including a delightful G major–E major juxtaposition. Moreover, the use of the parts marked for voices seems more deliberate and less casual than in earlier music. A reduction of the following section to voice and accompaniment reveals that the tenor line of a *coro grave* and the bass line of the *coro acuto* may develop the same theme, even if this makes for a slight infelicity in the layout of a chord.

'Buccinate in neomenia' was understandably included in both the 1615 collections. It is suitable for many a feast day, religious or national. In its astonishing sonority it is a work which the German pupils of Gabrieli could copy, and there are a number of Schütz's psalms, published just four years later, which show the same attitudes and technique. Among Gabrieli's own music, there are really only two comparable pieces, a motet 'Audite principes' and the huge setting of the Magnificat in seventeen parts. The motet is a Christmas piece for sixteen 'voices' arranged in three choirs, differentiated by range, as usual, and requiring instruments for the extreme parts. Which parts must be allotted voices, in fact, emerges from the structure, which is highly original. The lowest part, a tenor, of the first, upper choir opens with a cry for attention, 'Audite principes', to which the whole choir responds 'Et auribus percipite'. They develop the mood of rejoicing in a triple time section which comes to a cadence to allow the cantus (possibly a countertenor) of the second choir to call out 'Audite senes' to the opening musical phrase, and to receive the same reply, though the development into triple time now uses new music. After the cadence, a tenor from the third choir sings 'Audite patres' in the same terms, while the choir continues as before. But this time, instead of joyful dance measures, one of those passages occurs in which Gabrieli expresses the miracle of Christmas rather than its pompous ceremonial. Its rich flavour derives from its use of passing notes in dissonant combinations much as we find in 'O Jesu mi dulcissime' in the 1615 *Sacrae Symphoniae* and in a late motet by Croce 'In spiritu humilitatis' which comparisons may give us an idea of its intensity and mood (see Example 4).

The mood of glory is immediately resumed and though dignity interrupts in the shape of slower, steadier duples, the dialogue continues mainly in these joyful accents.

The Magnificat for seventeen voices is the largest of the six settings by Gabrieli which were published (doubtless there were others, since the need for them in Venice was frequent), and it epitomizes them all. If it does belong to the seventeenth century, as its free octave doublings and

occasional ornaments suggest, it is worth remembering that other attitudes were developing towards the treatment of the Song of the Blessed Virgin. Croce—in common with other sixteenth-century composers—had for a long time thought of it as a text which could be treated sectionally, using less than the tutti for its more intimate moments. Monteverdi took this a step further in both his settings in his 1610 volume of Vespers music, giving a new mood to each verse, so that the lowliness of the Lord's handmaiden was as clear as the power of God himself. Gabrieli has no such thoughts. Two *cori acuti* are set against the *coro grave* and *cappella* (even in 'Buccinate in neomenia' it had been the other way round) and although in the second of these he has marked two parts to be sung, they are the middle lines. Thus the outer parts are allowed the brilliance of continual extreme sonorities, the more especially since the bass is written for an instrument with a very low register and often seems to act as the foundation for both groups. It is an expansive work, repeating words in dialogue quite extensively and using the tutti a great deal, with an astonishing mastery of counterpoint. The only quieter passage of any size consists of some ten bars for the *cappella* alone at the words 'sicut locutus est'; which accentuates the effect of the massed forces immediately after. The doxology is set in a way Andrea would have been proud of; and the solemn chords at 'sicut erat' take us back to his Mass for four choirs.

The exhilaration of this Magnificat in fact belongs to a period long after the Lepanto era, which should remind us how dangerous it is to ascribe the mood of music too closely to the mood of a historical period. One sign of its later date is to be found in the places where the organ part ceases to be a mere *basso seguente* and provides an essential ingredient in the harmony. There are not many of them, yet they are enough to persuade one that the composer knew something of the concertante manner. Another sign is the occasional ornamental figure—semiquavers, or a dotted rhythm organized in the way of Bassano, not found in the vocal music published before the turn of the century. In most of the other grand works of the 1615 volumes, there are technical devices of this kind even when the basic shape and material is traditional. The mighty Christmas motet 'Salvator noster' may resemble 'Buccinate' at its opening; by its climax, the very look of the score, with its flurry of decorative quavers, makes the differences between the two obvious. The Kyrie of the Mass similarly departs from Gabrieli's earlier setting, which is clearly its model (just as that one in turn had taken Andrea's Mass in the *Concerti*) when virtuoso *passaggi* extract a vocal line from the held chords of instruments. Thus Giovanni's interest in the new, already demonstrated through his pupils, permeates his own music quite late in life, notwithstanding the fact that in church music, at least, there was no urgent reason for change.

The new style of ornamentation in Gabrieli's church music

Most of the 'innovations' found in the non-concertante motets (those which use the basso continuo in the new way are a different matter and must be discussed separately) are to be found in some form in the instrumental music and can here be taken for granted. The embellishment of melody is based on the same sources, and the same figures occur frequently. The 'fall' is as popular in the vocal as in the instrumental music:

and its variant, which seems to be the ancestor of the modern turn, is no less common, even if it comes more naturally to the fingers of a player than to the vocal chords:

Another kind of turn which fills the gap of a major third he finds equally useful, either in quavers or semiquavers or with bumpy dotted notes. The trill (*gruppo* in seventeenth-century terminology) has suggested a figure which enlivens the third descending; although in this form it cannot be quite accounted a trill since it is the upper note which belongs to the chord:

There are just a few others which are not the common stock of early seventeenth-century ornamentation. There is a nervous motif, almost a turn without its accompanying trill, reminding us of Gabrieli's profession of organist, the more especially since it involves very short note values:

Most extraordinary still is an oscillating third, obviously analogous to a trill which in performance seems very strange because the interval does not consist of adjacent notes. Though used as a special effect, it is worth quoting here to show that it is essentially part of the same process of integrating short, crisp figures into melodic lines:

With this integration of ornaments has gone any feeling for the smoothness and steady tread of the polyphonic melody as used by, say, the Roman composers of the time; and possibilities for sudden changes of direction, unthinkable in an earlier time, are increased by Gabrieli's enthusiasm for the tie. We have seen this new notational device in free use in the madrigals of his pupils. In some of his own motets it produces a quite startling melodic gait. Without a tie, the most rapid change possible lies in dotted figurations, where an exact relationship of three to one is no serious disturbance of the basic beat. In music where the tactus is to be counted in minims a tie enables long 'white' notes to be followed by the shortest of 'black' ones:

This is an extreme example, but there are many others where short and long are placed in unexpected juxtaposition. Even people used to madrigalian music where the device had come into constant use by the early years of the seventeenth century must have found this unusual, simply because there the crotchet beat reduces the temptation to combine very long with short notes. It is the extreme of the *note nere – note bianche* contrasts begun in the middle of the sixteenth century with which Gabrieli must have grown up as he was learning from his uncle and Lassus.

Dissonance in Gabrieli's later style

This kind of sporadic movement in melody has its implications for harmony. Ornaments, by their very nature, assume a somewhat cavalier attitude to consonance, and this is frequently reflected in Gabrieli's late motets. Sometimes the figuration seems to fit into a harmonic pattern quite neatly, so that there is a minimum of harshness, as in the following passage from the double-choir 'Cantate Domino', where passing notes form mellifluous thirds and sixths: the only severe dissonance is an old-fashioned clash of major and minor carried, as so often in sixteenth-century English and Venetian music, by melodic considerations (see Example 11).

At other times, the passing notes are themselves the cause of the asperity, as in the closing alleluja of 'Benedictus es Dominus' where the clashes between the various moving parts are momentary, but nonetheless real—

and, strictly speaking, unnecessary. It is unusual to combine notes in this way, by the standards of even the later sixteenth century, at least in a written-out form:

This is not a particularly dissonant passage, and significantly it sets a joyous word. It is quoted here to show that when the text does suggest extreme emotion, Gabrieli's new attitude to dissonance will allow full rein to his imagination. Sevenths, which it is not really possible to explain away as passing notes, are now quite common, as in an extensive passage at the opening of 'Vox Domini':

Equally there are ninths which sound like ninths. In the following example the G draws attention to itself as the climax of the phrase and as it ascends in sixths with the part below, the harmony sounds fascinatingly like the elements of two simultaneously announced chords, G and F, jumbled excitingly together (see Example 14).

Ex.14

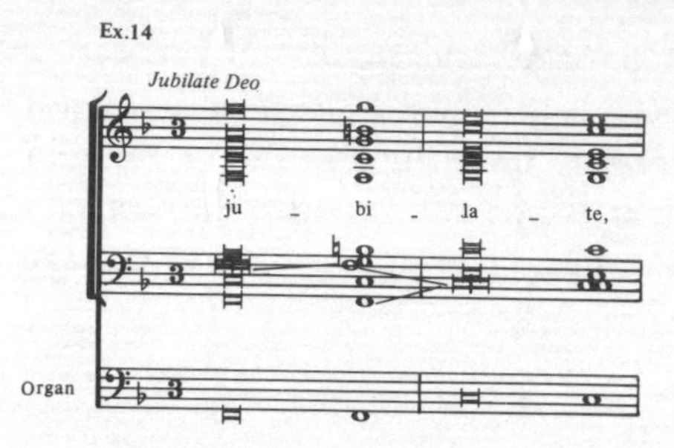

The use of ornaments in instrumental music led to an extensive use of harmonic and melodic sequences. They are found in church music too, and sometimes give a remarkable effect. The climax of 'Benedictus es Dominus' shows the solemn chords which often announce a doxology, made still more exalted in spirit not only by a chromatic change within the phrase but now by its simple repetition a tone higher:

Ex.15

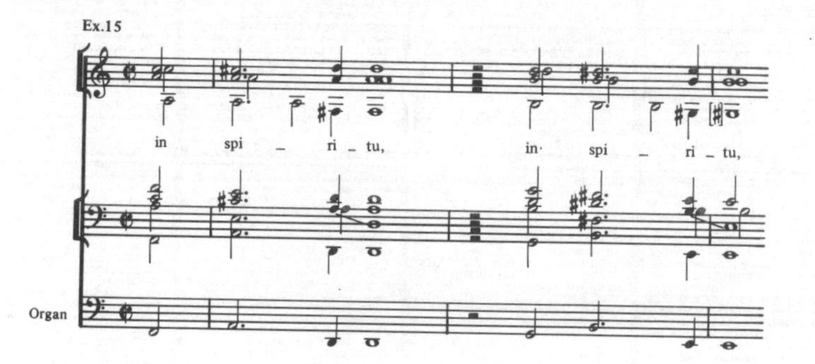

Not content with this, after four measures of glowing polyphony for the second choir, he repeats the whole process a fourth higher, to tremendous effect. There is a similar, if less dramatic, moment in 'O quam gloriosa', and a further one which is every bit as dramatic at the same emotional stage where the closing section begins in 'In ecclesiis'. The sequential progression is not confined to such places. It permeates whole sections as an organizing device, shaping a melody which has shed all the vestiges of contrapuntal development. Written in the trio notation which is its basic conception, the following passage from the double choir 'Hodie completi sunt' becomes evident as the direct antithesis of polyphonic writing of the old way, and the herald of much decorative trio writing of the later seventeenth century (see Example 16).

In this last passage the harmony does not always follow the sequential pattern and it sounds rather strange and inefficient when its bass and treble move in downward steps, while the middle parts do not fill in the chords

very convincingly to a modern ear. Gabrieli's harmonic idiom in these motets has altered radically from that of his earlier music. There are admittedly the same chains of 'perfect cadence' progressions, even in such a work as the 'Litany for the Blessed Virgin' the very length of which means that the fifths and fourths of the bass pall long before the end. And when sevenths become an integral part of the chords, a succession of these quasi-cadences can sound like the 'circle of fifths' which made harmony finally tonal in the music of Corelli and his imitators. What makes this different from such music of more than half a century later is the lack of a true overall modulatory scheme. It is not difficult to see how enlivened the 160 bars of the 'Litany', to take an extreme example, could have become by using the tonal centre of D as a base from which forays into related keys could be made. In the event, there is more than enough movement from D—to G, A, F, and their related dominants—but no feeling of an overall pattern. It was not a problem that had arisen before, and does not especially affect smaller-scale pieces or those which have a more varied texture. The change from *cori spezzati* and counterpoint to concertante interplay between single voices makes such harmonic considerations a pressing matter, and it was several decades before really satisfactory solutions were found.

Chromaticism

In the meantime, Gabrieli turned to other things to maintain harmonic interest: most particularly, to chromaticism. This now occurs very rarely in the linear form which Lasso had used, and which Gabrieli had followed in one or two early works. The concept is virtually always harmonic. There are, as we have seen in 'Benedictus es Dominus', grand moments when a chromatic chord progression seems to ascend to a climax, but these are less frequent than more casual changes of direction. In the 'Litany' they are not uncommon. A cadence in A major is followed immediately by a chord of F; a G is sharpened in mid-phrase to allow an intermediate cadence in A; the same is done to transfer the key centre quickly from G to D since the G sharp allows for a natural resolution in a dominant chord of the new key; and there are a host of false relations which allow the implications of a cadence to be abruptly turned aside. At the words 'Agnus Dei qui tollis peccata mundi' there is the device found in Gabrieli's early works and in those of other composers searching to enrich the sound of two chords, of juxtaposing one major chord with another major chord based on the root of a third below. This occurs sometimes as a direct confrontation (there is a splendidly uplifting example in 'Suscipe' and another in 'Vox Domini') and sometimes with passing notes intervening, as in 'Benedictus es Dominus' where a half-cadence on G turns to a moment of supreme glory, as the bass leads to E, allowing suspended dissonance to succeed suspended dissonance (see Example 17).

There are other places where a similar progression provides a break in regular patterns, as in the highly conventional triple section of 'Cantate Domino' to the words 'et benedicite nomen ejus', a C major—A major juxtaposition gives life to a succession of perfect cadences; and at the end of 'Confitebor tibi', a final summing up in some four bars of coda is made possible by an E flat chord denying the inevitable tonic of G major (a progression made all the more effective because some dozen bars earlier the tonic had been succeeded by a B flat chord in a similar situation).

All in all, there is a much greater freedom in this use of chromaticism than in Gabrieli's sixteenth-century music. Yet we must remember that the years of his maturity are those of Gesualdo and Monteverdi. Compared with any number in the former's *Il sesto libro de madrigali a cinque voci* (1611), or with the latter's 'Piagn'e sospira' from *Il quarto libro de madrigali a cinque voci* (1603), Gabrieli's most novel effects pale into insignificance. Giovanni Gabrieli was perhaps the most advanced composer in Venice in the first decade of the seventeenth century: but that is not saying very

much. Even in church music, the memory of Monteverdi's great Vespers psalms and Magnificats puts his originality in perspective. Even so the work of the avant-garde madrigalists helps to explain the details of the Gabrielian idiom, as the examination of his pupils' music has made clear. Partly it explains the new spirit which is all-pervading in these motets;

for what the madrigalists are attempting, so is Gabrieli. These 'innovations', the irregular rhythms in melody, the rapid changes of tonality implicit in his chromaticism, are meant to give the music less predictability and greater nervous energy. They are devices for giving sudden contrast. Contrast had no doubt been inherent in the *musica spezzata* from its inception, and yet its limitations are self-evident; in the end, a sophisticated composer will want more subtle means. Where better to look than in the modern madrigal?

Manneristic traits in the late motets

In discovering these new ways, Gabrieli discovered something else: a new attitude to the words. We may wonder whether it was a welcome by-product for his organist's abstract musical mind. Nonetheless, it could scarcely be ignored, and affected certain works in some depth. It is indeed tempting to describe the penitential motet 'Timor et tremor' as a sacred madrigal. It is almost a complete compendium of modern devices. Its opening is a vivid depiction of a verbal phrase. The jagged sixth leap is straight out of a Monteverdi madrigal; the gap in the melody is a 'sospiro', after Marenzio, a cliché of secular music; the ornament uses thirds in an eccentric manner; all these are the hallmarks of the final phase of the madrigal. The passage gains its full force if placed, as suggested by the late Manfred Bukofzer in a most perceptive comparison,[17] side by side with a setting of the same words by his uncle Andrea (see Example 18).

The passage which follows is necessarily less intense, but it is not in any sense conventional. Wide leaps express the words 'et caligo cecidit' (and darkness fell), and both chromaticism and dissonance maintain the atmosphere, create the vividness of Judgement Day. Finally come the words 'ne

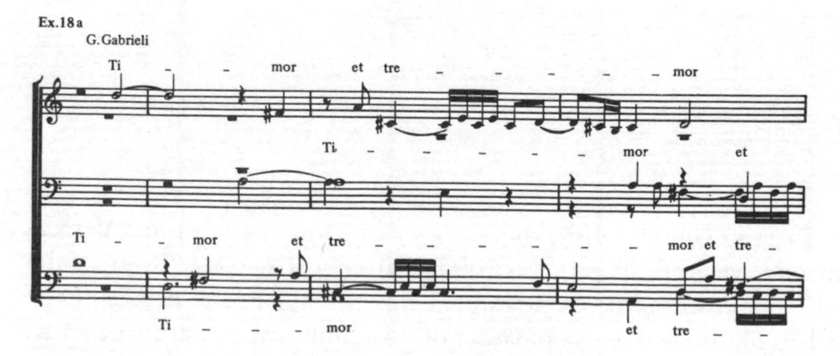

[17] M. Bukofzer, *Music in the Baroque Era* (New York, 1947), p. 22.

After Bukofzer, pp.22-3 (values in (a) reduced)

confundar in aeternum'. Gabrieli changes to triple time and uses a chromatic scale. The one produces its own confounding by syncopations, the other by strange harmonies:

Another comparison shows the astonishing mannerism of the style. The chromatic scale in another penitential motet of a quarter of a century earlier, Guami's 'In die tribulationis', is used in a similarly contrapuntal way, yet its measured tread and orderly development in long phrases are far from the almost neurotic fragmentation of Gabrieli's work. For all these reasons it is tempting to think of 'Timor et tremor' as a madrigal. It seems to be in the new Monteverdian style. But in performance it does not sound Monteverdian. We are very conscious of its sonorousness, and its central section is choral in a sense that very few of this mannered kind of madrigals are. Moreover, the proportions of the work are more ample than those of the highly concentrated madrigal of the early seventeenth century, none of which would have gone to the lengths of extension found in the triple section, nor have provided its expansive coda, which uses the sequence to act as a grand ritardando of both tempo and emotion. 'Timor et tremor' is madrigalian while remaining essentially a grand motet. It is yet another example of the Gabrielian compromise.

The mixture of traditional cori spezzati and mannerist techniques

There are many others. The festal setting of the psalm 'Exaudi me' for four choirs at first sight looks like an essay in the old ways. Two *cori gravi* and two *cori acuti* give no sign of any special instrumentation, and the lack of treble clefs suggests a modest sonority, as befits the sombre nature of the text. The first choir sets off in conventional enough counterpoint, even to the use of the 'canzona' rhythm; but at the beginning of the second phrase comes the word 'cogito', which duly receives an ornament; then, after some rather fine imitative counterpoint giving sustained dissonances, comes the word 'tremenda', for which a turn is developed throughout the parts. The second choir enters with smoother flowing melody, but this does not last long, for the word 'movendi' produces a double 'sospiro', two rests separating the three syllables. Choir IV enters with the most extensive piece of polyphony yet, lasting more than a dozen bars, and throwing into strong relief the adjacent music. For when the third choir comes in, it is to the word 'tremens', and to the musical figure of 'tremor' in 'Timor et tremor' (as in Example 9 above). The word 'timeo' again produces the 'sigh' motif. Then the dialogue is joined, the tuttis resound. The material expounded earlier is invoked and repeated in amplified forms until at the astonishing climax, the phrase 'quando caeli movendi sunt' receives its most graphic illustration, as the 'double sospiro' echoes through the choirs at half a beat's distance (see Example 20).

A substantial coda asserts order after this cataclysm, with a polyphonic web full of rich dissonance and ending with a grand plagal cadence. If we think back to Andrea's *Penitential Psalms,* or even those of Lasso, we realize the amazing intensity of Giovanni Gabrieli's late style. Only

Gesualdo or Monteverdi equalled this nervous tautness, and that in very different musical circumstances.

Comparison of early and late settings of 'O Jesu mi dulcissime'

A final comparison may throw light on the spiritual and musical development of Gabrieli. Two of his finest motets are settings of the Christmas text 'O Jesu mi dulcissime'. Both are for double choir, and indeed it is the earlier that is the more obviously enterprising in the disposition of its forces, with a *coro semi-acuto* and a *coro grave*, while the later is for two equal groups. But neither is really a study in sonority, and neither actually needs instruments. Both are shaped in the same way, long phrases for the individual choirs at the beginning, close dialogue for the words 'adoro te', rapture at the homophonic climax 'O Christe', an even mightier climax for tutti at 'O divina ergo proles', and exciting rhythms for 'ut veneremur'. The differences are thus less in conception than in detail, but these details make the later work much more emotional than the earlier one—which, in its turn, belongs amongst the richest of the *Sacrae Symphoniae* of 1597. It is not just the dotted-note ornaments[18] in the opening

[18] A comparison of the vocal parts with the *basso per l'organo* suggests that passages written with even quavers were sometimes performed with dotted rhythms.

phrase in the later setting, compared with the straightforward melody of the earlier, not even the advanced chromaticism which gives strength to its climaxes, though admittedly this helps to create an air of baroque sophistication by the side of which the sixteenth-century setting seems innocent. It is when dissonance, angular melody, and ornament all combine that we feel the full emotion made possible by Gabrieli's mastery of the new techniques (see Example 21).

These works possess an intensity that is quintessential Gabrieli. If they seem here to take pride of place among his later compositions, it is because they are unique in the history of church music, and also because their spirit is rarely lacking completely in the grander pieces of the 1615 collections.

Developments in the use of instruments in church music

In turning to works which are without doubt Venetian in their grandeur, this spirit of nervousness combined with faith and confidence often goes by unnoticed, sometimes because other features are more noticeable. Gabrieli's sense of instrumental sonority is the most obvious, as is shown by the markings on the pages of partbooks of several motets. In a number of them, indeed, the instruments are provided with symphonies or separate parts, which is still unusual enough in 1615 for their role to dominate our attention. More interesting than the mere existence of such markings and parts are what they reveal about Gabrieli's favourite sounds, which are not

quite those expected from reading Praetorius or even looking at Giovanni's own instrumental music. Not that the instruments themselves are unusual; cornetts, violins, and trombones are the staple fare, as is clear from the pay-books of the basilica. Their disposition is surprising, since the lower instruments usually predominate over the upper, making for a sound more subdued than brilliant. There is probably a technical explanation for this. With a choir relatively weak in the soprano register, and relatively strong in basses and tenors, a top-heavy application of instrumental sound would pose difficulties of balance. And if the choir was itself weaker than the instrumental ensemble, as seems likely, this would encourage a subdued tone-colour for the latter. Whether technical in origin or not, the comparative sombreness of some of these motets is undeniably impressive, and seems to fit the intensity of Gabrieli's last years.

Perhaps the finest example comes from the *Sacrae Symphoniae*, a motet in praise of St. John the Baptist, 'Suscipe'. Whether this was written for St. Mark's must be somewhat doubtful, since neither of the festivals of St. John the Baptist were among the important saints' days in the ducal chapel. Still, the resources deployed are those of the basilica, for the motet is conceived for two choirs, one of voices, the other of trombones. The uppermost voice is an alto, and not even a very high one. The deepest trombone plays the C below the stave as its lowest note. Thus the tonal range is restricted, the colours are anything but bright and gay, the mood anything but that of rejoicing. The technical problem of making such an ensemble effective is challenging. Voices cannot be matched on totally equal terms, and when the altos are not singing, it would be easy for the lower voices to be swamped even by the softer-toned trombones of the period. For the most part, Gabrieli does not try to match them on equal terms. When all the vocal lines are engaged he may use the same thematic material for both groups. Elsewhere he is careful either to reduce the number of trombones playing, or he gives the voices more ornamental material which will by its very nature attract attention. Nowhere does he shirk the problem by pitting the vocal group against the brass in the usual *cori spezzati* manner. The voices are virtually always accompanied by the trombones, and there are a series of duets, for pairs of altos, tenors, and basses. The skill in balancing these varied groupings goes far beyond that of earlier polychoral music, as can be seen at the first grand climax, where the instruments hold long notes, while the counterpoint of voices flourishes against them (see Example 22).

The sombre mood is reinforced by the devices of the 'mannered' motets already discussed. There are clusters of dissonances, ornaments with irregularly resolved passing notes, melody rendered unstable by sudden fast movements of semiquavers among sedate white notes, and expressive augmented and diminished intervals. The bass proceeds in the customary fourths and fifths, but the cadences are less often predictably in the major, and though there is a certain sprightliness in the setting of the last word of the phrase 'Tu solus Dominus altissimus' (the motif is almost always the same one Gabrieli had used for 'Ut vulnera' in the 1597 'O Domine Jesu Christe'), at the succeeding 'Jesu Christe' the slow-moving notes and emotional harmonies return.

The same darker tone is implied in the incomplete markings of 'Misericordia tua' where Gabrieli specifies voices for the uppermost parts of the three choirs, while all the lower parts are suitable for trombones. Again the voices stand out from the instruments by the use of ornamental figures, and by more flowing melody in the strangely indecisive alleluja, in which major chords on main accents are quite rare. This is more conventional in its *spezzato* design than 'Suscipe', and has something approaching the sheer power of the grand 'Sonata à 15' from the *Canzoni e Sonate*, beginning with and developing the canzona motto in much the same way. There are no instrumental indications at all in the even more superb Marian motet 'O Gloriosa Virgo', but by analogy with the other works it must require three voices—all tenors—and nine trombones. The voices are rarely extended beyond their middle ranges, and their frequent embellishments are passionate rather than brilliant, even though they include some virtuosic demisemiquavers; they nearly all reinforce the verbal idea—flourishes on such words as 'protege nos' or 'defende nos' and the cries of the tenors 'O gloriosa Virgo' at the end of the motet. But the emotional flavour of the work derives more from such touches as the chromaticisms when the sinner craves the intercession of the Blessed Virgin in his desire to have his sins forgiven, and the richness gained from delaying notes and their resolution:

'O Gloriosa Virgo' is a *spezzato* work, and uses that idiom with an incredible mastery. Long phrases mixed with quickly moving dialogue, repetitions of a whole section to give a sense of shape, interruptions of one choir by another, the grand tutti for the beginning of the final section, all sum up the idiom begun decades earlier. Indeed the grand tutti might have been the work of Andrea, except that the uppermost note of its choral exclamation 'O'[gloriosa Virgo] is middle C. The motet has an inward warmth, not the extrovert self-confidence of Andrea. Even with the unreliable text left us by Giovanni's legatee and editor, Grani, it is one of the finest Marian motets to survive from Venice.

'Jubilate Deo', in its ten part setting included in the *Sacrae Symphoniae*, is a festival piece, and 'Surrexit Christus' was clearly meant for Easter Day, when the full panoply of St. Mark's was on display. It is therefore surprising that these too are introverted works; but both are comparatively restrained, in orchestration at least. There are cornetts, it is true; but the only other 'upper' instruments are a pair of 'violins' (in fact the alto members of the family, what today we would call violas).[19] The lower parts are for trombones and a bassoon, while the necessary voices are a counter-tenor, tenor, and bass, with perhaps a soprano in 'Jubilate Deo'.

Both pieces are classical Venetian ceremonial music to the extent of being rondo motets, and 'Jubilate Deo', with its triple-time tutti refrain, seems very traditional. The main novelty in each is the addition of an instrumental *sinfonia*, which can be omitted at will for 'Jubilate Deo', but which is an essential in 'Surrexit Christus'. Both *sinfonie* are short—about the same size as an organ prelude or *intonazione*, from which the idea of using instruments to precede the voices may derive. Each uses the canzona rhythm at the onset and develops a contrapuntal point on a small scale. Neither attempts to exploit the full strength of the ensemble, and the *sinfonia* of 'Jubilate Deo' remains introductory in nature. That for 'Surrexit Christus', on the other hand, returns after the first vocal section, as though it were the refrain in a rondo structure. On its second appearance, however, the contrapuntal motif is developed at some further length, and has acquired by the cadence considerable emotional strength. Surprisingly, Gabrieli does not return to it throughout the motet. For this reason, 'Surrexit Christus' is not as impressive as other Easter Day motets; and perhaps the restraint of the instruments balancing the small vocal forces contributes to this feeling. The formal pattern is nevertheless significant. The accompanied solos between the refrains are akin to those in the *Sacrae Cantilene* of Croce, and even (though hymns of necessity offer a clearer

[19] See D. Boyden, *The History of Violin Playing* (London, 1965).

opportunity towards firm structures) Monteverdi's setting of 'Ave Maris Stella' in his Vespers music. Gabrieli's plan allows for greater variety in the 'episodes', deploying the individual voices in different combinations, and changing the accompaniment from a small group of instruments (there are only three for the first solo) to the grand tutti (in the ultimate trio). Nevertheless, the piece lacks the sheer energy of 'Jubilate Deo' which, after the initial *sinfonia*, is the more conventional work. Here the refrain is like those of many of the double-choir motets of the later period, its strength deriving not only from its rhythmic vitality but from the accumulation of passing notes on the unaccented parts of the bar. There is more octave doubling than hitherto, and not only between the bass lines. Hence the counterpoints are less complex, but there is no shortage of good part-writing in some of the sections in between the refrains. The greatest excitement, on the other hand, comes in the dialogue passages, very closely argued in some places, with crisply brief phrases, its dynamic syncopation made still more vivid by the alternation of opposite groups:

This alternation is obviously derived from *musica spezzata*, but now transplanted to music where contrast by spatial separation has been replaced by contrast in orchestral colour. Technically speaking 'Jubilate Deo' is not quite as enterprising as 'Suscipe', for it does not attempt a new relationship between voices and instruments. The uppermost line, though marked 'cornetto', is little different from the high soprano parts of other works, and if uncomfortable for a singer, is not utterly impossible. Two other motets in the volume face this problem more squarely and offer a different solution. These are 'Quem vidistis pastores' and 'In ecclesiis'. Both are marked 'a 14' in the index, but, as one modern editor has pointed out,[20] the latter, at least, is 'a 15', for its organ part is not a basso seguente, but a genuinely independent basso continuo; and without the organ in this new role neither makes musical sense.[21]

Quem vidistis pastores

The format of 'Quem vidistis pastores' is traditional. It is a motet for Christmas Day, incorporating within its text the words so beautifully set by Gabrieli in his earliest days at St. Mark's, 'O magnum mysterium'. The partbooks indicate a double-choir setting. Nor are the 'choirs' particularly unusual: cornett, trombones, and bassoon combined with countertenors, tenors, and basses. The *sinfonia* looks like a *canzona à 8* such as Raverii had published, quite large-scale and with considerable interplay between the opposing groups. So far the organ follows the harmony, and indeed the instrumental 'alleluja' in triple time looks utterly conventional. But then voices enter, and at once the organist becomes an accompanist, as first a tenor, then a countertenor, and then two more tenors sing solos. These take up nearly a hundred bars, and are followed by a series of ensembles in which the organ follows the lowest vocal line, but is nevertheless required to fill in otherwise sparse harmony. The solo sections take up much more than half the motet, and one is hard put to find a model for them. Viadana does not construct his concertos in this manner; Croce's concertante motets are more restricted in scope, and can hardly be compared with Gabrieli's, whose idiomatic writing for solo voice, with *passaggi* and chromatics, goes far beyond the simple quasi-contrapuntal vocal phrases of his *maestro di cappella*. A certain duet section suggests Gabrieli's model. At the words 'et natum carum pariter', the florid lines for tenors remind one of a madrigal in Monteverdi's *Quinto libro*, 'Ahi com'a un vago sol'. It is one of the six at the end of the book for which the continuo part was essential, and which most historians have regarded as a landmark in the history of the genre. We have seen that Gabrieli's pupils knew the volume, and presumably he too had studied it. His pupils, apparently, were directed towards the madrigals in which the continuo was 'a beneplacito', as stated on the title page, for none of them included such revolutionary pieces in their graduation volumes. Their master was more daring (see Example 25).

[20] F. Hudson in the preface to his edition of 'Quem vidistis pastores' (Zurich, 1970).
[21] As printed in Winterfeld III, p. 73.

Gabrieli again follows Monteverdi's continuo madrigals in closing with a tutti section. 'O magnum mysterium' becomes a grand climax, with passing notes providing richly clashing harmonies, and then the whole phrase repeated a tone higher, to increase its brilliance. Then come the chromaticisms, the embellished lines, the dissonances, the splendid sonorities which we have seen, for example, in the second setting of another Christmas text, 'O Jesu mi dulcissime', until the music bursts into one of Gabrieli's finest allelujas. No devotional plagal progression brings 'Quem vidistis pastores' to a close, but a grand perfect cadence, full of octave doublings to reinforce the release of tension when suspensions resolve, and with the delayed arrival of one part on the major third of the final chord, so that we retain the feeling of confidence to the very end.

In ecclesiis

The text of 'In ecclesiis' applies to no specific Venetian feast, and this is no doubt why it was found useful enough to be published in both the *Sacrae Symphoniae* and the *Reliquiae Sacrorum Concentuum*. There are three choirs, one of which is marked *cappella*; but the other two are not the *coro acuto* and *coro grave* of the Magnificats and Masses. Instead one is a four-part group, each line designated for a singer. The other is an instrumental ensemble, for three cornetts, a 'violino'—i.e. viola, and two trombones. It is a rondo motet, with traditional triple-time alleluja refrain, a *sinfonia*, and a grand climax, with solemn chords announcing the ultimate phase of the work. What is new is the way these devices are used. The piece is clearly sectional. It can virtually be divided into 'movements', each with its own resources, solo or ensemble, chorus or orchestra, normally finishing on a cadence which marks the division from its neighbour. But the *sinfonia*, instead of preceding the whole as an *intonazione* would, bursts in on the final chord of the second statement of the alleluja. The idea of solo sections probably came from Croce's pioneer work; but Croce never thought of making so strong a differentiation between solo and tutti as Gabrieli does. The differences arise in the first place in texture. These solo sections mostly have an organ accompaniment, implying a necessary filling in of harmonies. In addition, in many places, the voices are given ornaments to sing. The *cappella*, on the contrary, is written in solid chordal blocks, with a severe unembellished melody. The skills of the instrumental body are more fully extended; the cornettists in particular are given frequent 'backfalls' and other semiquaver figurations, and all are allowed to play the dotted rhythms which come so naturally to instruments which articulate with the tongue. This is truly concertante music, in which contrasts between resources and skills are assumed in the way of the later concerto; and at the same time in principle it is little different from the later Baroque cantata. The individual sections need broadening out and making into separate entities, the role of the orchestra enlarging, the insistance on a refrain removing, and there appears in embryo the work of J. S. Bach.

But 'In ecclesiis' is a typically Gabrielian masterpiece. The solo sections have the confidence of strong rhythms and short memorable phrases; the harmonies are clear-cut, and indeed in the opening section for soprano, a repeated figure in the bass reminds us of the ostinato patterns which were now beginning to be exploited, and which became so popular simply because they were easily remembered:

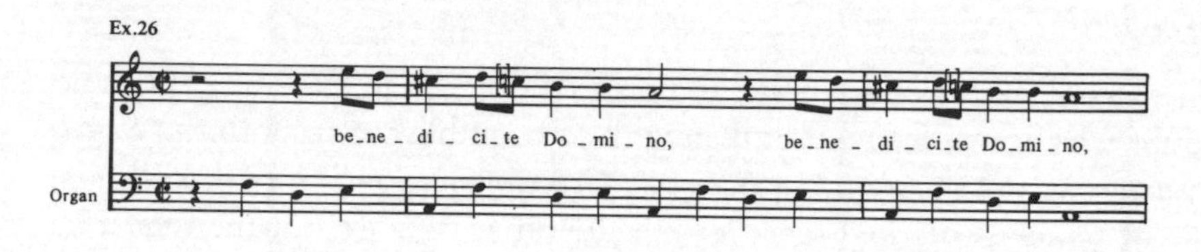

The *sinfonia* is another brief interlude rather than an extended canzona, though the 'motto' rhythm opens it; Gabrieli exploits the more brilliant register of the cornetts, and the capacity of trombones to hold bass notes firmly. The alleluja is remarkable for its varied repetitions, as the first

'vocal' choir opposes the *cappella*, initially with a single voice, then with two (alto and tenor), then with another two (cantus and bassus), finally with the tutti. At the powerful climax all the forces are assembled. There are block chords for the repeated 'Deus', now enhanced by the chromatic changes, F major—D major—G major—E major. These culminate in a short sustained passage on the words 'adjutor noster'. Then the 'Deus' chords return—B flat major—G major—E major—and the sustained music is then extended in sonorities which can scarcely be equalled anywhere else in Gabrieli's *oeuvre*, which outdo his uncle's music, and which even the Roman polychoralists such as Benevoli can hardly rival, for all their larger resources. There is a dominant pedal, held by trombones and the bass of the *cappella*, reiterated by the cantus of the *cappella* and the violins. Over it, the soloists of the first choir embellish rising scales, as also do the cornetts. All are placed in the most favourable part of their ranges (assuming male voices and a variety of cornetts) so that they make a full sound. In these conditions, the resolution on a tonic chord is awaited with a rising tension unequalled in music of the early seventeenth century (see Example 27).

Summing-up of Gabrieli's achievement in the new idiom

To end our discussion of Gabrieli's music with 'In ecclesiis' is fitting for many reasons. It is characteristic of Venetian grandeur. It uses the tradition of *cori spezzati* built up over three-quarters of a century, and could well have been splendidly performed by the virtuosi of Bassano's ensemble and perhaps Martinengo's new quartet in the galleries of St. Mark's, with the *cappella* 'sul palchetto' accompanied by Priuli at the *organo piccolo*. It is appropriate music for Doge and Senate, for it is music which is concerned to impress, to convey power and dignity. It is also undeniably personal to Gabrieli. It is music of immense technique, by a composer interested in shape and balance. It has variety in its unity; and because each 'choir' is treated idiomatically it no longer needs the particular circumstances of St. Mark's. The flourishes of the soloists over the held chords of a choir, the isolation of these soloists to be accompanied by the organ, the care not to obliterate them with the orchestra even when the latter is deeply involved, make 'In ecclesiis' possible for any large church. The particular has become general, devices have been modified into an established idiom. More than that, the Venetian stateliness has acquired a strong emotional tint. The plea 'Deus, Deus, adjutor noster' could have been set in a louder, more strident way if Giovanni had simply followed the manner of his uncle. It has instead a fierce joy which seems to sum up the belief of a devout man, whose mature years have been spent entirely in the service of his church. His desire for earthly glory has gone: the fashionable world of the madrigal and the theatrical entertainments of the rich North Italian courts have been well lost for the life of the organ loft, of the teacher and the security of the Venetian civil service. We shall never know if it had been a happy life: but we must be grateful for it, since the works it has left for us are among the glories of musical history, a fine testament to Venice, the Counter-Reformation, and the religious spirit of man.

Envoi

12 Agosto 1612
Il S. Zuanne Gabrieli d'anni 58 da mal de pietra g^{ni} 18 med^{o} il Cerchieri
S. Samuel.

Thus the Health Authority[1] recorded Gabrieli's death from a kidney stone. He had been ill at various times in the previous eight years, as we know from the Procurators' minute book, for they had had to find a substitute for him on several occasions. He was buried in the church of S. Stefano, where his confessor and now executor was one of the community of Augustines in the adjacent monastery. At the Scuola Grande di S. Rocco Priuli acted in his stead at the annual festival on 16 August, and eventually, after some disputation, Giambattista Grillo was given Gabrieli's sinecure there.[2] At St. Mark's there was no need even for the usual competition, since one of the substitutes of the past years, Gianpolo Savii, had been promised the post for the last two years.[3] His last pupil, Heinrich Schütz, to whom Gabrieli while dying had given his ring, left within a few months. By 1613 Giovanni Gabrieli was already being forgotten in Venice.

The amount of his unpublished manuscript music must have been extraordinarily large, for hardly any of the past fifteen years' work had yet appeared in print, and it might be thought that, just as Giovanni had performed this service for his uncle within a year of his death, so might some Venetian colleague have collected it together and seen it through the press. But it was three years before the motets and instrumental pieces were published by Magni; and then the editors were the executor Taddeo, and a pupil who was a member of the St. Mark's ensemble, Alvise Grani. Neither proved very competent at this task: both the *Sacrae Symphoniae* and the *Canzoni e Sonate* are full of misprints, in a way that the volume of *Concerti* of 1587 is not. The dedicatees of both volumes are Germans, the

[1] See D. Arnold, 'Towards a biography of Giovanni Gabrieli', *Musica Disciplina*, XV (1961), p. 207.

[2] Archivio di S. Rocco, Registro della Terminazioni, Reg. 4, f. 192v; entry for 28 August 1612 records the decision to elect Grillo. This was then challenged by supporters of Giovanni Picchi (one of whose works is contained in the Fitzwilliam Virginal Book) on 11 March of the following year. A new election was therefore ordered and the final decision confirming the election of Grillo was made 21 March 1614; ibid, f. 209v.

[3] Caffi, I, p. 211.

abbot of the monastery of SS. Ulrich and Afra at Augsburg, and the Duke of Bavaria. And in fact only in Germany, where his life as a composer had started, was Gabrieli's name kept alive, largely because his pupils could never forget him. In Venice his name occasionally appears in the list of organists of St. Mark's when a writer of a guide book wishes to extol the virtues of the basilica's musical history. There is no sign that his music was ever performed there again.

Attitude to the past in the early seventeenth century

The greatest composers of the early sixteenth century were, it is true, generally forgotten almost as soon as they died, but the early years of the seventeenth century were slightly different. A historical attitude was growing. Palestrina and his fellow Romans were not so completely put aside. St. Mark's even bought some of their music not long after Gabrieli's death,[4] and the tradition thus established continued in Venice throughout the Baroque period. Croce's music had been copied into choir books during his lifetime and certain of his works are still preserved in manuscript scores in the Biblioteca Marciana when they have not survived in printed sources.[5] Yet there is not a note of Gabrieli among the manuscripts of that library, and only an incomplete copy of the *Concerti* (1587) in its printed collection. Gabrieli seems to have been neglected completely in the last 180 years of the Venetian Republic. The most valuable body of unpublished music is to be found in the Murhardsche und Landesbibliothek at Kassel, a relic of the link between Gabrieli and the Landgraves of Hesse so firmly cemented by the studies of Heinrich Schütz. A less ample but scarcely less significant source is now in Vienna, where it has lain probably since Ferdinand II moved from Graz to take up the office of Holy Roman Emperor in 1619. And the only contemporary score of the first book of *Sacrae Symphoniae* was in the possession of the monastery of SS. Ulrich and Afra until it passed into the hands of the Staatsbibliothek in Augsburg. The manuscripts of keyboard tablatures now in Turin are in a German notation, while the works printed by the anthologists, Woltz and Schmid, confirm Gabrieli's transalpine reputation.

[4] A.S.V., Proc. de Supra, Registro 35, f. 1v.

[5] Although one must use the catalogue with considerable caution; Palestrina's Mass *Iste Confessor* is attributed to Croce in one manuscript.

New developments as the reasons for Gabrieli's declining reputation

The reason why Gabrieli's music faded into obscurity so rapidly in Italy is simply that musical style was changing so quickly. His compromise with the new methods of Viadana was not enough. Virtually all composers who took to the concertante manner were willing to break away from the past, the traditions of counterpoint or *cori spezzati*. The motet and mass for a few voices accompanied by organ had conquered completely by 1620. The musicians who were working in Venice were swept with the tide. Grani and Grandi of St. Mark's, Giulio Belli and Giacomo Finetti of the Frari, Grillo and Usper of the confraternities all composed in this medium. Monteverdi's position at St. Mark's ensured him the full range of resources available to anyone in Venice, and his experience included the composition of his Vespers music at Mantua, so that he might seem to be the obvious person to carry on the Gabrielian ways; yet he published no music in this style in the second or third decades of the century, and very little in his retrospective volumes at the end of his life. Then there was the changing orchestra. Bassano, master of the cornett, died in 1617, and an unknown Paduan took his place among the *piffari* of the Doge. Thereafter we hear little of cornettists among the records of the basilica until 1640, when the art has died out so thoroughly that a special bursary has to be offered to find someone willing to study it.[6] St. Mark's was not without virtuosi in the seventeenth century: they are violinists such as Biagio Marini and later Carlo Fedeli. The skill of the trombonists which had made Gabrieli's canzonas possible seems much less in evidence in the Venetian church music of Monteverdi; and certainly Cavalli's mid-century *Messa Concertata* does not call for it.

Spiritually, also, Gabrieli's kind of music became unfashionable. That religious intensity which we have seen to be so characteristic of his last phase disappeared from the artistic life of the Republic. It is significant that the so-called Jesuit architecture which flowers in the imitations (if that is not too strong a word) of the Church of the Gesù in Rome does not find much of a place in Venice at this time. Nor were the Venetian painters so interested in depicting the newly canonized saints, St. Ignatius, St. Charles Borromeo, and St. Teresa.[7]

[6] Caffi, II, p. 59.
[7] R. Wittkower, *Art and Architecture in Italy 1600–1750* (London, 1958), p. 17.

Monteverdi's influence in Venice

Monteverdi's own style was much calmer than it had been during his Mantuan period. Alessandro Grandi showed elements of extreme emotionalism in some solo motets published in the 1620s, but most of his larger-scale works are equally un-mannerist, and the concertante motets of his earlier Venetian years are not in the least Gabrielian. This mood may be connected with the disappearance of the Jesuits from Venice. During the interdict of 1606, they were banished from the Republic, which did not re-admit them for another fifty years. The fervour they were capable of creating wherever they went was thus lost to Venice. Certainly the cool though exhilarating church of S. Maria della Salute, the most characteristic monument of Venetian architecture built in the first half of the century, is quite different in atmosphere from their churches, just as Monteverdi's psalm settings for St. Mark's are quite different from the effusions of the grand Baroque, the colossal polychoral (but not Gabrielian) Masses of the Roman, Benevoli.

Gabrieli's surviving reputation in Germany

The Jesuits were very much in evidence, however, across the Alps. Around the turn of the century, the bishops of Salzburg, Breslau, Olmütz, Augsburg, Würzburg, and Passau had all been students at the Collegium Germanicum in Rome. Whether it was a result of this or whether this in itself reflects the fervour of the Church in Northern and Central Europe, there can be no doubt of the emotional intensity of much German church music. Not that this is confined to the Roman Catholic Church: Lutheranism also found value in sumptuous music. The considerable output of Michael Praetorius, much of it written for *cori spezzati*, Schütz's splendid *Psalms of David* published in 1619, a host of works which appeared in the twenty years after Gabrieli's death show quite clearly that all the churches desired to persuade their congregations of the glory of God by the use of all the musical devices known to man. This taste for the massive cannot be traced in more than a general way to the work of the younger Gabrieli. Even the psalm settings of Schütz, in spite of a host of details which tell of the composer's studies with his Italian master are quite different in effect.[8] In atmosphere, the path to the German 'colossal' Baroque seems to come more from the post-Lepanto works of Andrea, by way of Hans Leo

[8] See D. Arnold, 'Schütz's Venetian Psalms', *Musical Times*, CXIII (1972).

Hassler, Aichinger, and the less intense contemporaries of Giovanni in Venice.

Gabrieli's deep influence on German music of the seventeenth century

Nonetheless, the trail of pupils to St. Mark's had left its mark on German music. Though doubtless their royal masters had sent them to Italy to learn to compose in a way that would glorify them as Gabrieli's music did the Venetian Republic, the strongest impressions which these young Germans and Danes brought back seem to have been rather of the mannered madrigal. Italian madrigals were not, of course, very much use in their home territory. Their heavy-drinking, military monarchs were not likely to appreciate the subtlety of late Renaissance musical imagery. Gabrieli, on the other hand, had shown that church music could absorb both its idiom and its mood. It was no coincidence that 'Timor et tremor' was printed first in Nuremberg. It combined the attractions of modernity and utility: it was composed for church use, while a young musician could feel that he was keeping among the ranks of the avant-garde by imitating it. It was fervent music for a place where religious fervour was an essential ingredient of life. It offered a way of continuing that Counter-reformation tradition of the last years of Lasso, whose religious melancholy seems the logical result of the overwhelming devotion of his Bavarian masters.[9]

Schein, Schütz, and Demantius did not neglect the advances brought about by the basso continuo; yet they did take up this Gabrielian attitude.[10] The whole basis of the *Deutsche spruchmotette* lies in its realism, its word painting and symbolism, which is intensified, in Protestant music, by its use of the vernacular. The whole idea of these motets is to heighten the sensitivity of the listener, to shock him by sudden contrasts, to disappoint his expectations, to make melody proceed by strange leaps or impede its movement by seemingly illogical breaks, to take the harmony into strange paths. The very look of the page at the first climax of Schein's motet 'Die mit Tränen' shows the wildness of its feeling (see Example 1).

The Gabrielian features are obvious: the tied notes which, by connecting long to short, automatically heighten rhythmic contrasts, the use of the 'fall', the harmonic sequences which give shape to the whole, the dissonances arising from irregularly taken passing notes. Even nearer to 'Timor et tremor' is a passage from Schein's setting of Psalm 116, 'Das ist mir

[9] Wilhelm V abdicated to take up residence in a monastery in 1597.

[10] See F. Blume, *Die Evangelische Kirchenmusik* (Potsdam, 1931), p. 93.

Ex.1

lieb'. The falling tears of the psalmist are given exactly the same musical image that Gabrieli had found appropriate for his fear[11] (see Example 2).

There is more Gabrielian writing in the setting of the same psalm by Christoph Demantius, though here it does not lie in the use of ornament or violently unorthodox melody, but in the accumulation of suspensions which gives a Venetian richness of harmony. In fact the basic concept of

[11] See Chapter Eleven above.

Ex.2

the book from which these come, a collection of settings of this one psalm compiled by Burckhardt Grossman under the title of *Angst der Hellen und Friede der Seelen*, seems to belong to the Counter-reformation mood of the last phase of Gabrieli's church music (the verse from which the collection takes its title is translated in the Authorized Version 'The sorrows of death compassed me, and the pains of hell gat hold upon me'). The Venetian predilection for psalms, the agony of this particular one mirror Gabrieli's interests also, as revealed in 'Exaudi me' and 'Misericordia tua'.

This realistic, mannered music without doubt arrived in Germany through Gabrieli's pupils. They might have found something similar in the church music of Gesualdo, but there is absolutely no sign that his work was known in Germany. There are one or two pieces by Monteverdi that might have led the same way (in atmosphere rather than technique) but these were not chosen by the anthologist who introduced his church music to German-speaking lands. So clearly it was Gabrieli who set German music on this path. In Schein's *Israels Brünlein*, in Schütz's *Cantiones Sacrae* his memory is kept alive. Schütz lived on, indeed, for sixty years after his master's death and by then the path to J. S. Bach was well prepared. Bach too is a 'mannered' composer, concerned with the word and the musical symbol; he too has known the agony of contemplating death. His D trumpets are the descendants of the Doge's *piffari*, his expectation of virtuosity is that given to Gabrieli by Bassano and his company. So the last word is best left with a German. Schütz came back to Venice after fifteen years. He met Monteverdi and probably other famous musicians. He was not unmindful of their qualities, he learned from their new ways, and seemingly enjoyed Venice once more. But he could not forget

Gabrieli. In a dedication of a book of *Sacrae Symphoniae* (even Gabrieli's titles were still in his mind) he pays a tribute scarcely less moving than that embodied in his respectful imitation of Gabrieli's music:

At Gabrielius, Dij immortales, quantus vir But Gabrieli, immortal Gods, what a man!

Bibliography

G. d'Alessi, Precursors of Adriano Willaert in the practice of *coro spezzato*, *Journal of the American Musicological Association* v (1952) 187–210

C. G. Anthon, *Music and Musicians in Northern Italy during the Sixteenth Century* (Harvard thesis, 1943)

W. Apel, *The History of Keyboard Music* (Bloomington, 1972)

T. Antonicek, *Italienische Musikerlebnisse Ferdinands II. 1598* (Mitteilungen der Kommission für Musikforschung Nr 18, Graz 1968)

D. Arnold, 'Giovanni Croce and the Concertato Style', *Musical Quarterly* xxxix (1953) 37–48

'Instruments in Church: some facts and figures', *Monthly Musical Record*, 85 (1955) 32–38

'Ceremonial Music in Venice at the time of the Gabrielis', *Proceedings of the Royal Musical Association* lxxxii (1955–1956) 47–58

Articles on Andrea and Giovanni Gabrieli in *Die Musik in Geschichte und Gegenwart* (Kassel, 1956)

'Brass instruments in Italian church music of the sixteenth and early seventeenth centuries', *Brass Quarterly* i (1957) 81–92

'Alessandro Grandi, a disciple of Monteverdi', *Musical Quarterly* xliii (1957) 171–86

'Con ogni sorte di stromenti: some practical suggestions', *Brass Quarterly* ii (1959) 99–109

'Andrea Gabrieli und die Entwicklung der "cori-spezzati" Technik', *Die Musikforschung* xii (1959) 258–74

'Music at the Scuola di San Rocco', *Music and Letters* xl (1959) 229–41

'Towards a biography of Giovanni Gabrieli', *Musica Disciplina* xv (1961) 199–207

'The Monteverdian succession at St. Mark's', *Music and Letters* xlii (1961) 205–11

'Gli allievi di Giovanni Gabrieli', *Nuova Rivista Musicale Italiana* v (1971) 943–72

'Schütz's "Venetian Psalms",' *Musical Times* cxiii (1972) 1071–3

Giovanni Gabrieli (London, 1974)

Articles on Andrea and Giovanni Gabrieli in *Grove's Dictionary of Music and Musicians* (Sixth edition, London, 1979)

D. Arnold and N. Fortune ed., *The Monteverdi Companion* (London, 1968)

L. E. Bartholomew, *Alessandro Raverij's collection of Canzoni per sonare* (Michigan, 1963)

G. Bassano, *Ricercate, Passaggi et Cadentie* (Venice, 1585) modern edition ed. R. Erig (Zürich, 1976)

G. S. Bedbrook, 'The genius of Giovanni Gabrieli', *Music Review* viii (1947) 91–101

Keyboard Music from the Middle Ages to the Beginnings of the Baroque (London, 1949)

G. Benvenuti, 'Andrea e Giovanni Gabrieli e la musica strumentale a San Marco', *Istituzioni e Monumenti dell'Arte Musicale Italiana* i (Milan, 1932)

A. Bertolotti, *Musici alla Corte dei Gonzaga in Mantova dal Secolo XV al XVIII* (Milan n.d./R 1969)

F. Blume, *Die Evangelische Kirchenmusik* (Potsdam, 1931)

W. Boetticher, *Orlando di Lasso und seine zeit* (Kassel and Basel, 1958)
Aus Orlando di Lassos Wirkungskreis (Kassel, 1963)
C. Boito ed., *La Basilica di S. Marco in Venezia* (Venice, 1881–1888)
S. Bonta, 'The uses of the sonata da chiesa', *Journal of the American Musicological Society* xxii (1969) 54–84
D. Boyden, *The History of Violin Playing* (London, 1965)
W. Breig, 'Die Lübbenauer tabulaturen Lynar A1 and A2. Eine quellenkundliche studie', *Archiv für Musikwissenschaft* xxv (1968) 96–117 and 223–36
H. M. Brown, *Sixteenth-Century Instrumentation: The Music for the Florentine Intermedii* American Institute of Musicology, 1973)
'A cook's tour of Ferrara in 1529', *Rivista Italiana di Musicologia* x (1975) 216–41
Embellishing Sixteenth-Century Music (London, 1976)
Music in the Renaissance (New Jersey, 1976)
W. Brulez, *Marchands Flamands à Venise I (1568–1605)* (Brussels and Rome 1965) 658
M. Bukofzer, *Music in the Baroque Era* (New York, 1947)
F. Caffi, *Storia della musica sacra nella già cappella ducale di San Marco in Venezia dal 1318 al 1797* (Venice, 1854/R Milan, 1931)
P. Canal, 'Della Musica a Mantova', *Reale Istituto di Scienza, Lettere ed Arti* xxi (Venice, 1879) 655
G. Cesari, 'Le origini di Giovanni Gabrieli autori di canzoni a più strumenti', *Istituzioni e Monumenti dell'Arte Musicale Italiana* ii (Milan, 1932)
F. Chrysander, 'Lodovico Zacconi als Lehrer des Kunstgesanges', *Vierteljahresschrift für Musikwissenschaft* vii, ix, x (1891/93/94) 339–90, 249–310, 531–67
T. Coryat, *Coryat's Crudities* (London, 1611)
A. Curtis, *Sweelinck's Keyboard Music* (Leiden, 1969)
A. E. F. Dickinson, 'A forgotten collection. A survey of the Weckmann Books', *Music Review* xvii (1956) 97–109
'The Lübbenau keyboard books, a further note on faceless features', *Music Review* xxvii (1966) 270–86
G. Diclich, *Rito Veneto Antico* (Venice, 1823)
G. Diruta, *Il Transilvano* (Venice, 1593) modern facsimile reprint ed. L. Cervelli (Bologna, 1969)
N. Doglioni, *Le cose notabili et meravigliose della Città di Venetia* (1662 edition)
A. Dunning, *Die Staatsmotette 1480–1555* (Utrecht, 1969)
A. Einstein, 'Ein concerto grosso von 1619', *Festschrift Hermann Kretzschmar zum 70 Geburtstag* (Leipzig, 1918)
'Italienische Musik und italienische Musiker am Kaiserhof und an den erzherzoglichen Höfen in Innsbruck und Graz', *Studien zur Muzikwissenschaft* xxi (1934) 3–52
'Narrative rhythm in the madrigal', *Musical Quarterly* xxix (1943) 475–84
'The Greghesca and the Giustiniana of the sixteenth century', *The Journal of Renaissance and Baroque Music* i (1946) 19–32
The Italian Madrigal (Princeton, 1949) 3 vols
A. Einstein ed., *Denkmäler der Tonkunst in Österreich* xli (Graz, 1934/R 1960)
A. J. Ellis and A. Mendel, *Studies in the history of musical pitch* (Amsterdam, 1968)
C. Engelbrecht, *Die Kasseler Hofkapelle im 17. Jahrhundert* (Kassel, 1958)
H. Federhofer, 'Alessandro Tadei, a pupil of Giovanni Gabrieli', *Musica Disciplina* v (1952) 115–31

K. G. Fellerer, 'Church Music and the Council of Trent', *Musical Quarterly* xxxix (1953) 576–94

E. T. Ferand, *Improvisation in Nine Centuries of Western Music* (Cologne, 1961)

J. A. Flower, *Giovanni Gabrieli's Sacrae Symphoniae 1597* (University of Michigan thesis, 1955)

G. Giomo, 'Le Spese del Nobil Uomo Marino Grimani nella sua elezione a Doge di Venezia', *Archivio Veneto* 33 (1887) 443–54

O. Gombosi, 'About organ playing in the divine service c 1500', *Essays on Music in honour of Archibald Thompson Davison* (Harvard, 1957) 51–68

E. Harich-Schneider, *A History of Japanese Music* (London, 1973)

F. Hudson, 'Giovanni Gabrieli's Motet a 15, "In Ecclesiis", from the Symphoniae Sacrae, Liber II, 1615', *Music Review* xxiv (1963) 130–33

J. P. Jacobsen ed., *Dania Sonans* II and III (Copenhagen 1966 and 1967)

D. Kämper, *Studien zur Instrumentalen Ensemblemusik des 16. Jahrhunderts in Italien* (Cologne and Vienna, 1970)

W. B. Kimmel, *Polychoral Music and the Venetian School* (University of Rochester thesis, 1942)

O. Kinkeldey, *Orgel und Klavier in der Musik des 16. Jahrhunderts* (Leipzig, 1910)

E. Kenton, 'The late style of Giovanni Gabrieli', *Musical Quarterly* xlviii (1962)

Life and Works of Giovanni Gabrieli (Rome, 1967) 427–43

S. Kunze, *Die Instrumentalmusik Giovanni Gabrielis* (Tutzing, 1963)

'Die entstehung des concertoprinzips im spätwerk Giovanni Gabrielis', *Archiv für Musikwissenschaft* xxi (1964–1965) 81–110

R. Lassels, *The Voyage of Italy* (Paris, 1670)

H. Leichtentritt, *Geschichte der Motette* (Leipzig, 1908)

R. Lenaerts, 'La Chapelle de St. Marc à Venise sous A. Willaert', *Bulletin de l'Institut Historique Belge de Rome* xix (1938)

H. Leuchtmann, *Orlando di Lasso* i (Wiesbaden, 1976)

L. Lockwood, *The Counter-Reformation and the Masses of Vincenzo Ruffo* (Venice, 1970)

W. E. Mason, 'The Architecture of St. Mark's Cathedral and the Venetian Polychoral style: a clarification', *Studies in Musicology . . . in memory of Glen Haydon*, ed. J. W. Pruett (Chapel Hill, 1969) 163–78

J. Mattheson, *Das Vollkommene Capellmeister* (Hamburg, 1739) modern facsimile reprint ed. N. Riemann (Kassel and Basel, 1954)

H. J. Moser, *Heinrich Schütz: Sein Leben und Werk* (Kassel, 1936); English translation by C. F. Pfatteicher (St. Louis, Missouri, 1959)

W. Müller-Blattau, *Tonsatz und Klanggestaltung bei Giovanni Gabrieli* (Kassel, Basel, Tours, London, 1975)

A. Newcomb, 'Editions of Willaert's *Musica Nova*: new evidence, new speculations', *Journal of the American Musicological Society* xxvi (1973) 132–45

'The three anthologies for Laura Peverara', *Rivista Italiana di Musicologia* x (1975) 329–45

P. Nolhac and A. Solerti. *Il viaggio in Italia di Enrico III re di Francia, e le feste a Venezia, Ferrara, Mantova e Torino* (Turin, 1890)

C. Palisca, 'V. Galilei's Counterpoint Treatise: a Code for the Seconda Prattica', *Journal of the American Musicological Society* lx (1956) 81–96

Baroque Music (Englewood Cliffs, New Jersey, 1968)

A. Pirro, 'La musique des Italiens d'après les Remarques Trienniales de J. B. Duval (1607–1609), *Mélanges offerts à M. Henry Lemonnier* (Paris, 1913) 175–85
N. Pirrotta 'Gesualdo, Ferrara e Venezia' in ed. M. T. Muraro *Studi sul teatro veneto fra Rinascimento ad Età Barocca* (Florence 1971) p. 311ff
M. Praetorius, *Syntagma Musicum* (Wittenberg, 1615) modern facsimile reprint ed. W. Gurlitt (Kassel, 1959)
B. Pullan, *Rich and Poor in Renaissance Venice* (Oxford, 1971)
G. Reese, *Music in the Renaissance* revised edition (New York, 1959)
H. Riemann, *Handbuch der Musikgeschichte* ii (Leipzig, 1912)
G. Rota, *Lettera Nella Quale Descrive L'Ingresso Nel Palazzo Ducale Della Serenissima Morosina Morosini Grimani Principessa Di Venetia Co'la Ceremonia Della Rosa Benedetta, mandatale A Donare Della Santità Di Nostro Signore* (Venice, 1597)
A. Sandberger, *Beiträge zur Geschichte der bayerischen Hofkapelle unter Orlando di Lasso* (Leipzig, 1894–1895)
F. Sansovino, *Venetia Città Nobilissima* (Venice 1604 and 1663 editions)
C. Sartori, *Bibliografia della Musica Strumentale Italiana* (Florence, 1952)
A. Schering, *Geschichte der Musik in Beispielen* (Leipzig, 1931)
S. Schmalzriedt, *Heinrich Schütz und andere zeitgenössische musiker in der lehre Giovanni Gabrielis* (Neuhausen, 1972)
B. Schmid, *Tabulatur Buch von Allerhand ausserlesenen* (Strasburg, 1607) modern facsimile reprint ed. G. Vecchi (Bologna, 1969)
E. Selfridge-Field, *Venetian Instrumental Music* (Oxford, 1975)
L. P. Smith ed., *The Life and Letters of Sir Henry Wotton* (Oxford, 1907/R 1966)
A. Solerti, 'Le Rappresentazioni Musicali di Venezia dal 1571 al 1605', *Rivista Musicale Italiana* ix (1902) 503–58
O. Strunk, 'Some motet-types of the sixteenth century', *Papers of the American Musicological Society* 1939 (1944) 155–60
O. Ursprung, *Die Katholische Kirchenmusik* (Potsdam, 1931)
R. Wiesenthal, *Die Sacrae Symphoniae Giovanni Gabrielis* (University of Jena thesis, 1954)
C. Winterfeld, *Johannes Gabrieli und sein Zeitalter* (Berlin, 1834/R 1965)
W. Yeomans, 'The Canzoni (1615) of Giovanni Gabrieli', *Monthly Musical Record* 86 (1956) 97–103
'Andrea Gabrieli's Canzoni et Ricercari (Libro primo)', *Monthly Musical Record* 88 (1958) 16–21
L. Zacconi, *Prattica di Musica* (Venice, 1592) modern facsimile reprint (Bologna, 1967)

Archival Sources

VENETIAN STATE ARCHIVES (A.S.V.)

Procuratia de Supra Registri 3, 4, 5, 6, 35, 132, 133, 135, 137, 138, 140, 141, 193
Procuratia de Supra Busta 91, Processo 208
Procuratia de Supra Busta 67, Processo 148
S. Rocco Rubbrica Generale Index 6 Sonadori
S. Rocco 2ª Consegna, Libro di riceveri (1564–1623)
S. Rocco Filza 26, Polizze di Spese da 1500–1600, Busta 418
S. Rocco Buste 156, 157, 158, 159, 160, 423
Scuola della Carità, Notatorio (1581–1623)
SS. Giovanni e Paolo Registro 12

ARCHIVE OF THE SCUOLA GRANDE DI S. ROCCO, VENICE

Registro delle Terminazioni II and III
Registro delle Parti II
Registro 4
Rubrica Generale, Organisti
Mariegola

MUSEO CORRER, VENICE

Cicogna Op. P.D. 12594 and 11866–96
Cicogna 2587

BIBLIOTECA MARCIANA, VENICE

Mss Italiani, Classe VII, 553 (8812)

MANTUA, ARCHIVIO GONZAGA

Busta 402

Index of Works

[Titles with asterisks have a musical example from them in the text]

A Dio, dolce mia vita 10vv, 1587/2; CMM 6 (171–181); 110
*Ahi senza te 4vv, 1595/1; CMM 6 (8–11); 123
Alleluja quando iam emersit 6vv, 1615/3; a contrafactum of Scherza Amarilli; organ trans. in TGD; SDL III (20–22); 124, 264
Alma cortes'e bella 3vv, 1587/2; CMM 6 (1–3), AMI 2 (155–158)
Alti potentis Domine 19vv, only one part survives; K fol 62 F
*Amor dove mi guidi 12vv, 1590/1; CMM 6 (200–222); 111f
Angelicos cives 7vv, exists only in organ trans. in TDG; SDL III (27–30); 55
*Angelus ad pastores 12vv, 1587/2; CMM 1 (34–47), AMI 2 (177–192); 84f, 180
*Angelus Domini descendit 8vv, 1597/1; CMM (160–167), F (97–102); 100f, 105
Attendite popule meus 8vv, 1615/1 and 1615/3; organ trans. in 1617/1; CMM 3 (78–86)
Audi Domine hymnum 7vv, 1612/1, 1615/3 and K fol 55 D; DC 67 (7–14)
Audite coeli 12vv, K fol 55 F
*Audite principes 16vv, 1615/3; 266f
*Beata es Virgo Maria 6vv, 1597/1; W (29–31), CMM 1 (57–62), F (9–12); 79
*Beati immaculati 8vv, 1597/1; organ trans. in 1617/1; CMM 1 (121–128), F (65–70); 88, 94, 101f
*Beati omnes 8vv, 1597/1; organ trans. in 1617/1; CMM 1 (143–151), F (83–89); 93f, 95f
Benedicam Dominum 10vv, 1597/1; organ trans. in 1617/1; CMM 2 (55–61), F (220–226)
Benedictus 12vv, 1597/1; CMM 2 (173–176); 174f
Benedictus 12vv, 1615/1; W (42–45), CMM 4 (124–132)
*Benedictus es Dominus 8vv, 1615/1; CMM 3 (97–108); 271f, 274, 276
*Benedixisti Domine 7vv, 1597/1; CMM 1 (74–77), F (24–26); 74f
*Buccinate in neomenia tuba 19vv, 1615/1 and 1615/3; organ trans. in 1617/1; CMM 5 (188–210), ed. P. Winter (Frankfurt, 1960); 265f, 268
Cantate Domino 6vv, 1597/1; organ trans. in 1617/1 and TGD; CMM 1 (48–51), F (1–3), organ ed. SDL III (9–10)
*Cantate Domino 8vv, 1615/1; CMM 3 (87–96); 271f, 276

Canzonas

1597/1 Canzon Primi Toni a 8; IM 2 (1–13), Bk, F (168–177); 152f
*Canzon Septimi Toni a 8; IM 2 (14–29), Bk, F (178–188); 149ff
*Canzon Septimi Toni a 8; IM 2 (30–40), Bk, F (189–196); 148f
*Canzon Noni Toni a 8; IM 2 (41–51), Bk, F (197–204); OCM (6–8); 57, 158
Canzon Duodecimi Toni a 8; IM 2 (52–74), Bk, F (205–212)
*Canzon Primi Toni a 10; IM 2 (75–94), Bk, F (275–282); 58, 150ff
Canzon Duodecimi Toni a 10; IM 2 (95–117), Bk, F (283–290)
*Canzon Duodecimi Toni a 10; IM 2 (118–157), F (291–304); 157f
Canzon Duodecimi Toni a 10; IM 2 (158–179), Bk, F (305–312); 150

The following are two versions of the same work:
*Canzon in Echo Duodecimi Toni a 10; IM 2 (180–228 even page numbers), Bk, Ku (8–16), F (313–321); 154ff
*Canzon in Echo Duodecimi Toni a 10 sudetta accomodata per concertar con l'organo a 10; IM 2 (181–229 odd page numbers), Bk, F (322–339); 154ff, 236
Canzon Septimi e Octavi Toni a 12; IM 2 (230–246), Bk, F (437–448)
Canzon Noni Toni a 12; IM 2 (247–289), Bk, F (449–466); 237
Canzon Quarti Toni a 15; IM 2 (290–307), Bk, ed. D. Greer (London, 1968), F (509–521); 159, 162, 256
1608/1 Canzon 'La Spiritata' a 4; SDL I (27–29), ed. A. Einstein *Vier Canzoni* (Mainz, 1932, 4–7); 134, 234
*Canzon seconda; SDL I (30–32), Einstein ibid (8–12); 135f
Canzon terza; SDL I (33–35), Einstein ibid (13–16)
*Canzon quarta: SDL I (35–37), Einstein ibid (17–20); 135f
*Canzon 'Fa sol la re', in 1615/2 as Canzon IX a 8; Ku (36–43), Th, S (75–83); 67, 234f, 239, 246f
Canzon 'Sol sol la sol fa mi'; Ku (44–47); 234
1615/2 *Canzon 1 a 5; S (1–4); 236f
Canzon 2 a 6; Th, S (5–15)
Canzon 3 a 6; Th, S (16–22)
*Canzon 4 a 6; Th, S (23–30); 251f
*Canzon 5 a 7; Th, S (31–38); 237ff
*Canzon 6 a 7; Th, S (39–48); 239ff, 244
Canzon 7 a 7; Th, S (49–62); 253
*Canzon 8 a 8; Th, S (63–74); 247, 250f
Canzon 9 a 8; Th, Ku (36–43), S (75–83)
*Canzon 10 a 8; Th, S (84–95); 207, 241, 244ff
*Canzon 11 a 8; Th, S (96–108); 241, 248, 253
Canzon 12 a 8; Th, S (109–117)
Canzon 14 a 10; Th, S (127–136); 241
Canzon 15 a 10; Th, S (137–149); 207
Canzon 16 a 12; Th, S (150–168); 244
*Canzon 17 a 12; Th, S (169–184); 208, 244, 248ff
Schlossarchiv Aurolzmünster mss 212 (Vienna, Musikwissenschaftliches Institut der Univ.)
Canzon a 8, anon lute tablature, one choir only
TRF Vol. 3 *Canzon (1ª), unnamed in mss, in 1617/1 as 'Fuga colorata Adami Steiglederi'; SDL II (36–39); 56f
Canzon (2ª); SDL II (40–44); 57f
Canzon francese (3ª); SDL II (45–48)
*Canzon (4ª) a 4; SDL II (49–51); 58
Canzon (5ª); SDL II (51–53)
*Chiar'angioletta 8vv, 1590/1; CMM 6 (131–137), IM 1 (164–176); 143f, 233
Confitebor tibi Domine 13vv, 1615/1 and 1615/3; organ trans. in 1617/1; CMM 4 (167–199); 276
Congratulamini mihi 6vv, 1615/1; organ trans. in TDG; CMM 3 (12–21); organ ed. SDL III (31–33)

*Da quei begl'occhi 5vv, 1589/1; CMM 6 (57–60); 117, 119
Deh di me non ti caglia 4vv, 1595/1; CMM 6 (11–14); 123, 209
Deus Deus meus 10vv, 1587/2; organ trans. in 1617/1; CMM 1 (18–33), W (7–10); 84, 264
Deus Deus meus respice 12vv, 1615/3
Deus in nomine tuo 8vv, 1615/1; CMM 3 (66–77), DC 67 (15–32)
Deus qui beatum Marcum 10vv, 1597/1; CMM 2 (74–79), F (239–243); 177
Diligam te Domine 8vv, 1589/1; CMM 2 (1–6), F (117–121), DC 67 (1–6)
Diligam te Domine 7vv, 1600/1
Dimmi ben mio 5vv, 1589/1; CMM 6 (60–64); 116, 119
*Dolce nemica mia 7vv, 1587/1; CMM 6 (117–123); 112
Dolci care parole 5vv, 1589/1; CMM 6 (65–67); 116, 119
Domine Deus meus 6vv, 1615/3; organ trans. in TDG; SDL III (15–19); 55
*Domine Dominus noster 8vv, 1597/1; organ trans. in 1617/1; CMM 1 (151–159), F (90–96); 93, 97, 106
Domine exaudi orationem meam 8vv, 1597/1; CMM 1 (99–104), F (46–50)
Domine exaudi orationem meam 10vv, 1597/1; organ trans. in 1617/1; CMM 2 (62–66), F (227–230), W (15–17)
*Donna leggiadra e bella 5vv, 1583/1; CMM 6 (24–27); 16
Dormiva dolcemente 8vv, 1590/1; CMM 6 (138–146); 110
Dulcis Jesu patris imago 20vv, K fol 53 C
Ego dixi Domine 7vv, 1587/2; organ trans. in TFG; CMM 1 (6–10); organ ed. SDL III (33–35); 55
Ego rogabo patrem 6vv, 1590/2
Ego sum qui sum 8vv, 1597/1; CMM 2 (22–28), F (137–144); 180
*Exaudi Deus 7vv, 1597/1; organ trans. in 1617/1; CMM 1 (77–85), F (27–33); 75f
Exaudi Deus 12vv, 1615/1 and 1615/3; organ trans. in 1617/1; CMM 4 (1–23)
*Exaudi Domine 6vv, 1597/1; organ trans. in 1617/1 and TDG; CMM 1 (51–56), F (4–8), organ ed. SDL III (1–4); 55, 74
*Exaudi me Domine 16vv, 1615/1; CMM 5 (134–157); 280, 301
Exultate justi in Domino 8vv, 1597/1; organ trans. in 1617/1; CMM 2 (6–12), F (122–128)
Exultavit cor meum 6vv, 1615/1; organ trans. in TFG; CMM 3 (1–11), organ ed. SDL III (39–42)
Exultet jam angelica turba 14vv, 1615/3
Fantasias
1599/2 Fantasia in modo di Canzon Francese; SDL III (42–46)
BL1 *Fantasia IV toni; SDL I (47–48); B (20–21); 65f
BL1 Fantasia VI toni; SDL I (49–51); B (22–25); 60
Fuggi pur se sai 8vv, 1590/1, K fol 62 E; CMM 6 (147–161); IM i (136–163); 142
Fugues
BL1 *Fuga IX toni; SDL I (52–54), B (26–28); 63
M Fuga VIII toni; B (29)
TFG VI *Fuga prima a 4; SDL II (28–31); 64
Fuga seconda a 4, also in BL2 as Ricercar IX toni; SDL II (32–36); 65
*Gloria 12vv, 1597/1; CMM 2 (152–167), F (382–397); 172f
Hic est filius Dei 18vv, K fol 51 A
Hoc tegitur 8vv, 1597/1; CMM 2 (13–21), F (129–136)
Hodie Christus a mortuis 12vv, K fol 51 D

Hodie Christus natus est 8vv, 1603/1 and 1615/3; a contrafactum of 'O che felice giorno'; 109
*Hodie Christus natus est 10vv, 1597/1; CMM 2 (102–110), F (267–274); 178, 180ff, 233
Hodie completi sunt 7vv, 1600/1
*Hodie completi sunt 8vv, 1615/1; CMM 3 (44–56), DC 10 (9–19); 274f
*Inclina Domine 6vv, 1587/2; CMM 1 (1–5); 73
*In ecclesiis 14vv, 1615/1 and 1615/3; CMM 5 (32–55), HAM I no. 157, W (73–81), ed. F. Hudson (London 1963); 274, 291ff
In nobil sangue 5vv, 1587/2 by Andrea Gabrieli, pt 2 *'Amor s'è in lei' by Giovanni Gabrieli; CMM 6 (84–95), AMI 2 (201–214); 114f
In te Domine speravi 8vv, 1597/1; CMM 2 (29–36), F (145–150)
Intonations on the 12 tones, 1593/1; all these are in keyboard tablature in 1607/1 attributed to Andrea Gabrieli; *Intonazione del 10° tono; SDL I (1–11); B (37–42); 48f
*Jam non dicam vos servos 8vv, 1597/1; CMM 1 (136–143), F (77–82); 91f, 101
*Jubilate Deo 8vv, 1597/1; organ trans. in 1617/1 and TFG 4; CMM 1 (105–113), F (51–58), organ ed. SDL III (5–8); 88, 97ff
Jubilate Deo 8vv, 1613/1 and 1615/3; W (32–41); 263f
*Jubilate Deo 10vv, 1615/1; CMM 3 (163–192), ed. F. Hudson (Zurich, 1970); 274, 287ff
Jubilate Deo 15vv, 1597/1; CMM 2 (219–231), F (495–508)
Jubilemus singuli 8vv, 1597/1; CMM 2 (36–44), F (151–158); 180
Judica me Domine 10vv, 1597/1; CMM 2 (86–92), F (251–256); 178
Kyrie 12vv, 1597/1; CMM 2 (141–151), F (370–381); 174
Kyrie 12vv, 1615/1; CMM (97–115); 269
*Labra amorose e care 4vv, 1595/1; lute arr. in 1607/1; CMM 6 (14–18); 55, 123
*Laudate nomen Domini 8vv, 1597/1; CMM 1 (128–135), F (71–76); 88f
*Lieto godea 8vv, 1587/2; 2 lute arr. in 1601/1, German contrafactum in 1624/1; CMM 6 (124–130), AMI 2 (193–200), IM 1 (35–44), ed. P. Spitta *Heinrich Schütz Sämtliche Werke* Vol. 2 (Leipzig, 1886, 209–213); 142ff, 149, 158, 160 n50, 233
Litanie B. M. Virginis 8vv, 1615/1; CMM 3 (109–130); 275f
*Magnificat 8vv, 1597/1; CMM 2 (44–54), F (159–167), W (18–23); 95
Magnificat 12vv, 1597/1; CMM 2 (177–197), F (407–426); 175f
Magnificat 12vv, 1615/1 and 1615/3; CMM 4 (133–166); 247
Magnificat 14vv, 1615/1; CMM 5 (56–83); 264
Magnificat 17vv, 1615/1; CMM 5 (158–187); 266ff
Magnificat 18vv, Vn mss 16708 (incomplete); 261 n13
Magnificat 33v, Vn mss 16708 (incomplete); 261 n13
Maria Virgo 10vv, 1597/1; CMM 2 (66–74), F (231–238)
*Miserere mei Deus 6vv, 1597/1; CMM 1 (62–66), F (13–17), W (55–57); 77f, 237
Misericordias Domini 8vv, 1597/1; organ trans. in 1617/1; CMM 1 (114–121), F (59–64)
Misericordia tua Domine 12vv, 1615/1, K fol 51 O; CMM 4 (50–73); 285f, 301
Nunc Dimittis 14vv, 1597/1; CMM 2 (207–218), F (482–494); 186f
*O che felice giorno 8vv, 1590/1, K fol 57, a contrafactum, 'Hodie Christus natus est' in 1615/3; CMM 6 (162–170); 108ff, 144, 173
O Doctor optime 6vv, exists only in organ trans. in TDG; SDL III (11–19); 55
O Domine Deus meus 6vv, 1615/3
*O Domine Jesu Christe 8vv, 1597/1, organ trans. in 1617/1; CMM 1 (93–99); F (41–45), W (11–14), DC 10 (4–8); 101f, 178, 264, 284

O Fili Dei 7vv, 1600/1, identical with 'Sancta Maria succurre miseris'
*O gloriosa Virgo 12vv, 1615/1, K fol 51 C as 'O gloriose Jesu'; CMM 4 (24–49); 286f
*O Jesu Christe 6vv, 1615/3, organ trans. in 1617/1; 55, 263
*O Jesu mi dulcissime 8vv, 1597/1; CMM 1 (167–174), F (103–109); 103ff, 178, 281f
*O Jesu mi dulcissime 8vv, 1615/1; CMM 3 (30–43), DC 10 (20–28); 267, 271, 281f, 290
*O magnum mysterium 8vv, 1587/2; CMM 1 (10–17); 85f, 103f, 159, 178, 289
Omnes gentes plaudite manibus 16vv, 1597/1, organ trans. in 1617/1; CMM 2 (232–245), F (522–536), ed. P. Winter (Frankfurt, 1960); 185f, 265f
*O quam gloriosa 16vv, 1615/1; CMM 5 (112–133); 270, 274
O quam suavis es Domine 7vv, 1597/1, organ trans. in 1617/1; CMM 1 (66–73), F (18–23)
O quam suavis 8vv, 1615/1; CMM 3 (57–65), W (58–61); 264
O ricco mio thesoro 5vv, 1583/1; CMM 6 (27–31); 16
O sacrum convivium 7vv, exists only in organ trans. in TDG; SDL III (23–26)
Plaudite omnis terra 12vv, 1597/1, organ trans. in 1617/1; CMM 2 (111–125), F (340–354); 178f, 182
Quam pulchra es 8vv, 1599/1
Quando'io ero giovinetto 5vv, 1575/1; CMM 6 (18–24); ed. A. Einstein *The Golden Age of the Madrigal* (New York, 1942, 44–52); 14
Quando Laura 5vv, Vr; CMM 6 (31–38)
*Quem vidistis pastores 14vv, 1615/1; CMM 5 (1–31), ed. F. Hudson (Zurich, 1970); 289ff
*Queste felice herbette 5vv, 1589/1; CMM 6 (68–72); 116, 119, 214
*Quis est iste qui venit 10vv, 1597/1; CMM 2 (93–102), F (257–266); 88f, 177, 180ff
*Regina caeli 12vv, 1597/1; CMM 2 (198–206), F (427–436); 178, 180ff, 233
Ricercars
1595/2 VIII tone; B (4–6); as ricercare SDL I (38–40)
VIII tone; SDL I (14–18)
X tone; SDL I (19–23); B (7–11)
BL1 *VII and VIII tones; SDL I (41–43), B (14–16); 62
M II tone; B (17–19)
BL2 IX tone; SDL II (32–36) as Fuga (2ª)
B a 4 'a tre soggetti'; SDL I (38–40); 66f
a 4; SDL I (24–26), B as IX tone (12–22), W (65) as 'Canzone per l'organo'
TFG VI 1º a 4; SDL II (7–9)
2º a 4; SDL II (10–12)
3º a 4; SDL II (12–16)
4º a 4; SDL II (16–17)
5º a 4; SDL II (18–21)
6º a 4; SDL II (22–27); 60
Sacri di Giove augei 12vv, 1587/2; CMM 6 (182–222), AMI 2 (159–176); 114
Sacro tempo d'honor 5vv, 1586/2; CMM 6 (39–46), AMI 2 (149–154); 115f
S'al discoprir 5vv, 1589/1; CMM 6 (73–78); 116ff
*Salvator noster 15vv, 1615/1; CMM 5 (84–111); 269
Sancta et immaculata 8vv, 1587/1; CMM 1 (175–181), F (110–116)
Sancta et immaculata 7vv, 1615/1, organ trans. in TDG; CMM 3 (22–29), organ ed. SDL III (36–38); 264
Sancta Maria succurre miseris 7vv, 1597/1, organ trans. in 1617/1; CMM 1 (86–92), F (34–40), W (24–28); 78

Sanctus 12vv, 1597/1; CMM 2 (168–176), F (398–406); 174f
Sanctus 12vv, 1615/1; CMM 4 (116–132)
Scherza Amarilli 6vv, 1600/2, only available in Winterfeld's score, a contrafactum 'Alleluja quando iam emersit, in 1615/3; CMM 6 (110–116); 124, 264
Se cantano gl'augelli 6vv, 1592/1, a German contrafactum 'Quid mihi cum forma – Blandine meine schöne' in 1612/2; CMM 6 (105–110); 121, 214
Signor le tue man sante 5vv, 1586/1; CMM 6 (47–56); 115
*S'io t'ho ferito 6vv, 1591/1; CMM 6 (96–104); 120f
Sonatas
1597/1 Sonata pian e forte a 8 alla quarta bassa; F (213–219), HAM I no. 173, IM 2 (64–74), Bk; 159f, 209, 256
*Sonata octavi toni a 12; F (467–481), IM 2 (270–289), Bk; 161
1615/2 Sonata 13 a 8; Th, S (118–126); 253
Sonata 18 a 14; Th, S (185–215); 207, 253ff
Sonata 19 a 15; Th, S (216–240); 253, 256, 286
Sonata 20 a 22; Th, S (241–274); 253ff
*Sonata per tre violini; S (275–278), ed. W. Danckert (Kassel, 1950), OCM (9–13); 208f, 252, 261
Surrexit Christus 11vv, 1615/1; K fol 51 B with possibly a new symphonia; CMM 3 (193–212), ed. F. Hudson (Zurich, 1970), W (66–72); 287
*Surrexit pastor bonus 10vv, 1597/1; CMM 2 (80–86), F (244–250); 178f, 182
*Suscipe clementissime 12vv, 1615/1; CMM 4 (74–96), ed. F. Hudson (Zurich, 1970); 276, 284ff
*Timor et tremor 6vv, 1615/3; ed. J. Noble (Pennsylvania, 1968), A. Bank (Amsterdam, 1950); 270, 278f, 299
Toccatas
1593/2 Del secondo tuono, lute tablature in 1607/1; SDL I (12–13), B (34–36) AM 3 (137–140)
Vn mss 10110 Organ toccata
BL1 V toni; SDL I (44–46), B (30–33) as on the XI tone
TFG 2 a 4 (1ª); SDL II (54–55)
prima a 4 (2ª); SDL II (55–57)
primi toni a 4 (3ª); SDL II (58–61)
primi toni a 4 (4ª); SDL II (60–61)
a 4 (5ª); SDL II (62–63); 49
a 4 (6ª); SDL II (63–64)
a 4 (7ª); SDL II (65–66)
*a 4 (8ª); SDL II (66–67); 49f
*a 4 (9ª); SDL II (68–70)
*a 4 (10ª); SDL II (71–74); 50
*Udite chiari et generosi figli 16vv, K fol 57 H; CMM 6 (223–250); 124ff
*Vagh'amorosi 5vv, 1589/1; CMM 6 (79–83); 117
*Virtute magna 12vv, 1597/1; CMM 2 (126–140), F (355–369); 178f, 183
*Voi ch'ascoltate 4vv, 1575/2; CMM 6 (4–7); 13f
*Vox Domini 10vv, 1615/1; CMM 3 (131- 162); 270, 273, 276

Index of Works—Key

EARLY PRINTED SOURCES

1575/1 Il secondo libro de madrigali a cinque voci de floridi virtuosi . . . (Venice, Scotto)

1575/2 De Cipriano et Annibale madrigali a quattro voci . . . (Venice, Gardano)

1583/1 De floridi virtuosi d'Italia il primo libro de madrigali a cinque voci . . . (Venice, Vincenzi and Amadino)

1586/1 Musica spirituale composta da diversi eccellentissimi musici a cinque voci . . . (Venice, Gardano)

1586/2 Corona di dodici sonetti di Gio. Battista Zuccharini . . . (Venice, Gardano)

1587/1 Fiori musicali de diversi auttori a tre voci . . . (Venice, Vincenzi)

1587/2 Concerti di Andrea et di Gio. Gabrieli . . . libro primo et secondo . . . (Venice, Gardano)

1589/1 Di Andrea Gabrieli il terzo libro de madrigali a cinque voci . . . (Venice, Gardano)

1590/1 Dialoghi musicali de diversi eccellentissimi autori . . . (Venice, Gardano)

1590/2 Musica per concerti ecclesiastici di diversi autori . . . (Venice, Vincenti)

1591/1 La Ruzina canzone di Filippo de Monte . . . (Venice, Gardano)

1592/1 Il trionfo di Dori . . . (Venice, Gardano)

1593/1 Intonationi d'organo di Andrea Gabrieli, et di Gio. suo nepote . . . (Venice, Gardano)

1593/2 Il Transilvano . . . da penna del R. P. Girolamo Diruta . . . (Venice, Vincenti)

1595/1 Di XII autori vaghi e dilettevoli madrigali a quatro voci . . . (Venice, Amadino)

1595/2 Ricercari di Andrea Gabrieli . . . Libro secondo . . . (Venice, Gardano)

1597/1 Sacrae Symphoniae . . . (Venice, Gardano)

1599/1 Augustini Zineroni bergomensis . . . Missa, Beatae Virginis . . . (Venice, Amadino)

1599/2 Il secondo libro de intavolatura di liuto di Gio. Antonio Terzi da Bergamo . . . (Venice, Vincenti)

1600/1 Sacrarum symphoniarum continuatio diversorum excellentissimorum authorum . . . (Nuremberg, Kauffmann)

1600/2 Honori et amori Georgii Gruberi civis Norimbergensis . . . (Nuremberg, Kauffmann) [now lost]

1601/1 Florida sive cantiones . . . (Utrecht, S. de Roy and J. G. de Rhenen)

1603/1 Florilegium selectissimarum cantionum . . . collectum & editum studio ac labore M. Erhardi Bodenschatz, Lichtenbergensis . . . (Leipzig, Lamberg)

1607/1 Tabulatur Buch von allerhand ausserlesnen . . . Bernhard Schmiden . . . (Strasbourg, Zetzner)

1608/1 Canzoni per sonare con ogni sorte di stromenti . . . da diversi eccellentissimi musici . . . libro primo . . . (Venice, Raverii)

1612/1 Promptuarii musici . . . collectore Abrahamo Schadaeo (Strasbourg, Kieffer)

1612/2 Musicalische Streitkräntzelein . . . (Nuremberg, A. Wagemannu)

1613/1	Promptuarii musici . . . pars tertia . . . collectore Abrahamo Schadaeo (Strasbourg, Kieffer)
1615/1	Symphoniae sacrae . . . liber secundus . . . (Venice, Gardano aere Bartolomei Magni)
1615/2	Canzoni e sonate del Signor Giovanni Gabrieli . . . (Venice, Gardano appresso Bartolomeo Magni)
1615/3	Reliquiae sacrorum concentuum Giovan Gabrielis . . . Iohan-Leonis Hasleri . . . (Nuremberg, Kauffmann)
1617/1	Nova musices organicae tabulatura . . . Durch Johann Woltzen . . . (Basel, Genath)
1624/1	Erster Theil lieblicher, welscher Madrigalien . . . Valentinum Diezelium . . . (Nuremberg, Halbmayer)

MANUSCRIPT SOURCES

B	Berlin mss 191 of instrumental music, now lost
BL1 and BL2	Berlin Deutsche Staatsbibliothek mss Lynar A1 and A2, organ music copied by M. Weckmann
K	Kassel Murhardsche und Landesbibliothek music mss
M	Munich Bayerischen Staatsbibliothek
TFG	Turin Biblioteca Nazionale Universitaria Fondo Giordano, organ tablature, 8 vols
TRF	Turin Biblioteca Nazionale Universitaria Raccolta Foà, organ music, 8 vols
TDG	Turin Biblioteca Nazionale Universitaria Dono Giordano mss 4, Motetti de diversi autori, transcribed for organ
Vn	Vienna Österreichische Nationalbibliothek
Vr	Verona Accademia Filarmonica sacra musica mss 220

MODERN EDITIONS

CMM	*Giovanni Gabrieli Opera Omnia* ed. D. Arnold, Vols 1–6 (Rome, 1956–1974)
AMI	*L'Arte Musicale in Italia* ed. L. Torchi (Milan, Rome, 1897–1907)
IM	*Istituzioni e Monumenti dell'arte musicale Italiana* (Milan, 1931–1941)
F	*Giovanni Gabrieli 'Sacrae Symphoniae'* ed. V. Fagotto (Venice, 1969)
W	C. Winterfeld: *Johannes Gabrieli und sein Zeitalter* Vol. III (Berlin, 1834)
Ku	S. Kunze: *Die Instrumentalmusik Giovanni Gabrielis* (Tutzing, 1963)
SDL	*G. Gabrieli Composizioni per Organo* ed. S. Dalla Libera, Vols 1–3 (Milan, 1957–1959)
DC	*Das Chorwerk* (Wolfenbüttel, 1929–)
S	*G. Gabrieli Canzoni e Sonate* ed. M. Sanvoisin (Paris, 1971)
Th	*G. Gabrieli Canzoni e Sonate* ed. B. Thomas (London, 1972) with instrumental parts
B	*Giovanni Gabrieli Werke für Tasteninstrumente* ed. G. S. Bedbrook (Kassel, 1957)
Bk	*Music for Brass* ed. R. P. Block (London, 1972)
HAM	Davison and Apel: *Historical Anthology of Music* (Harvard, 1946)
OCM	H. Riemann: *Old Chamber Music* I (London, 1896)

Index

[Titles asterisked have a musical example from them in the text]

Agostin of the Frari (of the Minorite Order), 27, 33, 197
Aichinger, G., 299
Albrecht, Duke of Bavaria, 1ff, 15, 138
Alessandro (relative of Zuan), 190
Alvixe (son of Thomaxo), 190
Andrea (son of Pietro from Barena), 190
Andrea (son of our Pietro), 191
Andrea (son of Zuane), 190
Angelo (of Padua), 163
Angioletto (of the Minorite Order), 196
Antegnati, C., 42 n12
Anthon, C. G., 128 n5
Antonini, Marc 'Antonio, 17
Apel, W., 60 n31
Arcadelt, J., 60
Arnold, D., 6 n10, 18 n1, 36 n34, 82 n13, 114 n11, 128 n2, 181 n20, 182 n21, 211 n1, 260 n11, 261 n14, 295 n1, 298 n8
Arnold, F. T., 155 n45
Artusi, G. M., 214, 221
Ascension Day ceremonies, 21, 108
Augsburg, 10, 296

Bach, J. S., ix, 291, 301
Balbi, Z., 191
Baldini, V., 216
Bamberg, 1, 10
Banchieri, A., 41, 45, 148, 155, 160 n50, 233, 236
Barbarini, G., 204
Barbarino, B., 209f, *'O dulcissime'; *'Canite et psallite', 209f
Bartholomew, L. E., 232 n2
Bassano, G., 74, 136, 153, 236, 260f, 297, 301, compositions: *Fantasie a tre*, 35, 'Deus qui beatum Marcum', 177f, ornamentation treatises: 45, 144ff, 149f, 163, 209, 223f, 242, players: 127, 130ff, 137ff, 201f, 204, 294
Bataglia, F. dalla, 164
Batista (from Lagano), 191
Battista (of S. Pantalon), 33, 187
Battista (of Udine), 129
Bellavere, V., 28ff, 199f, *'Scendi O sacr' Himeneo', 28, *'Vidi speciosam', 30
Belli, G., 297
Bellini, G., 69
Benedict (Father), 202
Benevoli, O., 293, 298
Berenson, B., 22
Bergamo, A. da, 10
Berlin Singakademie, ix
Bernardino (of Vicenza), 42
Bernardo (of the Frari), 33
Bertolotti, A., 259 n6
Biblioteca Marciana (Venice), 296
bicinia, 3, 131
Biggs, E. Power, 42 n12
Blume, F., 299 n10
Boetticher, W., 1 n4, 3, 9 n19, 20, 10 n21, 72 n3, 142 n34
Boito, C., 20 n6
Bonardi (Bonardo), G., 186, 201
Bonelli, A., 233
Bonfante, M., 140
Bonta, S., 131 n11
Borchgrevinck, M., 212ff, *'Amatemi ben mio', 214
Borromeo (Archbishop, Saint) C., 71, 297
Bortolomeo, Father (from Padua), 202
Boscardo, G., 163
Boyden, D., 287 n19
Brachrogge, H., 212
Breslau, Königlich Akademische Institut für Kirchenmusik, x
British Library, 225
Brown, H., 258 n3
Brown, H. M., 113 n8, 141 n33, 144 n37, 193 n14
Bukofzer, M., 80 n8, 278 n17
Busoni, F., 44
Bustin, G. G., 163
Buus, J., 131
Byrd, W., 187, 221

Caccini, C., 216, 223, 230, 242ff
Caffi, F., 1 n3, 8 n17, 29 n21, 165 n6, 166 n11, 260 n8, 295 n3, 297 n6
Canale, Don F., 232f
canzona francese, 143, 180. *See also* Andrea and Giovanni Gabrieli
Capello, B., 28
cappella, definition of, 168
Casseller, G., 140
Cavalli, F., 210, 297
Cervelli, L., 43 n13
Charles, Archduke of Carinthia, 6, 114
Chioggia, 35
Chiozotto, Z., *see* Croce, G.
Christian IV, of Denmark, 217
Churches:
Amsterdam, Oude Kerk, 42
Augsburg, SS. Ulrich and Afra, 10, 296
Bergamo, S. Maria Maggiore, 128
Bologna, S. Petronio, 82
Brescia, S. Carlo, 42 n12, S. Maria delle Gratie, 232
Chioggia Cathedral, 43
Ferrara, S. Maria in Vado, 42
Nuremberg, Frauenkirche, 10
Parma, Steccata Chapel, 17
Rome, Cappella Sistina, 72, Gesù, 297, St. John Lateran, 2
Udine Cathedral (Chiesa Maggiore), 40, 42
Venice, Angel Raphael, 194, Frari, 297, Madonna of the Mercadente all'Horto, 194, S. Alvise, 42, S. Andrea, 194, S. Angelo, 42, S. Bartolomeo, 42, S. Bastian, 194, S. Geremia, 1, 27, S. Gerolamo, 42, Gesuati, 42, SS. Giovanni e Paolo, 22, 204, 211, S. Iseppo, 194, S. Maria Formosa, 36, 186, 188, S. Maria del Giglio, 42, S. Maria Maggiore, 194, S. Maria della Salute, 298, S. Marina, 20, St. Mark, *ceremonies:* 20ff, 69f, 139f, 163ff, 178, *choir:* 1, 18f, 32ff, 81, 164ff, 259f, *instrumental ensemble:* 7, 35, 82, 128ff, 137ff, 140f, 157, 186f, 201f, 294, *officials:* xi, 17, 25ff, 29, 31, 35f, 40f, 260f, 295f, S. Niccolò (Lido), 21, 194, S. Pantalon, 194, S. Stefano, 131, 194, 295, S. Stin, 194, S. Vito, 20, S. Zaccaria, 194
Cicogna, Doge P., 108, 163
Cima, G., 208
Clemsee, C., 212f
Collegium Germanicum (Rome), 298
Colombo, V., 42
Corelli, A., 241, 275
cori spezzati, 7, 25, 97, 105, 165ff, 261, 264ff, 275, 280ff, 297f
Coryat, T., 189f, 203ff, 209
Council of Trent, 71f
Cranmer, T., 71
Crequillon, T., 53
Croce, G., 33, 107, 122, 155, 182ff, 201f, 236, 259ff, 289, 291, 296, works: *Triaca musicale*, 36, *'In die tribulationis', 37, *'Virtute magna', 38, *Missa brevis*, 71, *'Omnes gentes', 97f, *'Ave Virgo', 99f, *Requiem Mass*, 165, *Missa Percussit Saul*, 175f, 255, *'Christe', 176, *Sacrae cantilene concertate a tre, a cinque et sei voci . . .*, 261, 287, *'Psallite, psallite', 262, *'In spiritu humilitatis', 267f
Curtis, A., 42 n11
Curzolari, battle of, 21

D'Alessi, G., 80 n9
Dalla Casa, Girolamo (Gerolamo, Hieronimo, also called Da Udine), 43, 55, 82, 149, 209, *Il vero modo di diminuir . . .*: 131, 144f, 153, instrumental ensemble: 129ff, 137
Dalla Casa, Giuseppe, 164
Dalla Casa, Nicolò, 204
Dalla Libera, S., 41 n3,4, 32ff, 42 n8,10, 49 n17, 50 n18, 60ff
Da Piove, *see* V. Rovetta
Da Ponte, Doge, 108
Dart, R. T., 15, 225 n9
Demantius, J. C., 299ff
Denmark, 212, 216
Diclich, G., 20 n6
Diedo, P. A., 30
Diruta, G., 43ff, 56, 60, 134 n18, **Il Transilvano*, 46
Doglioni, N., 41 n2
Domenego (from Stai), 191
Donato, B., 6, 31ff, 70, 155, 187, 196, *'Hei mihi', 34, 'Ahi miserelle ahi sventurate noi', 112
Donato, Doge Leonardo, 163, 258
Donington, R., 243 n8
Dowland, J., 107
Dunning, A., 69 n1

Einstein, A., 4 n7, 6 n10, 11, 8 n17, 12 n22, 112 n7, 117, 127 n21, 134 n17, 157 n46

Ellis, A. J., 76 n7
Erasmus, 72

Fabritio (of the Frari), 33
Faliero, M., 20
Fasuol, A., 33, 260
Fattorini, G., 45, 213
Fauretti, 201
Fedeli, C., 297
Federhofer, H., 212 n4
Fellerer, K. G., 72 n6
Fellowes, E. H., 76
Ferand, E., 52 n20
Ferdinand, Archduke (Holy Roman Emperor), 212, 232, 296
Fernando, M., 205
Ferrara, 3, 46, three ladies of, 72, 116
Festivals: Ascension Day, 21, S. Giustina, 20, S. Isidore, 20, 139, St. Mark, 20, 139, 192, S. Modestus, 20, St. Roche, 200ff, S. Vitus, 20
Fiammingo, Giovanni Antonio, 33
Finetti, G., 297
Florence, 46
Fortune, N., 18 n1, 211 n1
Foscari, Doge, 69
Francese, Guglielmo, 33
Frangipani, C., 25
Frankfurt, 2
Frescobaldi, G., 41, 67, 233
Frutariol, F., 7
Fugger family, 10, 114
Fuser, I., 146 n38

Gabrieli, A., *life:* visit to Munich, 1ff, relationship with Lasso, 3f, organist at St. Mark's, 4, relationship with Giovanni Gabrieli, 8, teaching methods, 9, music possibly played for visiting Japanese princes, 24, given a rent free house, 26, death, 28
Music, instrumental: organ toccatas, 47f, *'Toccata of the sixth tone', 48, organ canzonas, 51ff, 'Frais et Gailliard', 53f, *Ricercari ariosi*, 54, *fourth ricercar arioso, 54, ricercars, 59, *Canzon Francese detta 'Martin Menoit', 61, *Ricercar sopra 'Martin Menoit', 61, instrumental ricercars, 132ff, *'Ricercar del Primo Tono', 133, *'Ricercar del Sesto Tono', 133f, music for the increased ensemble at St. Mark's, 141ff, *battaglia, 141, *'Ricercar per sonar à otto', 142
religious: Cantiones Sacrae, 4, *giustinianae*, 4, *'Filiae Jerusalem', 26, *Motetti a 4 voci*, 26, motets for double choir, 82ff, *'Deus misereatur', 83, influence on music of Giovanni Gabrieli, 84ff, *Concerti* (1587), 165ff, *Mass* (1587), 171f, comparison with Giovanni Gabrieli's *Mass*, 174ff, 'Deus qui beatum Marcum', 182, *'Timor et tremor', 278f
secular: *'Felici d'Adria', 7f, *'Dunque il Comun Poter', 7, comparison with Giovanni Gabrieli as a madrigal composer, 111f, 'In nobil sangue', 114, *Il Terzo libro de madrigali a cinque voci*, 116, 'Amor mi strugge il cor', 131
Gabrieli, G. (see also index of works on p. 310), *life:* birth, 1, relationship with Andrea Gabrieli, 8f, years in Munich, 9f, return to Venice, 15, appointment at St. Mark's, 17ff, appointment at the Scuola Grande di S. Rocco, 200ff, as a teacher, 211, death, and neglect of his music, 295ff
music: influence of Guami, 31, influence of Bassano, 35, ability as an organist, 40f, music for pastoral plays, 108f, comparison with Andrea Gabrieli, 175f, comparison with Bassano, 177ff, alleluja refrains, 182f, comparison with Croce, 185f, possible works for S. Rocco, 207ff, influence on other composers, 231ff, ornamentation of vocal music, 269ff, chromaticism, 276, mannerist traits, 278ff, use of instruments in church music, 282ff
Gagliano, M. da, 227, 243
Galilei, V., 228
Galleazo (of Pesaro), 196
Gardano (publishing house of), 2, 154f, 216, 223, 236, 261
Gastoldi, G. G., 31, 71
Geronimo (son of Antonio), 191
Gerstenberg, W., 80 n10
Gerlach, C., 231
Gesualdo, C., xii, 216f, 221, 229, 276, 281, 301
Giacomo, Rev. Father, 202
Giacomo, Antonio (of the Crocieri), 33
Gibbons, O., 221
Giomo, G., 164 n1

Giovanni Battista, 202
Gistou, N., *'Quel augellin che canta', 214f
Giuseppe (player), 164
Gonzaga, A., 215
Gotterio, L., 27
Grabbe, J., 212, 223ff, *'Lasso, perchè mi fuggi', 224
Gradese rite, 20
Grandi, A., 210, 297f
Grani, A., 210, 287, 295, 297
Gratiora (from Padua), 205
Graz, 212, 261
Grillo, G. B., 157 n46, 204, 209, 233, 243, 295, 297
Grimani, Dogaressa, 164
Grimani, Doge Marino, 108, 163ff, 193, 258f
Groppo, A., 108 n4
Grossman, B., 301
Gruber, G., 10, 55, 124
Guami, F., 10f, 146
Guami, G., 11ff, 29ff, 37ff, 94, 233, 279, *'In die tribulationis', 12, *'Laetentur caeli', 13, *'La Novellina', 146ff
Guarini, G. B., 120, 213ff, 220
Gurlitt, W., 83 n14
Gussago, C., 232f, 243, *'Sonata 17', 233

Handel, G. F., ix
Harich-Schneider, E., 24 n13
Harman, A., 36 n33, 107 n1
Hassler, H. L., 29, 70, 124, 298f
Henri III, of France, 7, 25
Henri IV, of France, 259
Hesse, Landgrave of, 227, 296
Hieronimo (of the Carmini), 27, 33
Hitchcock, H. W., 243 n8
Homobon, Rev. Father, 197
Hudson, F., 289 n20

Jacomo (son of Matio), 191
Jannequin, C., *'Martin Menoit', 60
Japanese Princes, visit of, 24
Jeppeson, K., 200 n28
Jesuits, 15, 298

Kassel, 125
Kauffmann (publishing house of), 124, 231
Kenton, E., ix, 8 n17, 17 n25, 114 n10, 124, 126 n29
Kerll, J. C., 71
Kerman, J., 122 n15
Kiwi, E., 35 n31
Kolmann, H. J., 124
Kunze, S., 233 n3–6

Lantins, H. de, 69
Lassels, R., 21, 108 n2
Lasso, O. di, 72, 106f, 299, relationship with Andrea Gabrieli: 2ff, 54, 82, relationship with Giovanni Gabrieli: xif, 9ff, 92ff, 276
Laudis (Laudi), F., 10, 127, 140, 201
Laudis, M., 140
Lenaerts, R., 19 n3
Leo, L., ix
Leo XI, Pope, 258
Leoni, L., 213, 215ff, *'Dolci baci e soavi', 216
Lepanto, battle of, 6, 127, 132
Lindner, F. (publishing house of), 231
Liszt, F., 44
Locatello, G., 209
Lockwood, L., 71 n2
Long, J., 80 n10
Lupini, A., 198
Luzzaschi, L., 12, 79, 233

Magni (publishing house of), 295
Mantua, Duke and Duchess of, 164
Marascotti (publishing house of), 216
Marcolino rite, 20
Marenzio, L., xii, 11, 15, 36ff, 44, 70, 107, 115f, 120f, 216
Marini, B., 243, 297
Marsolo, P. M., 215
Martinengo, G., 260
Martinengo, G. C., 206, 260, 294
Martire, Father P., 211
Mason, W. E., 81 n11
Mattheson, J., 41f
Maximilian, Archduke, 212
Mazzocchi, D., 217
Mendel, A., 76 n7
Merulo, C., 5f, 8, 17, 25f, 39, 41, 43, 46ff, 67, 82, 154, 182, 200, 233, *Motetti à 6 voci*, 26, *'Adoramus te Domine', 27, 'La Zambeccara', 52, *'Petit Jacquet', 52f, 'Regina caeli', 181
Michael (violinist), 129
Milanuzzi, C., 131
Mischiati, O., 146 n38
Mocenigo, T., 69
Molinaro, S., 213

Molino, F. di, 7, 164 n5
Monte, C. de, 69
Monte, F. di, 120
Monteverdi, C., 1, 18 n1, 19, 188, 210f, 227, 229f, 243, 297, 301, madrigals: 120, 153, 213f, 216f, 220f, 235, 276, 289f, *'Ahi com'a un vago sol', 288f, Marian Vespers (1610): 184, 232, 244f, 268, 288, *Orfeo:* 109, 234
Moresca, 109
Morley, T., 35f, 70, 107, 122
Morosini, Battista, 35
Morosini, Bortolo, 202, 204, 207
Moser, H. J., 206 n35
Mosto, F. da, 137f, 153
Mosto, N., 140, 237
Mozart, W. A., 3
Munich, 2f, 9f, 15, 52, 74, 138
Murhardsche und Landesbibliothek (Kassel), 109, 296
musica reservata, 3f, 106

Naples, 2
Nasco, G., 80
Newcomb, A., 5 n9, 15 n24
Nicoleto (of Castello), 196
Nicolò (trombetta), 163
Nielsen, H., 212ff, *'Fuggi, fuggi, O mio core', 217, *'A la durezza vostra, al suo languire', 218, *'T'amo mia vita', 219, *'Ch'io non t'ami', 219
Nodari, G. P., *'Parlo misero taccio', 215f
Nolhac, P., 8 n15
Nozze di Hadriana (Le), 124
Nuremberg, 1, 10

Olizzi, J. di, 195
Ottavio, Father (from Padua), 202

Padovano, A., 41, 131, 141
Palestrina, G. P., x, xii, 12, 19, 38, 44, 81, 106f, 131, 165, 180, 182, 265 n16
Palisca, C., 229 n11
Pallavicino, B., 215ff, 223, *'Ch'io non t'ami', 219
Pasini, A., 20 n6
Patriarchino rite, 20
Paul V, Pope, 258
Pedersøn, M., 212, 216, 220f, *'Care lagrime mie', 221, *'Dimmi caro ben mio', 222, *'Madonn', amor ed io', 222, *'Lasso perchè mi fuggi', 224
Phalèse (publishing house of), 231
Picchi, G., 295 n2
Pidoux, P., 47 n16, 53 n21–25, 59 n28–30
Piero (da Oderzo), 139
Playford, J., 244 n11
Ponentin, P., 163
Praetorius, M., 83, 97, 168ff, 283, 298
Priuli, G., 166, 206, 209, 294f
Priuli, L., 188
Puliazzo de Petris, 27
Pullan, B., 188 n1, 191 n5, 192 n10, 193 n12

'Quem queritis', trope, 20

Radino, G., 232
Ragazzi, A., 36 n32
Ranke, L. von, x
Raverii, A. (publishing house of), 134, 232f, 243, 289
Reese, G., 72 n5, 116 n12
Reventio, Father, 202
Riemann, H., 243 n9
Riemann, M., 41 n5
Romano, A., 69
Romano, P., 33
Rore, C. de, 3, 5, 31, 120, 131
Rossi, S., 213, 243
Rota, G., 164 n4
Rovere, E. della, 205
Rovetta, G. B., 205
Rovetta, Vido (Da Piove), 205ff, 210
Rovigo, F., 232
Ruffo, V., 71

St. Ignatius, 297
St. Teresa, 297
Sandberger, A., 2 n5
Sansovino, F., 20 n7, 23 n12, 24, 41, 131, 164, 166
Santacroce, F., 80
Santini, F., 213
Sanuto, L., 121
Sarpi, P., 258f
Sartori, C., 131 n12, 211 n3
Savii, G., 295
Savioni, P., 163
Schein, J. H., 299ff, *'Die mit tränen', 300, *'Das ist mir lieb', 301
Schering, A., 243 n10

Schlesische Gesellschaft für Vaterländische Kultur, x
Schmid, B., 55 n26, 296
Schofield, B., 225 n9
Schütz, H., 212f, 225, 295f, 301f, 'Fuggi, fuggi, O mio core', 217, 'Ride la primavera', 227, *'O primavera', 227ff, *'Vasto mar', 227ff, *'Quella damma son io', 227f, *Psalms of David*, 266, 298
Schwab, H. W., 223 n7
Scotto (publishing house of), 19
Scotto, S., 140
Scuola Grande della Carità, 191
Scuola Grande di S. Rocco, xi, 188ff, 295
Selfridge-Field, E., 42 n6
Serafin, M., 198
Sigismondo (of SS. Giovanni e Paolo), 33
Simonetti, L., 205
Smith, L. P., 42 n9, 192 n9, 258 n1
Soderino, A., 232
Solerti, A., 8 n15, 25 n18
Spagnol (Spagnolo), A., 33, 196
Sponga, F., *'O se torni il mio sole', 215
Stagiera, A., 197
Stevens, D., 6 n12
Stivori, F., 122, 211
Strunk, O., 180 n18, 244 n11
Sugana, F., 29f
Sweelinck, J. P., 42f

Tadei, A., 212
Taddeo, P. F., 295
Tallis, T., 187
Tasso, T., 15, 214
Tenestrer, D., 198
Thaddeo, Father, 235
Tiburtino, G., 131
Tiepolo, Baiamonte, 20
Tiepolo, F., 164
Torchi, L., 265 n16
Treviso, 80
Trionfo di Dori (Il), 121f
Triumphs of Oriana, 121f
Trofeo, R., 232
Trojano, M., 4 n8
Tuscany, Grand Duke of, 28

Udine, 128
Udine, Girolamo da (*see* Dalla Casa)
Ursprung, O., 101 n15
Usper, F., 297

Val, J.-B. du, 203 n32
Vale, G., 40 n1, 42 n7, 129 n6, 260 n10
Vecchi, G., 55 n26, 107
Venice, 6ff, 21ff, 69f, 108f, 113, 163ff, 258
Venier, Doge, 128
Vento, I. de, 10
Ventura (violinist), 140
Viadana, L., x, 148, 208, 215, 232, 236, 248, 261, 265, 289, 297
Vido, D., 202
Vidue, H., *'Io vo piangendo', 11
Vicentino, N., 80f
Vienna Staatsbibliothek, 260 n13
Vincenti (publishing house of), 155, 236, 261

Wert, G. de, 38, 79, 92, 110, 116, 213, 220, 225, *'Misera non credea', 92
Wilhelm, Duke of Bavaria, 12, 15, 141, 299 n9
Willaert, A., 4f, 80ff, 88, 107, 165, 231
Winterfeld, C. von, ixff, 124, 263 n15, 289 n21
Wittkower, R., 297 n7
Woltz, J., 55, 296
Wotton, Sir H., 42 n9, 192, 258
Würzburg, 2

Zacconi, L., 9
Zarlino, G., 5, 8, 11, 13, 17, 25, 27, 30ff, 38, 44, 66, 70, 220
Zelter, C., ix
Zenck, H., 80 n10
Zuccarini, G. B., 28